BUYI

Buying versus renting: how large a mortgage? • Lev money • Equity buildu value • interest rates: "Points" • Balloon pay payment rights on your mortgage • Refinancing your home • First and second mortgages • Condos and co-ops: what do you really own? And what can you do with it? • Why inflation does not guarantee increasing value in your home • Selling your home and tax deferral

INVESTING IN COMMERCIAL PROPERTY

Credit and non-credit real estate: the differences, and which is a better investment for you • Tax benefits: how you can lose and still win • Understanding tax shelters, and which ones might be good for you • The magic of depreciation • When to sell a property • Shopping centers and office bulidings: how mixed tenancies affect your return • 8 checkpoints on a partnership or REIT investment • Limited partnerships and limited liability • General partners: how much should they cost you?

THE REAL ESTATE BOOK

"If you want one book to answer all your real estate questions, this is it."—*Newark Star Ledger*

"A solid, fact-filled guide that will be useful for years to come."—*Publishers Weekly*

ROBERT L. NESSEN is an investment banker, a founder and senior editor of the *Eton Journal of Real Estate Investment,* and chairman of March-Eton Corporation, a real estate consulting and investing firm. He is also a partner in the law firm of Nessen, Goodwin & Segersten, and a lecturer at Boston University School of Law. He is the author of *How You Can Have More Money Now: How to Keep What You Make Through Tax Shelters.*

THE REAL ESTATE BOOK

A Complete Guide to Acquiring,
Financing, and Investing in a
Home or Commercial Property

Revised and Updated

by Robert L. Nessen

A SIGNET BOOK
NEW AMERICAN LIBRARY

NAL BOOKS ARE AVAILABLE AT QUANTITY DISCOUNTS WHEN USED TO PROMOTE PRODUCTS OR SERVICES. FOR INFORMATION PLEASE WRITE TO PREMIUM MARKETING DIVISION, NEW AMERICAN LIBRARY, 1633 BROADWAY, NEW YORK, NEW YORK 10019.

A Robert Wool Book

SIGNET TRADEMARK REG. U.S. PAT. OFF. AND FOREIGN COUNTRIES
REGISTERED TRADEMARK—MARCA REGISTRADA
HECHO EN CHICAGO, U.S.A.

SIGNET, SIGNET CLASSIC, MENTOR, PLUME, MERIDIAN AND NAL BOOKS are published by New American Library, 1633 Broadway, New York, New York 10019

First Signet Printing, May, 1983

2   3   4   5   6   7   8   9   10

PRINTED IN THE UNITED STATES OF AMERICA

With love, to
Susan, Julie, Betsy, Ethan, and Dick

ACKNOWLEDGMENTS

I owe an unpayable debt of gratitude to Susan W. Nessen, Richard N. Goodwin, and Robert Wool. Without their encouragement and guidance, I doubt that I could have undertaken or completed this book. Their patience with me over the past two years would, on a more exalted battlefield, have earned them a peace prize.

There are several others whom I have to thank. My colleague Robert H. Segersten has not only taken the time to read the manuscript and comment on it, but has also given me the time to write it.

I have been fortunate to have as my editor at Little, Brown, Mary Tondorf-Dick, who has been unfailingly helpful and constructive. And I will always be grateful to Robert E. Ginna, a fine gentleman, for taking a chance on me.

Others in the real estate and tax fields who have read sections of the manuscript and have been generous with their advice are Jack Barry Gould, David Hewitt, Jeffrey W. Haupt, Hans C. Mautner, Saul O. Nessen, Frederick Pratt, Marshall Rose, Jeffrey Rosenhouse, and William Wildhack.

This book has required extensive research and I am indebted to Kathleen Stone, Deborah Goldman, Rhonda Kaplan, and Patrick Spain for helping me undertake this task with skill and diligence.

Finally, I want to thank Joan Harris. Without her help, there would have been no book.

CONTENTS

Chapter 5 Condominiums and Cooperatives (continued)

tages • Rights and Obligations • Condominium government • Neighbors • Restrictions on your right to sell • Difficult developers • The ground lease • The recreation lease • Condos under construction

Cooperatives: The ownership structure • Advantages • The blanket mortgage • Financing • Defaulting neighbors • Exclusivity and selling your interest

One

THE HOME

One

THE HOME
AS AN INVESTMENT

ON AN APRIL EVENING IN 1960, MY WIFE AND I WERE HAV-
ing our first public fight. We'd had many fights before, but
this was the first one in front of an outsider—a real estate
agent.

The fight was over whether to move from our rented apartment on West 116th Street in New York City and buy a 45-
year-old Victorian-style house in Montclair, New Jersey.
There was no dispute over the quality of the house—it suited
our needs and our tastes. It was, in the then-favored expression of real estate agents, in "mint" condition; and if
someone had made us a gift of the house, we would have
been like the blissful couple in a 1940s movie walking hand
in hand toward their new home—like Adam and Eve invited
back into the Garden of Eden. The problem was, of course,
that no one was giving it to us. If we wanted the house, we
had to pay for it.

Even though I was a lawyer, and had had at that time
about two years of real estate experience, I was still a bundle
of fears (my wife was pretty solid): How much should we
pay for the home? Can we get mortgage financing? Can we
afford it? And, of course: Is this the first step toward financial ruin? In short, I asked the questions that have, over the
years, dissolved the most sophisticated, cool, and mellow men
into puddles of tears. Perhaps, with my background, I should
have behaved better. But in fairness, I was sharing a universal experience, when it comes time to buy a home: letting
emotion subvert reason and superstition overtake knowledge.

We did buy the house and lived happily in it for several

3

years. But I know that for other people the outcome is not always so pleasant. Recently, a young man from the West Coast whom I wanted to hire came east with his wife to look for a house. They had been renting a small apartment in Los Angeles for three years. His dream house was an old colonial located in the middle of a field. Hers was a Frank Lloyd Wright creation on top of a mountain. But until they were about to make the move, they had never discussed their conflicting preferences. Through their house-hunting experience, as he explained it, they got to know each other. He turned down the job, and they got a divorce.

Dollars vs. Emotions

The trauma of buying a home (and there is always trauma) is understandable when you recognize that it is not simply a financial decision. It is also a matter of aesthetics, which do not easily lend themselves to the niceties of logic. Aesthetics are intuitive and emotional. And this is as it should be. Buying a home is not like buying a share of General Motors. A home, particularly the first home, reflects the yearnings, the hopes, the fears, and the pride of a lifetime. As a poet laureate of the real estate agents once said, "It is investing with your heart."

No one, from an aesthetic standpoint, can tell you which house is best for you, no more than he can tell you who will make the best wife or husband. But, as you have been told, a house is not a home—or at least not only a home. It is also a financial investment. If, when I bought the Montclair house, I had imagined myself as the great real estate entrepreneur William Zeckendorf entering into a tough, hardheaded negotiation over a piece of property, much of the tension and probably very little of the romance would have disappeared. And this would not have been a foolish flight of fancy. The purchase of a home involves, for most people, the single largest capital outlay they will ever make. In my case, measured as a percentage of my income and capital, it had the proportions of an investment made by a Stavros Niarchos or an Aristotle Onassis in a fleet of oil tankers.

It is from this perspective—the home as an investment—that you should begin to look at the problems of buying a home.

Conventional wisdom tells us that the first step when buying a home is to figure out whether or not you can afford it. Conventional wisdom is not correct. Even so, this widely held misconception prevents many people from making sound judgments and sensible choices.

Cost

Eventually, of course, you will have to face the issue of what you can afford, but the first question you should ask yourself is: *How much will it cost?* Only after you answer that question can you decide whether or not you can afford it. This is neither a quibble nor as obvious as it may first appear.

My brother called me several years ago about a house for sale in a small college town in New England. He said that the seller would not take less than $45,000, and all he could afford was $40,000. I responded, with the accumulated wisdom of my mistakes, "You can't possibly know whether you can afford it until you know what it will actually cost." And to help him figure what the house would really cost, I needed certain information. Here is what he told me:

At a purchase price of $45,000, he would have to make a cash down payment of $10,000, slightly more than 20%. A local bank would give him a mortgage loan of $35,000 covering the balance. The loan would have to be repaid over 25 years, and the interest rate would be 10%. Property taxes were $800 a year. He was, at the time, renting a house of comparable size for $330 a month and was also paying for insurance, utilities, repairs, and maintenance.

These facts raised most of the issues that had to be considered in deciding whether buying the home would be a good investment. Even further, they raised many of the issues that should be considered when analyzing any real estate opportunity. Buying a home is a microcosm of real estate investing, and almost all principles applied in analyzing a home purchase can also be applied (with appropriate modifications) to shopping centers, office buildings, and apartment projects. This will become clearer as I discuss such matters as how much to borrow, interest rates, repaying the mortgage, tax effects, and measuring the return on investment. But for the moment, I want to consider only the basic question of cost.

The down payment. There are two major components of cost: the down payment and carrying costs. My brother's down payment—his initial cash investment—would be $10,000. There would also be about $500 in incidental, or closing, costs (as discussed in chapter 7), such as attorney's fees and a property survey; so his total initial cash outlay would be $10,500.

Carrying costs. His carrying costs—the money that he would have to pay out each year (by custom calculated on a monthly basis) in order to own and operate the home—would consist of mortgage installment payments, property taxes, utility expenses, insurance premiums, and charges for repairs and maintenance.

Furthermore, he would be losing potential interest on the money he used to make the down payment and to cover the incidental costs. For unless he had stashed this money under a mattress or, applying the contemporary investment equivalent, unless he was keeping it in a noninterest-bearing checking account (which is probably worse than the mattress because historically mattresses have not deteriorated as quickly as banks), he was no doubt doing *something* with the money: investing it somewhere to earn more money. My brother had it in a savings account with a local bank where it was earning interest at the rate of 5% a year, or roughly $525 on $10,500.

Rental costs vs. carrying costs. Juggling all these facts, my brother analyzed the investment like this:

First, he was willing to make the initial cash outlay of $10,500.

Second, he compared his annual cost of renting—$3,960 ($330 per month times 12)—with the significant carrying costs. His payments on the $35,000 mortgage, at an interest rate of 10%, would be $3,816 a year (you'll see later how he arrived at this figure), or, dividing by 12, $318 per month. His property taxes would probably stay at $800 a year. And he added to this the $525 in interest he would be losing on his savings account. He did not include the costs of utilities, insurance, maintenance, and repairs in the comparison because, in his particular situation, they would be about the same whether he owned or rented.

He thus determined that the total annual carrying costs

would be $5,141 if he owned, as compared with $3,960 if he continued renting. His calculations are summarized in table 1.

TABLE 1

Calculating Ongoing Cost of Owning vs. Renting

	Yearly	Monthly
Mortgage payments	$3,816.00	$318.00
PLUS		
Property taxes	800.00	66.67
PLUS		
Loss of interest on savings account	525.00	43.75
Total owning costs	$5,141.00	$428.42
MINUS		
Total renting costs	3,960.00	330.00
Total difference	$1,181.00	$ 98.42

Looking at these figures, my brother concluded that owning was too expensive. It would cost him $1,181.00 more each year, or $98.42 more each month.

His reasoning was simple, seductive—and wrong.

In trying to understand why he was wrong, put aside for the time being some of the long-term and, perhaps, speculative advantages of ownership, such as the possible appreciation in value of the home over the years (which becomes increasingly important in times of inflation). Instead look at the numbers solely from the point of view of current carrying costs.

Everyone has heard that there are two inevitabilities in life—death and taxes. While no one has definitively proved that "you can't take it with you," it is abundantly clear, under our tax system, that you can't take it *all* with you. Taxes pervade life, death, and the ownership of a home. And it was taxes—the "aftertax" effect of his investment—that my brother failed to consider.

Tax Considerations

My brother's taxable income was $20,000. Based on the tax rates at the time, he had to pay $2,050 in federal income taxes, after taking his exemptions into account. (The tax rates have gone down since then.) However, the Internal Revenue Code, for better or for worse, gives tax advantages to homeowners that are not available to those who rent. Under the Code, my brother could have deducted mortgage interest and property taxes—thereby reducing his income-tax obligations. He could not, on the other hand, have deducted his rent payments.

As I mentioned, his annual mortgage payments would have been $3,816. Of this amount, about $3,500 would have been interest in the first year (you will see why later). His property taxes would have been $800. Since both interest and property taxes—a total of $4,300—would have been deductible, his taxable income would have dropped from $20,000 to $15,700 ($20,000 minus $4,300). On this $15,700, he would have had to pay a tax of $1,184, instead of $2,050 on $20,000. Thus, the deductions for mortgage interest and property tax would have allowed him to save $866 in taxes ($2,050 minus $1,184). His carrying costs would have been reduced from $5,141 (see table 1) by this $866 tax saving, to $4,275.

Furthermore, he would have had to pay a tax on the interest income from his savings if he had kept the $10,500 in the savings account. The tax would have been about $25. Thus, he would not have been losing the full $525 in interest on his savings account by using the $10,500 for his initial cash outlay. Rather, he would have been losing $500. This would, in turn, have reduced his carrying costs by another $25, to $4,250.

Putting this all together: His annual rent would have remained at $3,960. But his carrying costs (including the after-tax interest he would have been losing on his savings account) would have been $4,250, not $5,141. Owning would have cost him only $290 more than renting in the first year ($4,250 minus $3,960), as you can see in table 2.

The great lesson is that in calculating the cost of a home, you must consider the tax effects. The raw numbers cannot tell the entire story. In my brother's case, the apparent cost was the $10,500 initial outlay payment plus carrying costs of $5,141. But after taking taxes into account, the carrying costs in the first year would actually have been $4,250. Furthermore, he would have been building value as he paid off his mortgage, and there is the distinct possibility that he would

TABLE 2

Calculating Aftertax Cost of Owning vs. Renting

	Yearly	Monthly
Total pretax owning costs (from table 1)	$5,141.00	$428.42
MINUS		
Tax saved (homeowner deductions)	866.00	72.17
MINUS		
Tax saved (savings account interest)	25.00	2.08
Total aftertax owning costs	$4,250.00	$354.17
MINUS		
Total aftertax renting costs	3,960.00	330.00
Total difference	$ 290.00	$ .24.17

have been able to sell his home in the future for more than he paid for it.

Despite this analysis, my brother made an unfortunate choice. As much as he and his wife wanted the home, they did not buy it. I asked him why.

"Because," he said, "I can't afford it."

Real Estate Myths

This brought me back to square one; and it was at this point that I should have given up. But I had to know how he arrived at his decision. It was based, he told me, upon the ultimate authority: our father.

Our father told him he should pay no more than two times his income for the house, or $40,000. I assured my brother that this was not a rational conclusion. It was a myth or, worse, mysticism. But a father is a potent force, and in the end he prevailed. His ability to hold sway over my brother was a victory of the mythology that pervades real estate. Throughout this book I will examine and, I hope, dispel some of these myths, starting with two rules of thumb (each of which has many variations) on buying a home: *Never pay more than two times your income for your home*, and *The monthly payments on your home should not amount to more than one week's salary*. My answer to these "rules" is: Why not, if you are willing to give up other things?

Besides, you may get a raise. Obviously, if your salary is $500 each month and the monthly payments on your home are also $500, you cannot afford to make the payments, unless you are willing to accept the alternative—starvation— and in any case the bank will not make the loan to you under those circumstances.

But what you can or cannot afford—particularly during these times of high prices and record interest rates—is more a matter of priorities than of arithmetic. Vegetarians should be better able to afford more-expensive homes than meat eaters, nondrinkers better able than alcoholics, and bicyclists better able than sports-car enthusiasts.

In deciding whether or not to buy the home, my brother should have been governed by the following questions.

First: *Is this the home I want to live in?* It was.

Second: *Do I have enough money to make the down payment?* He did.

Third: *How do the carrying costs compare with the cost of renting* (after taking into account the effect of federal income taxes)? They compared favorably.

Furthermore, by owning, he would have reaped the benefits of any increase in value of the home.

But my brother became a victim of real estate mythology. The source of this mythology, as with all mythic tales, remains unknown; but it is my guess that it arises out of the compulsion of certain kinds of men—usually fathers, uncles, elder brothers, and successful sons-in-law—to give advice. These myths are not easy to break down, and their existence interferes with sound investment analysis—not only in the case of a home, as we have seen, but with other real estate as well. I will try to untangle real estate investing from these myths by examining each element of the investment—using the home as a starting point.

Two

THE DOWN PAYMENT—OR, HOW MUCH TO BORROW

SEVERAL YEARS AGO A YOUNG MAN WAS ELECTED GOVERNOR of a northeastern state in what was described as a "tide of fiscal morality"—a term best defined by a question he asked when he learned that his annual salary was going to be close to $50,000:

"What will I do with so much money?"

For those of us who had supported the governor in his campaign and who were similarly situated—married, about the age of forty, and with two or three children—his comment was startling. The governor was either lying about his circumstances (which we doubted) or he was living in a reality separate from ours (on another planet, a friend suggested). Whatever doubts we may have had about his sincerity were, however, resolved by a second incident.

The governor bought, shortly after taking office, a "stripped down" Plymouth Volari for about $3,700—all cash. He got the money by closing out his savings account—because, as he proudly told the reporters who accompanied him to pick up the car, "I have never bought anything on time in my life."

While that was rather obviously a statement designed to assure his constituents of his thrift and sense of responsibility, it did, in fairness, apparently come from his soul. And it was not without some appeal, since most Americans have grown up in a "credit" society where personal debt has become a routine burden of daily life.

But after balancing the governor's principles against my

11

needs, I decided that while I might buy a used car from this man, I would never let him handle my financial affairs.

In thinking about how far the governor would be willing to extend his golden rule—Never buy anything on time—I remembered the Frank Capra movie, made in the 1940s, *It's a Wonderful Life*. It's about a would-be suicide who is hypothetically granted his wish never to have been born, and about what his town would have been like without him. I tried, using Capra's device, to imagine what the governor's home life would have been like if he tried to buy a house for all cash—a modest, "stripped down" house, accommodating a family of four or five, and costing, at today's prices in suburban Boston, around $90,000.

To play out the fantasy, you should know certain facts about the governor: he has his share of talent; he is hardworking; and he is ambitious. This potent combination of character traits adds up, however, to no home. No matter how his home life would have turned out, it would not have been in a house that he owned—he could not have afforded it. Ninety thousand dollars in cash is a staggering amount of money to have been saved by a person in his thirties or early forties with a family but without an inherited fortune to accompany it. Even if it would have been possible to have saved the $90,000, *thrift* would have been a pale word in describing how he did it. *Privation* would come closer to the mark.

The governor's abhorrence of borrowing may, arguably, be a virtue when buying a car, a washing machine, or a television set, but it becomes an absurdity when applied to buying a home. For most people, necessity demands that they borrow at least some part of the cost. Borrowing to buy a home is also, in most cases, a sensible investment decision, and the issue is not (either as a matter of morality or money management) *whether you should borrow, but rather: How much should you borrow?*

How much to put down? As broad as this question may appear, there are two important limiting factors. The first is: *How much money do you have available to make the down payment?*

In the apocrypha of real estate, the old-time investors like to tell the story of a legendary real estate developer and his son riding down Fifth Avenue past the Empire State Building.

"Wonderful news, Dad," exclaimed Junior. "We can buy the Empire State Building for ten million dollars, and we only have to put up a hundred thousand dollars in cash!"

His father frowned.

"What's wrong, Dad?" his son asked. "Don't you think it's a good deal?"

"It's fine, but where are we going to get the hundred thousand?"

Perhaps the saddest words of all, "It might have been," were inspired by the words even sadder: "You can only spend what you've got."

How much will the bank lend? The second limitation on how much you should borrow is: *How much can you borrow?"*

In most cases, a conventional lending institution (such as a bank) will not lend more than 80% of the purchase price of a home (even if it has the authority to lend more). And in times of so-called tight money, such as Americans began going through in the late 1970s, and continuing into the 1980s, when banks do not have much money to lend, the loan will probably be closer to only 70% or 75%, requiring a down payment of 25% to 30%. (In specifying these percentages, I am assuming that the price you pay does not exceed the value of the home. Generally speaking, the purchase price is the same as the value and, in fact, usually establishes the value. But if the bank, in making an appraisal of the home, decides that you are overpaying, the 80% limitation will apply to its determination of value.)

There are exceptions to the 80% ceiling. As you'll see in chapter 4, if the mortgage is insured by the Federal Housing Administration (FHA), the Veterans Administration (VA), or a mortgage insurance company, it may be as high as 90% or more, and the down payment as low as 10% or less. However, a conventional loan on, for example, a $90,000 house will typically not exceed $72,000, or 80% of the purchase price. With an 80% loan, the down payment has to be at least $18,000. So, the decision to be made is limited by this—the $72,000 loan and the $18,000 down payment.

The Alternative Use of Money

Returning to the example of the governor, if he has only

$18,000 in cash, his decision is easy. If he wants the home, he will have to use the $18,000 for the down payment.

But assume that the governor has the entire $90,000, whether from an inheritance, excess campaign funds, a winning lottery ticket, cheating, stealing, or some other windfall. He would now have the freedom, and all the dilemmas accompanying it, to make some choices.

There are several considerations, but the key one involves the investment principle I call the "alternative use of money."

In the example, the governor has to use $18,000 of his $90,000 in savings to make the down payment, leaving him with $72,000. The balance of the cost of his home (after making the down payment) is also $72,000; and he can pay this balance in one of two ways: First, he can borrow the $72,000 from the bank and use his $72,000 in savings for something else, such as investing in General Motors. Or, second, he can use his $72,000 in savings to pay the balance of the cost of his home and not borrow anything from the bank. His decision will, all other things being equal, depend upon what he can earn by investing his savings as compared with what it will cost him to borrow.

Assume that the bank charges 10% interest on $72,000— $7,200. (As I make this assumption in the fall of 1982, I recognize that mortgage interest rates are closer to 15% than to 10%. Nevertheless, I have two reasons for selecting 10%. First, rates appear to be coming down, and I believe that the prevailing rate will be nearer to 10% than 15% within a year to 18 months. Second, it is an easy number to work with. And if I am wrong about where rates ultimately settle—if they keep going up—all you may have to do with my numbers is multiply by two. Moreover, the principles I am discussing are applicable whether mortgage rates drop to 5% or rise to 20%.)

Also assume that the governor can invest his savings of $72,000 with General Motors for a return of 11% and earn $7,920 a year—$720 more than the bank will charge him for a loan at 10% interest. In this example, he will make $720 (the difference between 10% and 11%) by borrowing the $72,000 from the bank and investing his savings in GM. Conversely, if he can invest his savings with GM at only a 9% return (or $6,480) and his cost of borrowing remains at 10%, he will be losing $720 by borrowing the $72,000 and investing his savings—the difference between 9% and 10%. (These numbers do not take into account the impact of income taxes. Interest earned on savings invested in GM will be taxable, while the interest paid on a home mortgage loan will be deductible. The tax impact will increase as your tax bracket gets higher. More on this in the next chapter.)

Invest in a home, or elsewhere? When I speak of the "alternative use of money," I am asking the question: *What is the best use of your money?* And it is a question that brings you to the threshold of sophistication in making an investment analysis—even in a discussion limited to the purchase of a home. Are you better off, as measured by the return on your money, investing in your home or investing in something else, like common stocks, commodities, or corporate bonds?

The decision cannot be based solely upon the numbers. In the mix of considerations, there are factors that are not easy to measure, or not even measurable. They can be broadly discussed in terms of "risk" and the "tolerance for risk."

How much risk? In the example of the $90,000 house, I assumed "all other things being equal." This means that the expected return (whether 9% or 11%) on the governor's invested savings was presumed to be as certain as the 10% interest that had to be paid on the loan from the bank—equal certainties of risk. But all things are rarely, if ever, equal. There is never an exact equivalence of risk. An 11% return from a General Motors bond seems very secure; much less secure on a Chrysler bond; and somewhere in between on a Ford bond. Yet, in an age of rapid technological change, every General Motors is an incipient Penn Central.

Each of us would, undoubtedly, like to be blessed with the Midas touch, without any of its liabilities. But there are no paradises for investors. Even for the most prudent and knowledgeable, there is a delicate balance between heaven and hell. There are no absolute guarantees of return. If you want something, you have to risk something. Faced with these realities, you have to recognize that everyone has a different tolerance for risk.

In my case, for example, my risk tolerance in money matters was put to the test in 1965, when I moved my family from Montclair to Concord, Massachusetts.

I bought a house that today would cost about $90,000. (It actually cost about $70,000.) I had savings, at the time, of $25,000. I could have put down all of the $25,000 and ob-

tained a $65,000 mortgage, or I could have put down 20%
($18,000) and obtained a $72,000 mortgage. If I had chosen
the second alternative, I would have been able to keep $7,000
of my savings—$25,000 minus the $18,000 down payment.
Whether I should have made only the $18,000 down payment
(and borrowed the full $72,000 balance) should have de-
pended upon what I could have done with the $7,000. In
other words, this was the time to apply the principle of the
"alternative use of money."

If I had borrowed the full $72,000 at 10% and made the
$18,000 down payment, I would have had to pay interest in
the first year of $7,200 (10% of $72,000). If, instead, I had
used the "excess" $7,000 to increase my down payment to
$25,000 and reduce my mortgage to $65,000, my interest
payment in the first year would have been only $6,500—an
interest saving of $700 ($7,200 minus $6,500). Therefore,
my question should have been: Can I earn more than $700
by investing the $7,000? For example, if I could have invest-
ed the $7,000 at 15%, I would have earned $1,050 (15% of
$7,000)—or $350 more than if I had applied the $7,000 to
my down payment. Even if I could have invested it for 10%
and made $700, I would have broken even. But instead of
employing either alternative, I did something rather original.

I did borrow the full $72,000 at 10% and made the $18,000
down payment. But instead of investing the $7,000 at more
than 10%, I left it in a savings account with my bank, on
which I was paid 5%. Since I was borrowing at 10% and was
investing at 5%, this meant, as an absolute certainty, that I
had to lose money—the difference between what I received in
interest from the bank and what I had to pay in interest to
the bank on the loan of the additional $7,000. I was receiving
5% on $7,000, or $350. I was paying the bank 10% on the
additional $7,000, or $700. The net result was a loss of $350
—$700 minus $350.

When my wife found out what I had done, she was furi-
ous. My accountant appeared surprised (the only display of
emotion I can remember him ever making). My lawyer was
amused. What was my defense? I had several excuses that ran
from safety to the need for liquidity, which I summed up by
saying, "The $7,000 is my nest egg."

My lawyer replied, "You can't hatch it by sitting on it."

Only my bank, needless to say, was delighted. Perhaps a
friend had the real explanation:

"With your low tolerance for risk," he told me, "you had the psychological need to find someone in whose eyes *you* could be a hero—and you chose your bank."

If this were a book on religious instruction, I would stop at this point and set forth the first catechism: *Always borrow as much as you can, if you can invest it for a higher return.* This is another in the series of real estate myths, and it's as helpful as telling you, "Always bet on the winning horse— never on the losing one." The problem with this real estate dictate is that you can usually assume that when you invest for a higher return you are investing at a greater risk—which reduces the certainty of the return.

Leverage

Aside from the financial considerations, there is one good reason for borrowing as much as you can: You can buy a better home. While I did not consider the possibility when I moved to Concord, I could have bought a $125,000 home by using my $25,000 savings as a down payment (assuming that the bank was willing to lend me 80% of the cost, or $100,000, and also assuming that my income was and would continue to be sufficient to pay off a $100,000 mortgage). This raises the principle of *leverage*—a marvelous word for its graphic description of what is happening.

Leverage is buying something with a small amount of cash by borrowing a large amount of cash. If, for example, I can buy a $125,000 home with only $25,000 of my own money as a down payment, I have leverage of 4 to 1—for every dollar I put down, I can borrow $4. Leverage is not only a principle for increasing pleasure—allowing you to buy things, such as a home, that you could not otherwise afford—it is also the principle followed in making, and losing, great fortunes in real estate.

In addition to considerations such as leverage (the $90,000 home versus the $125,000 home) and the alternative use of money, I should have asked three other questions before deciding upon how much of my $25,000 to use in making my down payment.

Liquidity

First: *Do I need any part of the down payment for liquidity?* Real estate is not a liquid asset—it cannot be sold quickly, like common stock, and turned into cash. By making a $25,-000 down payment, my $7,000 "nest egg" would have been tied up in the home and, to that extent, my liquidity would have been diminished. A wise investor should have a reserve, either in cash or some other form readily convertible into cash, in order to meet emergencies and other immediate needs.

Best Use of Your Money

Second: *Is this the best possible use of my money?* The answer to this question required more than an analysis of the relative return on my investment. I also had to decide: How important is my home to me? What is the value of design quality, charm, and room in which to spread out, and what am I willing to pay for it? If my behavior had been dictated solely by the necessity of maximizing my return (the fullest application of the principle of the alternative use of money), instead of buying a $90,000 or $125,000 home, or any home for that matter, I might have forced my family to move into a cold-water flat.

What Can You Afford?

Third, returning to my brother's original question in chapter 1: *Can I afford the home?* The answer depended, primarily, on whether I could afford to make the payments on the bank loan. (I also had to be concerned with other costs, such as utilities, insurance, and property taxes, but assume for the moment that these costs represented no change for me.) If I bought a $90,000 house (with an $18,000 down payment and a 25-year bank loan of $72,000 at 10% interest), the payments I would have had to make on the loan would have been about $7,850 a year ($654.17 a month). On a $125,000 house (with a $25,000 down payment and a $100,000, 25-year loan at 10% interest), the payments would have been about $10,900 a year ($908.33 a month), a difference of $3,-050 each year ($254.17 a month).

As I noted earlier, what anyone can afford is more a matter of personal priorities than the application of any rule of thumb. Obviously, if I make $30,000 a year, I cannot afford a $1 million estate. But barring the absurd, whether or not I can afford the $125,000 home depends, in great part, upon what I am willing to give up.

In these days of increasing costs for homes, we frequently hear the dire conclusion that America is a place where "most people can no longer afford a home." This is not so much an economic conclusion as a state of mind. Too often a person cannot afford to buy a home because he cannot bring himself to sacrifice something he wants more: a sports car, a winter vacation, expensive restaurants, or a work of art.

Perhaps the best advice on what you can afford was given by Hubert Humphrey to his son-in-law:

"I told him you won't like a house you can afford. Get something with a couple of big mortgages and then work like the dickens to pay it off. When you're fifty they'll [the children] all be gone. Enjoy it now."

In deciding upon your down payment and how much to borrow, you will be limited, first, by the amount of cash you have.

Next is the question of how much you can borrow. Under ordinary circumstances, a bank will not lend you more than 80% of the cost of your home.

The other considerations are not so simple, and will vary from person to person. From the point of view of investment strategy, are you better off putting your cash into a home or investing it elsewhere (alternative use of money)? And in order to answer this question, you have to factor in your tolerance for risk—a subjective but, nonetheless, very real consideration.

How much liquidity do you need?

And, finally, there's the question of what you can afford—which is, as I have suggested, intimately involved with your personal preferences and priorities.

If your financial situation is similar to that of the governor, borrowing $72,000 at 10% on a $90,000 home and making an $18,000 down payment is probably a balanced decision. This assumes that you have savings of $25,000 and an annual salary of $50,000. On that salary, the payments on the $72,000 loan should not be unduly burdensome. And by using only $18,000 of your savings for the down payment, you are leaving yourself with $7,000 to cover emergencies or to use for other investment opportunities that may arise.

Unfortunately, such a balanced decision won't always be a perfect decision. It may not give you everything you want. If, instead, you want a $125,000 home, you may decide to make a $25,000 down payment. You will end up with a better home—but only by giving up liquidity. You cannot, in this case, have both.

But any final conclusion on how much to borrow and how much to put down on a home is premature until you learn more about the mortgage and the mortgage process.

THE MORTGAGE

> They will purchase the hollow happiness of the next
> five minutes, by a mortgage on the independence
> and comfort of years.
>
> *William Hazlitt*

OVER THE PAST TWENTY YEARS, I HAVE BECOME A MODEST
representative of the American success story, having pro-
gressed to bigger homes and bigger mortgages. In 1960, I
bought the house in Montclair for $30,000; in 1965, I bought
the house in Concord for $70,000; and in 1972, I moved
across town into my present home in Concord, which, after
making improvements, cost around $125,000.

With this upward movement, I seemed to be following the
advice of Hubert Humphrey to get a larger mortgage. But I
lacked his élan. I am a worrier, and as my mortgage payments increased, I began to feel that the words of William
Hazlitt set forth above had been written, over one hundred
years ago, as a warning just to me.

I was brought up to view a mortgage as an unwholesome
burden. So, when a investment adviser told me that the $90,-
000 mortgage I had taken out on my $125,000 home was too
small, I was perplexed. For a long time I had been uneasy
about the size of my mortgage, feeling a mixture of fear and
guilt. Now I was being advised by a man whose judgment in
money matters I respected to increase it to at least ·$100,-
000—more, if possible. Was I becoming the man "whose au-
tumn is mortgaged before the spring is over?" Or was I so
entangled in moralistic and cultural attitudes about thrift that
I was incapable of rational judgments in these matters?

Despite my misgivings, a mortgage does not have any eth-

ical attributes. Nor is it an instrument of terror. It is simply a
legal document, defining the rights and obligations of the borrower (the homeowner) and the lender (the bank). In chapter 2, I examined personal and investment factors that go into
deciding how much to borrow when you buy a home. Now, I
want to look at the nature of your obligation when you do
borrow.

Your Mortgage Obligation

When I bought my $125,000 home in Concord, I borrowed
$90,000 from a local bank, making a down payment of $35,-
000. In return, I gave the bank my promissory note for $90,-
000. This was my "IOU"—my promise to repay the loan
with interest.

The bank also had a mortgage on my home, which bound
both me and my home to the loan. I was under a firm legal
obligation to repay the loan with interest—an obligation secured, or collateralized, by the mortgage.

Default. If I defaulted, the bank had the right to take my
home from me and sell it in order to recover any unpaid balance of the loan. This might be a frightening prospect, but it is
also a remote one. Banks do not like to dispossess a person from
his home and will take that step only as a last resort. It is bad
for their image and worse for their financial statements. We
have come a long way from that old-time melodrama in
which the arch villain gives the chaste widow the dreaded
choice between dispossession and loss of virtue.

Principal. The $90,000 that the bank loaned me is called
the "principal" of the mortgage. (The term *mortgage* typically refers to the promissory note and the mortgage collec-
tively, as if they were one document. While this is not
technically correct, to simplify, I'll follow that custom unless
I indicate otherwise.) The principal has to be paid back to
the bank over a specified period of time, usually between 20
and 30 years.

Maturity date. In my case, I had to repay the principal over
25 years, after which time the mortgage would be said to
"mature." The maturity date of a mortgage is the final date
by which it has to be repaid in full. If my 25-year mortgage

were given on January 1, 1972, the maturity date would be December 31, 1996.

I also agreed to pay the bank interest on the mortgage. In this case the rate was close to 10% per year. This is, in effect, the fee I have to pay the bank for the use of its money.

Installment Payments

The payments on the mortgage are made in equal periodic installments that include *both* interest and repayments of principal. The amount of each installment payment does not change, but the proportion of interest and principal contained in each installment changes every time a payment is made.

When all of this was explained to me by my lawyer, I listened with respectful but inert silence. But then he said the magic words: *"And the composition of installment payments will affect your taxes."* These were words of passion, reviving my "greed glands." I was eager for instruction.

Interest and principal "shift." First, you have to understand the shift between interest and principal. On my $90,000 mortgage, with interest at 10%, the annual installment payments each amount to $9,915.13. This is what I have to pay each year for 25 years in order to repay fully the mortgage principal plus interest. (I am, for ease of illustration, assuming that mortgage payments are made in equal annual installments. Sometimes they are, but traditionally they are made monthly. Nevertheless, the principles I am discussing are the same whether I use monthly, quarterly, or annual installments.)

You can pick up published tables that will show you what the installment payment will be on any mortgage, whatever the amount, interest rate, and maturity date. They are available, at no cost, from almost every real estate broker and bank, or you can find them at most stationery stores for a few dollars.

In the year that I borrowed $90,000, the first year's interest was $9,000—10% of $90,000. Thus the total annual installment payment of $9,915.13 was mostly a payment of interest. This left a balance of $915.13. ($9,915.13 minus interest of $9,000), which was applied to the repayment of principal, reducing the amount of the unpaid mortgage to $89,084.87. You see why it is that people say the first year's payment is mainly interest.

In the second year, the interest rate was still 10%, but was paid on $89,084.87, not on $90,000.00, since I repaid $915.13 of principal in the previous year. Therefore, interest was only $8,908.49 (10% of $89,084.87), leaving a balance of $1,-006.64 to be applied to principal—the difference between $9,-915.13 and $8,908.49.

This shift from interest to principal accelerates each year as more of the mortgage is repaid. You can track the shift in table 3, which breaks down the payments for the first five years of my mortgage and every fifth year thereafter.

Around the fifth year, you will probably begin to feel the way my wife did when she said: "My God, are we ever going to pay off this mortgage? We keep paying and paying, and we have so much of it left. Does it ever end?"

It does, of course, come to an end, and if you begin to lose faith, look again at table 3 and you can see that by the twenty-fifth year, interest is only $901.34 and principal repayment is $9,013.44.

TABLE 3

Payment Breakdown on a $90,000 Mortgage
(25 Years at 10% Interest)

Year	Unpaid Mortgage Principal	Installment Payment	Interest on Unpaid Mortgage Principal	Portion of Installment Payment Applied to Principle
1	$90,000.00	$9,915.13	$9,000.00	$ 915.13
2	89,084.87	9,915.13	8,908.49	1,006.64
3	88,078.23	9,915.13	8,807.82	1,107.31
4	86,970.92	9,915.13	8,697.09	1,218.04
5	85,752.88	9,915.13	8,575.29	1,339.84
10	77,573.01	9,915.13	7,757.30	2,157.83
15	64,399.25	9,915.13	6,439.93	3,475.20
20	43,182.78	9,915.13	4,318.28	5,596.85
25	9,013.44	9,915.13	901.34	9,013.44

Amortization. The repayment of principal is sometimes called "amortization," and schedules, called "amortization schedules," showing the changing allocation of interest and principal on any mortgage, can be purchased for about $5 from financial-service companies. Frequently, the bank from which you obtain your mortgage will provide you with one.

In brief, the mortgage is not stable, even though the installment payments and the rate of interest are fixed over its full term. Like a radioactive element, it is in a constant process of change. And this, as I said earlier, has tax implications that affect your cost.

When the bank told me that the interest rate on my mortgage was 10%, I was outraged. This seemed an unconscionable price to pay, and my first instinct was to keep my mortgage as low as possible. But I was forgetting the aftertax cost of interest—the lesson I was later to give my brother.

Taxes and interest deductions. Assume that the top $15,000 of my income was taxed by the federal government at the rate of 40%. (Not all of my income will be taxed at 40% because the federal income tax is a graduated tax—that is, the first dollar I make will be taxed at a lower rate than the last dollar. You can find your tax rate by looking at the tax tables sent to you by the Internal Revenue Service each year along with your tax return.) Based upon a 40% rate, $6,000 of this $15,000 in income would be taken from me by the government in taxes, leaving me with $9,000 after taxes.

However, the interest paid on a mortgage is deductible. Since I could, then, deduct the first year's interest of $9,000, this $15,000 of my income would be reduced to $6,000 ($15,000 minus interest deduction of $9,000). Therefore, I would only have to pay a tax of 40% on $6,000 ($2,400), instead of a tax of 40% on $15,000 ($6,000). As a result, I would be saving $3,600 in taxes ($6,000 minus $2,400).

The fact that my interest deduction would be saving me $3,600 in taxes meant that the true first-year cost of interest on my mortgage would not be $9,000. Rather it would be $9,000 minus the tax saving of $3,600—or $5,400. And if my "aftertax cost of interest" was $5,400, then my installment payment would, in effect, be less than $9,915.13. It would be $6,315.13, consisting of $915.13 in principal plus $5,400 in aftertax interest.

Since interest declines in each subsequent year, my interest deductions and tax savings would also decline. Correspondingly, the aftertax cost of my future installment payments would increase; but they would never be as high as $9,-915.13. This can be seen in table 4, which assumes that my income is taxed at the 40% tax rate.

TABLE 4

Tax Effect on Installment Payments
($90,000 Mortgage, 25 Years at 10% Interest, 40% Tax Bracket)

Year	Installment Payment (pretax)	Interest Cost		Portion of Installment Payment Applied to Principal	Aftertax Cost of Installment Payment*
		Pretax	Aftertax		
1	$9,915.13	$9,000.00	$5,400.00	$ 915.13	$6,315.13
2	9,915.13	8,908.49	5,345.09	1,006.64	6,351.73
3	9,915.13	8,807.82	5,284.69	1,107.31	6,392.00
4	9,915.13	8,697.09	5,218.25	1,218.04	6,436.29
5	9,915.13	8,575.29	5,145.17	1,339.84	6,485.01
10	9,915.13	7,757.30	4,654.38	2,157.83	6,812.21
15	9,915.13	6,439.93	3,863.96	3,475.20	7,339.16
20	9,915.13	4,318.28	2,590.97	5,596.85	8,187.82
25	9,915.13	901.34	540.80	9,013.44	9,554.24

*Aftertax interest cost plus portion of installment payment applied to principal.

I was learning that in a world with taxes, two plus two never equals four. Nothing is ever quite what it seems—10% interest is never 10%; it is always less. And it might be even lower than the figures show in table 4 if I were living in a city or state like New York that has an income tax similar to the federal system.

Tax bracket and aftertax cost. Furthermore, the "aftertax cost" of the mortgage payment varies with the tax bracket. The higher the bracket, the less the cost, a reaffirmation of what has been called one of the unwritten amendments to the United States Constitution—"The rich get richer."

Table 5 shows what someone is really paying on a $90,000 mortgage at 10% interest, if he is taxed at the 30%, 40%, or 50% rate.

The right to deduct interest applies, of course, whatever your income-tax bracket—whether it is 30%, 40%, or 50%. And this fact should put today's mortgage rates—scandalous as they may be—in better perspective.

If I had to pay $15% on a $90,000 mortgage, interest in the first year would be $13,500. However, if I am taxed at a 30%

TABLE 5

Effect of Tax Bracket on Installment Payments
($90,000 Mortgage, 25 Years at 10% Interest)

Year	Interest (pretax)	Aftertax Interest Cost			Aftertax Cost of Installment Payment		
		30% Bracket	40% Bracket	50% Bracket	30% Bracket	40% Bracket	50% Bracket
1	$9,000.00	$6,300.00	$5,400.00	$4,500.00	$7,215.13	$6,315.13	$5,415.13
2	8,908.49	6,235.94	5,345.09	4,454.25	7,242.58	6,351.73	5,460.89
3	8,807.82	6,165.47	5,284.69	4,403.91	7,272.78	6,392.00	5,511.22
4	8,697.09	6,087.96	5,218.25	4,348.55	7,306.00	6,436.29	5,566.59
5	8,575.29	6,002.70	5,145.17	4,287.65	7,342.54	6,485.01	5,627.49
10	7,757.30	5,430.11	4,654.38	3,878.65	7,587.94	6,812.21	6,036.48
15	6,439.93	4,507.95	3,863.96	3,219.97	7,983.15	7,339.16	6,695.17
20	4,318.28	3,022.80	2,590.97	2,159.14	8,619.65	8,187.82	7,755.99
25	901.34	630.94	540.80	450.67	9,644.38	9,554.24	9,464.11

rate, my aftertax interest cost is $9,450, or 10.5% on $90,000. In the 40% bracket, it is 9%, and in the 50% bracket it is 7½%.

Effect of interest rates. Another point should be made about today's high interest rates. If they are sustained at their current level, the cost of carrying or operating a home has to go up. This may make it more difficult to obtain a large mortgage, since the bank will want to be sure, as always, that the person it is lending the money to will be able to make the higher mortgage payments.

If the banks start giving, instead, relatively small mortgages (which means a higher down payment), it will become painful, if not impossible, to pay the high prices for homes experienced over the past few years.

One of two things must then occur. The first possibility is that no one will be able to sell a home because no one will be able to buy one. But if you agree with me that this takes you past the point of the ridiculous, you figure that this cannot happen. If there is any meaning left to the concept of the "free market," what has to happen is that prices will go down in response to high interest rates. Moreover, you should be able to get better terms from your seller on the way you have to pay for the home—for example, through the increased use of a second mortgage (which I'll discuss in chapter 4).

None of this is a defense of a 15% interest rate. At best, such a rate is discomforting—initially for the buyer, and eventually for the seller. The only perfect cure for high interest rates is low interest rates. Nor am I trying to justify a monetary policy that allows mortgage rates to reach this level—I do not even understand it. But contrary to the emerging prophecies of doom, a rate of 16% is not fatal so long as mortgage interest is tax deductible and market forces compensate for these rates through lower prices.

Interest is the first part in the dynamics of the mortgage process. The second part is the repayment of principal and the buildup of equity.

Principal payments and equity. Interest and principal act in counterpoint. As interest declines, principal payments increase by a corresponding amount (see table 3). While principal payments are not deductible, they do increase the equity in your home. *Equity* is, in a real estate context, a word of art that means the amount of money you have invested in your home over and above the mortgage. The down payment is both your equity and initial investment in your home. And as you repay the principal, you are increasing both your equity and your investment.

When I bought my home for $125,000, I made a down payment of $35,000 (borrowing $90,000 from the bank). I had an equity of $35,000—an investment in my home that was $35,000 above the mortgage. If I had resold my home for $125,000 on the day I bought it, I would have gotten back the $35,000, with the remaining $90,000 being used to pay off the mortgage.

Equity buildup. As the principal of the mortgage declines each time I make an installment payment, the equity in my home goes up. By the fifteenth year, for example, I would have paid about $25,600 of principal, with the unpaid balance of my mortgage being approximately $64,400 (see table 3). My equity would have been $60,600—the $35,000 down-payment plus the $25,600 in principal repayments. So, if I sold my home in the fifteenth year for $125,000 (assuming no decline in its market value, a reasonable assumption in today's economy), the money would be divided up like this: $64,400 would go to the bank to pay off the balance of the mortgage; $35,000 would reimburse me for my original down payment; and $25,600 would be the buildup of equity, which would also go to me.

The importance of equity buildup is too often overlooked in evaluating an investment in a home. In Arthur Miller's *Death of a Salesman*, Willy Loman's wife adds almost unbearable poignancy to the last scene when, at Willy's graveside, she says: "I made the last payment on the house today. . . . We're free and clear. We're free. We're free . . ." She was right in saying that they were "free and clear," but she was wrong in thinking that it happened all at once. It didn't. It was a process. Each mortgage payment was reducing the mortgage and increasing their equity. If Willy and his wife could have understood that over the years they had been building value, it might have wreaked havoc with the dramatic impact of the play, but it would have relieved them of much of the financial strain that drove Willy to his death.

When selling a home, you can recoup principal payments

because of built-up equity; but interest, even though deductible, is gone forever.

Once I began to grasp these dynamics of the mortgage, I was not sure what to do with my newly acquired knowledge. My lawyer, a man of constant patience (not, I have always suspected, out of a natural benevolence, but because he is paid by the hour), explained that I then had to decide upon the length, or maturity, of my mortgage. That would determine my total interest-obligation and the rate of my equity buildup.

Interest vs. equity. The earlier the mortgage matured (20 years, for example, instead of 25 years), the faster my equity would grow and the less interest I would have to pay, because I would be repaying the principal sooner. The corollary of this, however, was that my periodic installment payments would have to be larger because principal would be repaid over a compressed period of time.

If the mortgage matured in 30 years rather than 25 years, I would have to pay more interest, because I would be using the bank's money for a longer period of time. Therefore, I would be paying more in total dollars; but with these five extra years, my individual installment payments would be smaller. Table 6 on the following page illustrates this.

In trying to make up my mind, I thought of the words of a famous football coach: "The future is now." If I wanted to keep my installment payments as low as possible, I would be better off with a longer mortgage. My total cost would be more, but my immediate cash drain would be less. I would, in a sense, be trading the present for the future. This might enable me to buy a more expensive home or give me more cash to invest in something else—applying, once more, the principle of the alternative use of money. But there were other factors that I had to consider before making a final decision.

Tax brackets and the maturity. The tax effect had to be taken into account. As you have seen, the aftertax cost of the installment payments will decline as the tax bracket gets higher, because of the interest deduction. Table 7 shows the effect of various tax brackets on the total cost amount of the installment payments for each of the mortgage lengths I was considering.

TABLE 6

Effect of Maturity on Installment Payments ($90,000 Mortgage at 10% Interest)

Maturity (in years)	Installment Payment Yearly	Installment Payment Monthly	Total Cost of Payments (pretax)	Equity Buildup 10 Years	Equity Buildup 15 Years	Equity Buildup 20 Years
20	$10,571.37	$880.95	$211,427.40	$25,043.59	$49,926.32	$90,000.00
25	9,915.13	826.26	247,878.25	14,584.82	29,075.95	52,414.07
30	9,547.13	795.59	286,414.01	8,719.84	17,383.68	31,336.87

TABLE 7

Effect of Maturity and Tax Bracket on Cost of Installment Payments
($90,000 Mortgage at 10% Interest)

Maturity (in years)	Total Pretax Cost of Payments	Total Aftertax Cost of Payments		
		30% Bracket	40% Bracket	50% Bracket
20	$211,427.40	$174,999.18	$162,856.44	$150,713.70
25	247,878.25	200,514.78	184,726.95	168,939.13
30	286,414.01	227,489.81	207,848.41	188,207.01

The cost difference between a 20- and a 30-year mortgage narrows considerably as the tax bracket increases. But before acting on these tax considerations, I needed to be aware of at least two caveats: tax brackets can change; and so can tax laws.

For reasons that I may not be able to foresee, my income may go down. Among the many cruelties of age, there is the sad fact that when most people go past the age of sixty their earning power declines, lowering their tax bracket. As a result they lose some of the advantages of the interest deduction. Even further beyond their control is the possibility of congressional action that will limit or eliminate this deduction on home mortgages.

Equity as an asset. Equity buildup was another factor to be weighed when I considered my mortgage. Equity is an asset that can be very valuable in the future. It can be the source of funds that will put my children through college or may provide me with the money I need to retire. (My wife discourages this line of thinking, telling me: "I love our house, and never want to sell it." This is hard to argue with, considering my affection for her and the fact that the house is owned in her name.)

Equity is, however, an asset that takes time to grow. And that time is in the future, with all of its risks and contingencies. You may find it hard today to believe that home values can decline, particularly when you consider that the average cost of a new home in the United States in 1970 was $35,500 and in 1982 it was around $90,000. For existing homes it was $30,000 in 1970 and approximately $70,500 in 1982. But there is no ironclad rule of economics or politics that says home values cannot decline. And if they do, your equity buildup will erode.

Built-up equity is, moreover, not liquid. Assuming that the value of my home remains stable, I will eventually receive this equity. But no mechanism has been devised, as yet—by the real estate industry, the banks, or anyone else—to let me convert equity buildup into cash as it is growing, unless I am willing to take one of two major and dramatic steps: sell my home or refinance my mortgage (which requires paying off the current mortgage and obtaining a new one, as I'll discuss later).

There is also the question of whether equity buildup will reflect a real increase in the worth of my home or simply inflation. Despite the mass of data available on the subject, this is an extremely difficult distinction to make, befuddling both accountants and economists. However, the extent to which equity buildup derives from inflation will be an important factor in deciding whether or not I can afford to sell my home sometime in the future, as I shall discuss in chapter 6.

Deciding on Mortgage Length

Typically, the range of mortgage maturities has been 20 to 30 years. I chose 25 years. This might appear to be a compromise choice stemming from indecisiveness. It wasn't. It was a sensible middle ground for me or anyone else in a similar position—between the ages of thirty and forty, with a young family, and making between $35,000 and $70,000 a year.

The 25-year mortgage kept my installment payments within comfortable bounds, relieving me of cash pressures. At the same time, I was putting a reasonable amount of my income into the buildup of equity (which is sometimes spoken of as a "forced savings"), and was taking advantage of the tax dispensation afforded me by the federal government on interest payments.

A mortgage with a shorter maturity (20 years, for example) would have been the least acceptable alternative. It would have accelerated the rate of equity buildup and required the payment of fewer total dollars over the mortgage term; but, as I have shown, the mathematical imperative of shorter maturities is higher installment payments. This would have imposed too great a monthly financial burden on me,

and would not have allowed me to take proper advantage of
the interest deduction.

At the other end of the range, the 30-year mortgage is better suited for those with a large income and those with only a
modest one. (I was somewhere in between.) This does not
mean that there is a kinship of the rich and the poor. They
have different needs and goals, which happen coincidentally
to be met best by a long-term mortgage.

If you are in a 50% tax bracket, the tax benefits to be
derived from the interest deductions are a compelling reason
for choosing a long maturity. The bank will be getting more
interest, but in effect the government will be paying at least
half of it.

If you are making between $20,000 and $30,000 a year,
minimizing the amount of your installment payment is a vital
factor in being able to afford a home. This is accomplished
by a longer maturity, a fact that has been recognized by the
government in most of its housing programs. Under these
programs, the mortgages usually mature in 30 years or more.

Banks and Your Mortgage

There is another party to the mortgage process—the bank.
When you speak of mortgages, you are talking about the
bank's money; and in negotiating with the bank, the final
result rarely emerges as the bargain between equals, unless
you are a Rockefeller or a J. Paul Getty. But the bank is not
in total control. It has one commodity to sell—money. If its
terms are unreasonable, either you cannot or will not buy. It
is like the boy who owns the bat and ball. If you do not play
by his rules, he may go home—you may not get to play, but
neither does he.

This was not as clear to me as it should have been when I
went to the local bank to borrow money on my first home. It
was an intimidating experience, both physically and emotionally. There the bank stood, an imposing centerpiece of
Montclair—Greek-revival architecture, a citadel of stability
and tradition. The bank was a Goliath, but I was no David.
In discussing how much and how long I could borrow, and at
what interest rate, the bank's loan officer made me feel like a
wavering virgin being lectured by a maiden aunt secure in the
virtue of her chastity. I knew what Harry Truman meant
when he described bank policy as a willingness to lend you

money when you did not need it and an unwillingness to lend it to you when you did.

This experience prompted me, years later, to complain about the inflexibility of banks and their policies to a friend who is the director of a major national bank. I told him my story, and also the story of a colleague:

He was passing a branch of the bank that held the mortgage on his home and where he had a checking account. The place was offering a free piggy bank to anyone who opened a new checking account.

He went in and told the bank teller he was a customer of the bank and wanted a piggy bank for his daughter. She explained that the offer was limited to new customers. He said that this was a ridiculous policy and "as an old and loyal depositor, I should be treated as well as a new one. So give me the piggy bank." She refused, and he asked to speak to the bank manager. They went through the same routine, with the manager holding firm—no piggy bank. So my colleague, then and there, withdrew all his money, and immediately opened a new checking account at the same bank. He got his piggy bank.

My friend, the director, told me that the bank manager should have been fired. But, he explained, a bank is similar to the Army. "We [the directors] set policy, and the loan officer is our sergeant. We want him to implement and not make policy. If he wants to make exceptions, he has to come to us for permission—something he is not likely to do. This is not as arbitrary as it may seem. Remember our policy governs the use of millions, many millions, of dollars—our stockholders' and depositors' dollars—and if every loan officer could vary that policy whenever he thought the facts of a particular situation warranted it, the bank would become unmanageable. We do leave him some room to make trade-offs. If he gets a large down payment, for example, he can be more liberal about the maturity of the mortgage and the credit standing of the customer. But we don't want him tinkering with interest rates or the security for the mortgage."

Shop around for terms. In negotiating for your home mortgage, however, you are not limited to dealing with a single bank. Policy among banks is not the same, and one bank may provide more acceptable terms than another. You can "shop" among banks much as you shop for a car.

⌂ CHECKLIST

THE COMPOSITION OF THE MORTGAGE

Although the annual mortgage payments remain constant throughout the term of the mortgage, they are made up of both interest and principal; the ratio of interest to principal shifts every time a payment is made.

There is a direct relationship between the installment payments and the maturity date of the mortgage—the longer the maturity, the smaller the installment payments; and the shorter the maturity, the larger the installment payments.

Interest on the mortgage:
- is the major component of the payment in the first years but will gradually decline as the principal of the mortgage is repaid. The rate of decline will vary with the maturity of the mortgage; the earlier the maturity, the faster the decline.
- is tax deductible. The aftertax cost of interest will depend upon the tax bracket of the borrower. The higher his bracket, the lower his aftertax cost.

Principal payments on the mortgage:
- gradually rise in proportion to the decline in interest payments.
- are not tax deductible, but build up equity in the home that may be converted into cash by selling the home or refinancing the mortgage.

I am using the term *bank* to refer to lending institutions that provide money for real estate mortgages, and, in the case of home mortgages, particularly to refer to savings and loan associations, mutual savings banks, and commercial banks.

Savings and loan associations; mutual savings banks. Savings and loan associations and mutual savings banks are major sources of money for home mortgages. Their funds come primarily from the savings of individual depositors, and they are the most likely place to obtain a mortgage upon the most reasonable terms.

Commercial banks. Commercial banks include such giants of the banking industry as Citicorp, Bank of America, and Chase Manhattan. While they engage in many other areas of lending, including commercial loans to major industrial companies and equipment loans for oil tankers and aircraft fleets, they are also a significant source of money for mortgages on one- to four-family homes.

Other institutions. There are other financial institutions such as insurance companies, pension funds, and real estate investment trusts, which give or invest in real estate mortgages (including home mortgages); but their mortgages are primarily for large apartment projects and other commercial properties.

Mortgage companies (sometimes referred to as mortgage bankers) also arrange home mortgages, particularly mortgages insured or guaranteed by the Federal Housing Administration and the Veterans Administration. However, they are not usually the actual lenders. Instead, after originating the mortgages, they normally sell them to various lending institutions and government agencies, which thereby provide the money to fund these mortgages.

Bank laws and flexibility. Beyond any internal policies banks might have, they are subject to federal and state statutory and regulatory restrictions on the size and maturity of home mortgages and on the interest rates they can charge (although restrictions on interest rates, known as usury laws, have in most jurisdictions been lifted or liberalized).

Despite these restrictions, the banks have considerable leeway in their lending practices; and it is important that you are aware of what terms are negotiable, what the "trade-offs" are, and how and whether these trade-offs should be made.

Mortgage Terms to Negotiate

The major terms of the mortgage you will be negotiating with a bank are:

- the down payment,
- the interest rate,
- the amount of each installment payment,
- the maturity date,

- the right to pay off the mortgage before it matures (referred to as the prepayment right),
- points,
- balloon payment, and
- assumption of your mortgage.

Each time I bought a home, I made at least a 20% down payment, not because I am a traditionalist or a conservative, but because the bank insisted upon it. With a few exceptions, the bank will not give more than an 80% mortgage (even though it may be authorized by law to lend more than 80%).

I could have made a down payment of more than 20% and there would have been some advantages. It certainly would have made my bank happier, increasing its security for the loan. But unless I was an uncommon altruist, with rather questionable feelings of affection toward the bank, I should have demanded more for my money. With a large down payment (more than 20%), the bank might have been willing to extend the length of the mortgage by as much, possibly, as five years, and so reduce the amount I had to pay to them each month. The bank might also have agreed (although with much more reluctance) to a slight reduction in the interest rate.

Larger down payment. Assume, for example, you made a $20,000 down payment, or 20%, on a $100,000 home. The mortgage would be in the amount of $80,000, at 10% interest, with a 25-year maturity. If you had made a $30,000 down payment, or 30%, you might have been able to extend the maturity to 30 years and reduce the amount of the installment payments on the mortgage. You might also have persuaded the bank to lower your interest rate to 9.875%. However, I doubt whether it would have been worth tying up an additional $10,000 of your money by making the larger down payment in return for these benefits—keeping in mind that the difference between 10% and 9.875% on each $10,000 of the mortgage is only $12.50 a year before taxes; for someone in the 40% bracket, it is $7.50 after taxes. And the annual installment payment for each $10,000 of a 30-year mortgage at 9.875% is $1,049.75, as compared with $1,101.68 on a 25-year mortgage at 10%—a difference of only $51.93, even without considering the aftertax effect of the payment.

Mortgage interest rates. Interest rates are much more difficult to negotiate with the bank. "When it comes to how much you put down and how long we will give you to pay off your mortgage," I was told by the lending officer of a savings and loan association, "we can be reasonably sympathetic to your problems. But not when it comes to interest rates. Here we've got to look at it from our point of view—our cost of money and of doing business. We also have to consider how much money we have to lend. Interest rates are our bread and butter. We've got to hang tough on them. I wish people would understand this. I am a nice man, and I get tired of being looked at as the enemy."

I, too, am a nice man, and after this appeal I tried to empathize with him and look at interest rates from his point of view. His problems start with the fact that the interest rate has to cover his bank's cost of money.

The bank has to "buy" most of the money it invests in home mortgages by borrowing from its depositors. Their savings deposits are short-term loans on which the bank has to pay interest. However, the interest the bank has to pay on these deposits (in order to attract and retain them) will fluctuate, rising and falling with changes in the economy. By contrast, the interest rate on your mortgage has, traditionally, been fixed. If you obtain a 10% mortgage from the bank, interest remains at 10% over the full term of the mortgage (which may be as long as 30 years), despite the fact that the interest the bank has to pay on savings deposits may, at some time in the future, exceed 10%. So, the bank has to set mortgage interest at a rate that is higher than is necessary to cover its cost of money today.

In other words, mortgage interest is not simply a reflection of conditions as they now exist; it is also a prediction of the future. And you can expect the bank to err on the side of overestimating rising costs rather than underestimating them. Banks are, however, moving away from fixed mortgage-interest rates, in an attempt to keep mortgages in phase with savings deposits (more on this in chapter 4).

The mortgage-interest rate also must cover the bank's other costs of doing business—its administrative and operating expenses, and compensation for taking a credit risk (the possibility that you may default—fail to make the mortgage payments). Furthermore, the banks want to make a profit. A bank, like General Motors and IBM, is not a charitable institution. It is in business to make money—as much money as the marketplace and government regulation will allow.

Mortgage-interest rates are also a function of supply and demand. Money is a commodity. The more money a bank has to invest in mortgages in relation to demand, the lower its interest rate will be. The converse is, of course, also true. The lower the supply in relation to demand, the more the bank will charge for interest.

The federal government (particularly through the Federal Reserve System) is the prime force in determining the money supply. Through various mechanisms the government can control the amount of money that will be available to the banks for lending. When the government constricts the money supply (a policy which is supposed to curb inflation), it is said that the economy is in a period of "tight money."

Whether or not this policy effectively combats inflation (or, as I suspect, adds to it), it can create intense competition for money, which in turn drives up interest rates on home mortgages—precisely what the country has witnessed and suffered through during the late 1970s and early 1980s.

These several factors cannot be put into a simple or precise formula that will tell you, at any given moment, what the interest rate will be. Indeed, if there is a formula, it is one of the bank's better-kept secrets. It is more likely that the mortgage interest rate set by the bank ultimately will be determined by what the marketplace will tolerate.

Setting these rates has become more of a problem for banks in recent years because the demands of depositors have become increasingly volatile. They will quickly withdraw their funds if they can get a better return on their money elsewhere (by investing, for example, in government or corporate securities). As one frustrated banker put it: "Depositors have become more sophisticated about the workings of the money market. Some of my colleagues seem to admire this. Maybe they're right, but I think our banking customers are developing all the virtues of dogs, other than loyalty."

Despite the needs and problems of the bank, I was advised by a fierce critic of the banking system that "it takes the emotional strength of a saint to sympathize with the banks' control over interest rates. Whenever you start to feel sorry for the banks, just remember that you're the one who has to borrow. It's the banks that have the money. You don't, and you've got to dance to their tune. The banks are like the president of a major corporation who pulls out a salary of over one million dollars, yet complains about the high cost of labor."

There is one situation in which the bank may be willing to reduce the interest rate: if you pay "points." Points are, in effect, interest paid in advance—on the day you get your mortgage.

Points. Each point is 1% of the amount of the mortgage; so on a $80,000 mortgage, one point is $800. Paying one point means that you are prepaying $800 of interest. As a matter of mathematics, one point on a 25-year mortgage at 10% interest ($800 on a $80,000 mortgage) is the equivalent of approximately 0.13% in interest rate. (It will be the equivalent of slightly more on a 20-year mortgage and slightly less on a 30-year mortgage.) Therefore, the 10% rate of interest being charged by the bank can be reduced to 9.87% (a reduction of 0.13%) by paying the bank one "point."

Points and tax deductions. The advantage of points is that they are usually tax deductible in the year you pay them, so long as the mortgage is on your principal residence and the number of points is not excessive—that is, they do not exceed the amount generally charged on home mortgages in your geographic area and the payment of points is an established business practice in that area. So if you pay one point on the $80,000 mortgage, you can deduct $800 extra in the first year. Assuming that interest would have been 10% without points, your interest deduction in the first year would have been $8,000 (10% of $80,000). If you reduce the interest rate to 9.87% by paying one point, your total interest deduction that year would increase to $8,696—9.87% of $80,000 plus $800 (1% of $80,000).

In succeeding years, the interest deduction would be less on a 9.87% mortgage than on a 10% mortgage. But by paying the point, you have accelerated both your interest payments and your tax savings; and one of the immutable laws of money is that one dollar of tax savings today is always worth more than a dollar of tax savings next year.

Disadvantages of points. But there are disadvantages to paying points, and I was alerted to them by my lawyer, when he said: "Remember, you don't win them. You pay them." You increase your "up-front" costs by paying points, just as you would by making a larger down payment. But unlike the down payment, points do not increase the equity in your home. They are usually interest, not principal.

Whatever your preference, the bank may insist upon the payment of points. They are a device for increasing the bank's effective return on the mortgage without having to change its publicly stated interest rate. The bank may want to charge you more than the state rate (either because you are more of a credit risk than the average homebuyer or because it perceives that interest rates in the marketplace are going to rise in the near future); but for reasons of competition or public relations it may prefer to act indirectly, increasing its profits without raising its stated interest rate.

The president of a local savings bank once told me that every bank wants to appear to be a leader in the community, except "when it comes to raising interest rates. On taking the lead in raising rates, we are all cowards—shameless and abject cowards. Unlike the infantry commander who says, 'Follow me,' we abjure heroics and live by the rule: 'After you.' "

The way for the bank to have its cake and eat it is to charge points and leave the interest rate alone. In the example of the 25-year, $80,000 mortgage, the bank may want to keep interest at 10%, but get a return of 10.26%. The solution is to charge two points, or $1,600.

As you have seen, the amount of each installment payment on the mortgage and the maturity date are closely connected. While most home mortgages mature within 20 to 30 years, many banks are increasingly insisting upon shorter maturities (15 years or less) in order to cut down the period over which they are "locked into" fixed interest rates. If the bank does require a short maturity, the installment payments can and should, nevertheless, be kept low—as if the mortgage were for 20 to 30 years. This is how it is done:

The annual installment payment on a $80,000 mortgage bearing interest at 10% will be $8,813.45 if it matures in 25 years, and $10,517.90 if it matures in 15 years—a difference of $1,704.45. The bank may want the 15-year maturity, but you may not be able to afford the increase in each installment payment.

Balloon payments. The solution is to provide that the amount of each installment payment will be the same as it would have been on a 25-year mortgage ($8,813.45), even though the mortgage matures in 15 years. At the end of the fifteenth year, $26,000 of the principal will have been repaid, and there will be a balance due on the mortgage of approximately $54,000 ($80,000 minus $26,000). The $54,000 is called the "balloon payment"—the amount of the principal that remains to be paid at maturity. This approach helps to accommodate conflicting goals—the bank's desire for a shorter maturity, and yours for reasonable installment payments.

Does that mean that you will have to pay the bank $54,-000 in one lump sum? The answer is yes. But before you faint, let me show you how painless reality can be.

I am not a stranger to this type of mortgage. When I bought my first home, in Montclair, my bank required a 15-year maturity. It was, the bank explained to me, a "compromise." Maybe it was, but for me it was an intimidating compromise. The balloon payment was a specter that accompanied me until I finally sold the house. What was going to happen to me at the end of 15 years?

Among other things, inflation happened to me—helping to hold up the value of my home so that, when I sold it, the selling price covered my mortgage balance by a comfortable margin. But until then, I had worried that the value of my home would go into a steep decline.

How valid was my concern? A look at the trend of housing costs over the past ten years shows that my fears were unfounded. The probabilities are that the value of your home, like mine, will increase or at least remain stable. In this event, you will have no trouble making the balloon payment: you should be able to get either a 10-year extension of the mortgage from your bank or a new mortgage from another bank having at least a 10-year maturity (although, probably, at a different interest rate).

If the cost of your home had been $100,000 with a $80,000 (or 80%) mortgage and a $20,000 down payment, then, after 15 years, when the mortgage reached maturity, the equity in the house would have grown to $46,000 (the original $20,000 down payment plus the $26,000 of equity buildup). You would, in effect, be able to use this $46,000 of equity as a down payment in obtaining a new mortgage of $54,000 (a mortgage of almost 50% of the original cost of your home); and the proceeds of the $54,000 mortgage would be used to pay off the balloon payment. A bank will rarely miss the opportunity to lend against such comfortable security. However, there is no certainty that home values will not go down over a 15-year period. Therefore, there is always some risk, which you should be aware of, that the value of your home will not cover the balloon payment. You will, nevertheless, still have to pay it.

A less remote risk with the 15-year balloon-payment mortgage is that you may have to pay more than the original 10% interest rate on the extended or new mortgage. That revised interest rate will reflect market conditions existing 15 years from the time of purchase. The bank, by shortening the maturity, will thus get "another look" at interest rates—but, keep in mind, so will you.

Prepayment. Actually you can get more than one extra look at interest rates, if you have the right to pay off—or "prepay"—your mortgage before it matures.

The prepayment right is your trump card; and you should not give it up in negotiating with the bank—particularly in times of high interest rates. A client once said to me, when we completed negotiations with his bank for a mortgage: "I feel like I have just been to a gambling casino. I was playing against the house and the house never loses." But in his irritation, he forgot to extend the analogy. He has two advantages: the casino can't throw him out, and he can always leave voluntarily and go to another one.

Similarly, the bank is bound to the mortgage (and a fixed interest rate) until the maturity date; but with the prepayment right, you can monitor interest rates and choose the best time to pay off the mortgage.

There are at least three situations in which you may want or need to exercise this right.

The first relates, of course, to interest. If you have a mortgage at 10% interest and interest rates decline below 10% over the next few years, you can take advantage of the lower rates by prepaying your existing mortgage and obtaining a new one either from your present bank or another bank. (This advice becomes more compelling if the interest rate you start with is 15% rather than 10%.) This combination of steps—prepaying your existing mortgage and replacing it with a new one—is known as "refinancing."

Assumption of your mortgage. Second, you may want to sell your home. This may not be possible unless you can prepay the mortgage, since the purchaser may want his own mortgage if he can get better terms elsewhere. And even if he were willing to accept your mortgage, you would (unless the bank released you) continue to be bound on an obligation that, after the sale, would be on someone else's home. In this connection, you should try to get your bank to agree that if you sell your home before the maturity date, your buyer can take over, or assume, your mortgage—even if you have to remain liable for it. Banks are increasingly reluctant and resistant to allow this and, in fact, may require that you repay the mortgage at the time you sell your home. If, however, a buyer can assume your mortgage it will be much easier to sell your house during periods of high interest rates. If, for example, your mortgage interest rate was 10% when you bought your home and, since then, market rates have gone up to 15%, you will be able to command a higher price from your buyer if you can deliver to him, along with your home, your mortgage at 10% interest.

Third, you may want to prepay in order to turn your equity buildup into cash. For instance, on a $100,000 home with a $80,000 mortgage that over 15 years has been paid down to $54,000 of remaining principal, the buildup of equity is $26,000. By refinancing—prepaying the $54,000 balance of your existing mortgage by obtaining a new mortgage of $80,000—you will net $26,000 from the transaction ($80,000 minus $54,000). A new $80,000 mortgage may put you back to square one, but you will be standing there $26,000 richer.

Refinancing. Refinancing has been described as "one of those dreams where you find money lying around on the street, waiting for you to pick it up and stuff it in your pocket." It can be more than a fantasy, if the value of your home has gone up. In the example of the $100,000 home and the $80,000 mortgage (an 80% mortgage), let us assume again that the mortgage has been paid down to $54,000 and the value of your home has appreciated to $125,000. If the bank applies the same ratio of mortgage to value (80%), you should be able to obtain a new mortgage of $100,000 (80% of $125,000), and, after paying the $54,000 balance on the original mortgage, you will keep $46,000 in cash. You will, of course, have to make larger installment payments on the new mortgage, and the interest rate may be higher.

You may want to refinance in order to cover the cost of renovations or other improvements. If, for example, you renovate your kitchen for $25,000, you may be able to borrow all or most of the cost by prepaying your existing mortgage and obtaining a new one. In this situation, the amount a bank will lend you will depend upon your equity in the home and its value as renovated. The terms of the new mortgage will reflect current market conditions, and you may have to pay a higher rate of interest than you are now paying. While you should explore your refinancing plans with several banks in order to get the best mortgage terms, you should first approach the bank holding your existing mortgage. It may be more willing than the others to offer you concessions on interest and other terms when your reason for refinancing is to renovate your home.

There are other approaches to financing home improvements. You may be able to get a personal loan from the bank. Typically, it will be for not more than $5,000 to $15,000, will mature within 5 to 10 years, and will carry an extremely high interest rate, although you may be able to get better terms if you are using the money for insulation or other energy-related improvements. (You may also be entitled to an income-tax credit of up to $300 if you install an energy-saving device in your home, such as insulation and storm windows and storm doors. Additionally, if you install a solar device or other renewable energy source on your property, the credit can be as high as $4,000. Your accountant can tell you whether you are eligible for the credit. If you are, the credit can be subtracted from the income tax you would otherwise have to pay.)

Some banks may also give you a second mortgage for home improvements—although they are frequently unable or reluctant to do so—but it will be at a very high rate of interest and will generally mature within 10 to 15 years. (I'll discuss second mortgages further in chapter 4.)

Another way of dealing with renovations is to plan them at the time you purchase your home. For example, if you buy a $75,000 home that needs $25,000 worth of improvements (making the total cost $100,000), your bank may be willing to give you a mortgage based upon the $100,000 total. In this case, however, the bank will probably advance the money in stages. If you take an 80% mortgage ($80,000), the bank may give you 80% of the initial $75,000 purchase price ($60,000) when you purchase the home, and advance the remaining $20,000 as the renovation progresses.

Whether you refinance in order to convert your equity buildup into cash or in order to cover the cost of improving or renovating your home, you will undoubtedly incure additional administrative and legal fees and other incidental costs in obtaining the new mortgage.

"Prepayment privilege" and fees. Furthermore, you will, in many cases, have to pay a fee or premium when you prepay your exising mortgage (whether or not for the purpose of refinancing). The right to prepay is often referred to as the "prepayment privilege." And when I used this expression, I was told by someone wiser and more experienced that I was letting the terminology confuse me. " A privilege," he told me, "is a gift—something you get for nothing. And banks don't give gifts. Why should they? You pay for the right to prepay." The amount of the premium will vary depending upon the type of bank and where it is located; but it will often be equal to two to six months' interest on the unpaid balance of the mortgage. The bank may also restrict your right to prepay for a minimum period of time, if it is not prevented from doing so by the laws of the state in which your home is located. For example, it may not allow prepayment for a year or two after you have obtained the mortgage, particularly if your reason for prepaying is to refinance at a lower interest rate.

Purchase Conditioned Upon Obtaining Mortgage

One other consideration to keep in mind is that you are not going to start serious negotiations with a bank for a mortgage until you find the home you want to buy. Therefore, there should be a provision in the purchase-and-sale agreement with your seller that your obligation to purchase the home is conditioned upon your obtaining a commitment from a bank to give you the mortgage. While timing can be a delicate issue with the seller, you should insist upon at least three to four weeks in which either to find an acceptable mortgage or to terminate your agreement to buy. If you have to terminate, any deposit you have made on the home should be returned to you.

⌂ CHECKLIST

EIGHT POINTS YOU SHOULD BE PREPARED
TO NEGOTIATE ON THE MORTGAGE

Down payment   Usually between 20% to 30% of
the purchase price. If you can afford the monthly installment payments on the mortgage, try to keep it
closer to 20%.

Interest   You may be able to get a lower rate, if you
make a larger down payment.

Installment payments   The lower your interest rate
and the longer the maturity of your mortgage, the
smaller these payments will be.

Maturity   Avoid a maturity of less than 25 years
and, if you want to keep your installment payment
low, try for 30 years.

Prepayment   Never give up this right, even if you
have to pay a premium to exercise it.

Points   From a tax standpoint you may be better off
if, in return for paying points, you can get a lower interest rate.

Balloon payment   Paying this shouldn't worry you
unless there is a sharp decline in the value of your
home.

Assumption of your mortgage   Try to get your bank
to agree in advance that a buyer can assume your
mortgage, because it should make it easier for you to
sell your home during periods of high interest rates.
Banks are increasingly reluctant to let you have this
right.

There is, of course, another side to this problem. You may be the seller instead of the buyer. You should make sure that your buyer is not being fanciful about the terms of the mortgage he is trying to obtain. If his purchase is subject to getting a 10% mortgage when current rates are 15%, he won't get it and both you and he will be wasting time. But if he is realistic, you will not be taking any undue risk by waiting; and, in this case, you probably would be unwise to accept a lower price from someone else just because the second prospect is ready with his check.

For the vast majority of men and women, owning a home would be an unattainable dream if the bulk of the cost could not be borrowed. Borrowing to buy a home is, like death and marriage, a common experience; but also like death and marriage, it remains intensely personal. When you obtain a mortgage, you are making a commitment that will bind you for at least several years; and it is a commitment that will, to a great extent, define your priorities and limit your other financial activities and options. Therefore, it is a step having serious implications that can extend far beyond the purchase of a home. Perhaps, in an imperfect world where any choice constrains others, it is a step that has to be frightening—but it is not a step that should or has to be dominated by fear. Knowledge of the mortgage process—breaking it down into its separate parts—can go far in alleviating the inevitable pain and tension that are part of buying a home, and can help to make it an intelligent investment.

Four

CREATIVE FINANCING— VARIATIONS ON THE MORTGAGE THEME

ALTHOUGH I WAS NOT AWARE OF IT AT THE TIME, MY first purchase of a home, in 1960, was more than a private act. I was helping to fulfill a long-standing goal of public policy. At least as far back as 1932, when Franklin D. Roosevelt decried the fact that one-third of the nation was ill-housed, the single-family home has been part of the American Dream. And it is the rare politician who disputes its inviolability, despite the fact that the word *Dream* more nearly describes the reality than the actual physical facts.

By some estimates only about 15% of all families in the United States today can afford to buy an average home, as compared with 30% ten years ago. By the same token, I would guess that proportionately more people can afford a second car and a color television set today than could a decade ago. I am openly skeptical about estimates of what people can or cannot afford because this frequently is an issue of what they are willing to give up. Today, you may have to give up more than you had to ten years ago; but whether it will be worth the sacrifice is probably more a matter of personal priorities than of statistical analysis.

Nevertheless, one fact seems clear: For most people the accessibility of a single-family home will depend upon the availability of mortgage financing on reasonable terms. With few exceptions, unless a person can borrow at least 70% to 80% of the cost, a home will be beyond his means. This becomes a more severe problem when interest rates are rising, because a bank may be less willing to lend a high percentage of the cost (75% or more) if it feels that the mortgage payments will create too great a financial strain on the borrower. Therefore, his down payment may have to be more.

In view of this need to borrow in order to buy a home, a major concern of federal and state governments has been how to encourage banks to invest in home mortgages and how to get them to increase the amount they will lend. Among the approaches have been the so-called low-down-payment mortgages and the alternative mortgage instruments.

As you saw in the last chapter, when you negotiate a mortgage with a bank, you are negotiating over specific terms. But the area of negotiation has been (and continues to be) relatively narrow, with most mortgages covering between 70% and 80% of the cost, a fixed interest rate, a maturity of between 20 and 30 years, and equal installment payments that consist of interest and principal.

These terms may, however, be too confining, for both you and the bank. As a result, variations of the standard mortgage have been and are being developed, and are becoming more available. The most important of these are:

- the VA mortgage (guaranteed by the Veterans Administration),
- the FHA mortgage (insured by the Federal Housing Administration),
- the privately insured mortgage (insured by a private mortgage-insurance company),
- the variable-rate mortgage,
- the roll-over mortgage (also called the renegotiable-rate mortgage),
- the graduated-payment mortgage,
- the reverse-annuity mortgage,
- the shared-appreciation mortgage,
- the growth-equity mortgage,
- the second mortgage.

Some of these mortgages (such as the VA and the FHA mortgages) have existed for many years; others are relatively new and, in some cases, are still in the experimental stage.

Insured Mortgages

Insured mortgages—mortgages insured by the Veterans

Administration, by the Federal Housing Administration, or by private mortgage-insurance companies—are designed primarily for the person who is unable to make a large down payment. These mortgages will, ordinarily, cover between 85% to 95% of the cost of a home (depending upon the type of mortgage), so that the down payment can be less than 20%.

While each of these types of mortgage is different, they have several features in common. You actually obtain an insured mortgage from a bank; it is not given by the Veterans Administration, the Federal Housing Administration, or a private mortgage-insurance company. The VA, FHA, and the private companies are insurers—they do not lend money to you or the bank. They insure the bank against loss in the event that you default on the mortgage. The form of the insurance, and the protection it affords to the bank, will differ with each type of mortgage; but, in each case, the insurance (referred to as a guarantee in the case of a VA mortgage) adds significantly to the bank's security. As a result, the bank may be able and willing to give you more than an 80% mortgage without violating any legal restrictions or its own policy.

The VA and FHA mortgage may also be obtained from a mortgage company (a "mortgage banker"), particularly in the case of a newly built home. The mortgage company is known as a financial intermediary; that is, it will usually not be putting up the mortgage funds for more than a short period, but will sell the mortgage to a bank or other lending institution, including an agency of the federal government. You can find out about a mortgage company from your bank, your real estate broker, or the person selling you the home.

VA Mortgages

Irving Berlin might have modified his lament in the song "You're in the Army Now" if he had known that Congress, in 1944, was going to pass legislation that would allow banks to give World War II veterans "low-down-payment" home mortgages that would be guaranteed by the Veterans Administration. Later these VA mortgages were extended to veterans of the Korean conflict. Today they are available to all veterans who have been in active service, including Vietnam veterans.

VA mortgage eligibility. In order to be eligible, a veteran of

World War II, the Korean conflict, or Vietnam must have served at least 90 days of active duty. All other veterans must have served on active duty for more than 180 days. (Others eligible for the mortgage benefits include any person who has been disabled during service or as a result of a service-connected disability; and the spouse of any person who was killed or is missing in action, who died from a service-connected disability, or who has been a prisoner of war for at least 90 days.)

Someone once referred to VA mortgages as the "country's way of saying 'thank you' to our boys who have served with honor." Despite its unctuous flavor, the statement is accurate. But the VA mortgage is more than just a symbolic thank-you—it can be a very attractive method of financing.

I am a veteran, having served honorably from 1956 to 1958 in the suburbs of Chicago. This entitles me to a VA mortgage, which can be issued in any amount so long as it does not exceed the reasonable value of my home. In 1981 the average VA mortgage value was approximately $55,000. Although you may have to make a 5% to 10% down payment, a VA mortgage can, by law, cover 100% of the cost of your home; and in many cases you may not have to make any down payment, even though your purchase price exceeds $100,000.

Under the Veterans Administration's limited guarantee, the VA agrees to reimburse the bank for a loss resulting from a default on the mortgage. The amount of the guarantee is 60% of the mortgage or $27,500, whichever is less; and the bank bears the risk of any loss not covered by the guarantee.

With the protection of a VA guarantee, the bank can be liberal in granting mortgage terms—particularly with respect to the down payment. A VA mortgage customarily matures in 30 years. The veteran can, at any time, prepay all or any part of the mortgage without penalty. And, adding proof to the old refrain that "the best things in life are free," neither the veteran nor the bank has to pay a fee or premium to the Veterans Administration for the guarantee.

The VA mortgage is not, necessarily, a "low-interest" mortgage. While the stated interest rate (which is established by the Veterans Administration) is normally below the market rate charged on conventional home mortgages, the bank can narrow or eliminate this difference by charging points.

The bank can charge only one of these points to the

veteran as a loan-orientation fee (which, in this form, will not be tax deductible). But the bank can, and frequently does, circumvent this restriction by charging additional points to the seller. And in times of rising interest rates, the bank might charge as many as eight to ten points if the Veterans Administration is slow to increase the maximum rate that can be charged on a VA mortgage and it thus lags behind market rates.

In this situation, the price charged by the seller will undoubtedly reflect the cost to the seller of having to pay points.

In refusing the opportunity to get a VA mortgage, I suffered from a deep-seated (and irrational) fear of retaining any connection with the United States Army, which can probably be understood only by those who have been involuntarily drafted into the armed services. But, in so refusing, I overlooked the several advantages of a VA mortgage—the low down payment, a maturity that can be as long as 30 years and 32 days, the right to prepay without a penalty, and the fact that the Veterans Administration does not charge for the guarantee.

I even could have taken advantage of a VA mortgage more than once. If I had sold my home and satisfied my mortgage obligations, I would have been eligible for another VA mortgage on any home I bought in the future.

VA drawbacks. One drawback of a VA mortgage, as mentioned, is the effect points may have on the purchase price of a home. Furthermore, it may take longer to process a VA mortgage than a conventional mortgage. By some estimates it may take 30 days or more because of the administrative detail involved. Nevertheless, a VA mortgage can be one of the best ways to finance your home—even a home that costs over $100,000—so long as you are willing to join the armed services in order to be eligible.

FHA Mortgages

An FHA mortgage also allows for a low down payment. You get the mortgage from the bank, and the FHA insures the bank against any loss arising out of your default. This insurance protection enables the bank to accept a down payment that is usually around 5% to 10%. (The mortgage can be as high as 97% of the first $25,000 of value of your home and

95% of the value in excess of $25,000. It can even be somewhat higher if you are a veteran.)

Unlike my rejection of a VA mortgage, I did not refuse an FHA mortgage. Rather, I never even considered one. I assumed, sharing in a widespread misconception, that it was a "poor folk's mortgage." I was wrong. This mortgage—known as a "Section 203(b)" mortgage—is normally available to anyone who can meet the ordinary credit requirements of the bank.

FHA ceiling. However, there is a ceiling on an FHA mortgage. The maximum mortgage on a single-family home that the FHA will insure under the section 203(b) program is $67,500. The FHA is, however, authorized to increase this ceiling to as high as $90,000 on single-family homes in those areas of the country where middle- and moderate-income persons have limited housing opportunities as a result of the high cost of homes. You should check with your local FHA office to find out which ceiling applies to your area.

In 1981 the average FHA mortgage was approximately $43,000 for an existing home and $55,000 for a new one.

The maturity of an FHA mortgage is usually 30 years, and may be as long as 35 years for a home under construction. The mortgage may be prepaid without penalty.

FHA and points. As with a VA mortgage, the stated interest rate will usually be below market rates, but again, points can eliminate this apparent advantage by being reflected in the purchase price for the home when market rates move too far ahead of the FHA rate. (And like a VA mortgage, only one of these points can be charged directly to the buyer, in the form of a loan-origination fee.)

Unlike the VA guarantee, the insurance on an FHA mortgage is not free. The FHA customarily charges an annual insurance premium of 0.5% of the outstanding principal amount of the mortgage. As a result, when you combine the interest, points, and insurance premium, your effective cost can be more than that on a conventional mortgage. (The FHA has recently been authorized to charge a one-time fee for the insurance, instead of periodic premiums.)

The obvious benefits of an FHA mortgage are the low down payment, the long maturity, and the prepayment right.

FHA drawbacks. These benefits may be tarnished by several facts: FHA insurance premiums add to your carrying costs; points can increase your purchase price; and, as with a VA mortgage, it may take more time to process an FHA mortgage than a conventional one.

Privately Insured Mortgages

Charles Wilson, President Eisenhower's Secretary of Defense and former president of General Motors, made the statement, "What's good for the country is good for General Motors, and vice versa." Nothing he did or said, before or after this remark, brought him closer to immortality. It was his affirmation of the proposition that private industry was more effective than the government. Without arguing the merits of his contention, it is clear that private industry has come up with an alternative to the VA and FHA mortgage—the privately insured mortgage.

This type of mortgage is actually a conventional mortgage, with one exception. You can make a down payment of less than 20%—usually 5% to 15%; and there is usually no ceiling on the principal amount of the mortgage other than that imposed by or upon the bank. You get such a mortgage from your bank, and it is insured by a private mortgage-insurance company (instead of the VA or FHA).

The coverage will usually insure the first 20% to 25% of the mortgage. If you default on a $60,000 mortgage, the insurance will protect the bank against up to the first $12,000 of loss in the case of 20% coverage, or up to the first $15,000 of loss in the case of 25% coverage. The bank itself still suffers that part of a loss exceeding the insured amount.

You will have to pay for the insurance, and the premiums will be added to your mortgage installment payments. While there are a variety of premium payment plans, the premium on a 90% mortgage with 20% coverage is customarily between 0.5% and 1.0% of the original mortgage amount in the first year, and 0.25% of the mortgage balance in each subsequent year.

The bank may not require continued insurance coverage once the balance of the mortgage drops below a certain level—for example, below 80% of the value of your home.

A privately insured mortgage may be more expensive than a VA or FHA mortgage, and the amount of the down payment may be somewhat larger. However, you do not have to

⌂ CHECKLIST

SIX CONSIDERATIONS IN CHOOSING AMONG THE LOW-DOWN-PAYMENT MORTAGAGES

Insurance premiums   If you are a veteran, the VA mortgage is the best bargain because, unlike an FHA or privately insured mortgage, you don't have to pay a premium.

Down payment   Again, the VA mortgage may be the best choice because you may not have to make any down payment. With an FHA mortgage, the down payment will usually be about 5% to 10%, and in the case of a privately insured mortgage it will usually be 5% to 15%.

Mortgage amount   The FHA mortgage is limited to $67,500 (although it may be higher in many areas of the country). There are fewer restrictions on the size of a VA or a privately insured mortgage.

Maturity   The FHA and VA mortgage usually have about a 30-year maturity, which helps to lower your installment payments. The maturity of a privately insured mortgage will generally depend upon bank policy and legal requirements.

Points   Points may be charged on an FHA or VA mortgage in order to narrow or eliminate the difference between the allowable interest rate and the market rate. Keep in mind that these points may be reflected in the price you pay for the home.

Processing time   The advantage, in this case, belongs to the privately insured mortgage. The processing time will usually be shorter than for an FHA or a VA mortgage.

join the Army, Navy, or Air Force to be eligible for it, and there are few restrictions on the size of the mortgage that will be insured. Obtaining such insurance is also a model of simplicity. If you meet the bank's standard credit requirements, a commitment for private mortgage insurance can usually be obtained within a day or two of applying for it. Private mortgage-insurance companies will also insure many of the newer types of mortgage (which I will discuss shortly), whereas the FHA and VA are more restrictive in the coverage they provide.

The volume of privately insured mortgages has increased dramatically over the last several years. In 1970 about 7% of all insured mortgages on one- to four-family (nonfarm) homes were privately insured. In 1981 this percentage reached approximately 53%.

In addition to the insured mortgages, several new forms of mortgage have recently become available to home buyers in many parts of the country. This has moved an officer of a Boston savings bank to complain that "the changes taking place in the home mortgage market make me feel like I am in the middle of the first major revolution since the Bolsheviks took over Russia."

I can sympathize with him, given the onslaught of acronyms reminiscent of the New Deal—ROMs (roll-over mortgages), VRMs (variable-rate mortgages), GPMs (graduated-payment mortgages), RAMs (reverse-annuity mortgages), SAMs (shared-appreciation mortgages), and GEMs (growth-equity mortgages). And these types of mortgages, although they each serve a different purpose, are lumped together under the collective label "alternative mortgage instruments"—which, in further desecration of the English language, has been compressed into "AMIs."

The roll-over and variable-rate mortgages are sometimes known as adjustable mortgage loan instruments, and they deal with the bank's problem of being locked into a fixed interest rate on a long-term mortgage. Under these instruments, the bank can, within defined limits, vary the interest rate to correspond with fluctuations in the marketplace.

The graduated-payment mortgage and the reverse-annuity mortgage are designed to meet the changing needs of people at different financial stages. The graduated-payment mortgage appeals, primarily, to the young family with a modest income today, but with "great expectations" for the future. It provides for low mortgage payments in the early years, which rise (or "graduate") in later years. The reverse-annuity mortgage is directed to the older person (usually in his sixties) who bought a home many years ago and has built up a substantial equity. Under this mortgage, he receives periodic payments from the bank that are secured by his equity buildup.

The shared-appreciation mortgage allows the bank to share in any appreciation in the value of your home.

The growth-equity mortgage is a technique enabling the bank to have the mortgage repaid over a relatively short period of time through increasing principal payments.

If these new mortgage instruments have brought about a revolution, it is not because they represent a new technology. It is because they allow for choices. As another banker told me: "It's not like going from propeller-driven airplanes to jet aircraft. These mortgages are simply variations of the mortgages we have always used. What is new is that we are beginning to give our customers a choice."

As we shall see, however, this array of alternatives may, in some cases, allow the bank—and not you—to do the choosing. For example, many banks are unwilling to give conventional mortgages (unless they are required to do so by law), insisting that you accept either a variable-rate or roll-over mortgage. Your choice, in these circumstances, is limited to going to another bank.

Before examining the alternative mortgage instruments, you should recognize that they are still in the experimental stage. They are not available everywhere; and, in some states, they are encountering considerable resistance. But the trend is clear: These mortgages are growing in acceptability and some of them will become, in time, part of the orthodoxy of home-mortgage financing.

There are literally hundreds of variations on these mortgages, particularly since recent federal regulations have liberalized the terms that can be imposed by federal savings and loan associations and federal mutual savings banks. While I have set out the general form of each, you should be aware that the terms can vary within a wide range.

Variable-rate mortgages. The variable-rate mortgage is one of the most common alternative mortgage instruments.

In most respects, variable-rate mortgages are similar to conventional mortgages; the terms and requirements of both regarding principal amount, down payment, maturity, and credit standing of the homeowner are comparable. But there is one important difference, which has become the center of a controversy: The interest rate on the variable-rate mortgage can be increased or decreased to correspond with changes in market conditions.

When you obtain a conventional mortgage, it has a fixed rate of interest for the entire term. With the variable-rate mortgage, the interest rate may change as often as once or twice a year, which led one businessman to complain: "I wouldn't take one of those damned mortgages. It's enough 'hat I have to worry about the line of credit for my business very time interest rates change. When I get home, I want to ¦lax. I don't want to have to bob and weave with interest tes on my own home."

While the provisions of any particular variable-rate mortgage may differ, the mechanics are generally as follows:

When you obtain the mortgage, the initial interest rate may be about 0.25% to 0.50% lower than that on a conventional mortgage (although the banks are reluctant to give this interest concession while mortgage money is scarce). So, if interest is 10% on a conventional mortgage, then it may start at between 9.50% and 9.75% on the variable-rate mortgage.

Let's assume that you and the bank agree that there will be no change in the rate for six months. Thereafter, the bank may adjust the rate periodically—as often as monthly—with no limit on the total increase or decrease except to the extent you and the bank may have negotiated a ceiling or a floor on the rate that can be charged.

The only limit (other than one negotiated between you and the bank) is that the rate adjustments are tied to an index, which you can readily verify and which is beyond the control of the bank; that is, it cannot be manipulated by actions or policies of the bank. Interest moves up or down with changes in the index, like a thermometer reacting to changes in the weather.

A downward movement in the index *requires* the bank to lower your interest rate. On the other hand, if an increase in the rate is indicated, the bank does *not* have to make the change. The bank might, for instance, waive the increase in order to avoid a prepayment of the mortgage (as discussed below) or to maintain good customer relations.

If the bank decides to increase the interest rate, it must

give you between 30 and 45 days' notice, and you customarily have a number of options.

First, you can accept the increase, and your future mortgage installment payments will be modified. Using the example of the variable-rate mortgage beginning at 9.5%, assume an original principal amount of $60,000 and a maturity of 30 years. Your mortgage installment payments (if they are calculated annually) will be approximately $6,100.84. If the rate is increased to 10% at the end of the first year, then, beginning with the second year, these payments will be $6,-360.90—an increase of $260.06 each year.

Second, instead of revising your installment payments, the bank may agree to extend the maturity of the mortgage for a period of up to 40 years. As a result, the additional cost of the rate increase will, in effect, be paid after the thirtieth year. Under this option, if the interest rate rises from 9.5% to 10.0% (using the same example), the installment payments would remain at $6,100.84, but the maturity of the mortgage would be extended by about 10 years (from the thirtieth to the fortieth year).

Third, you can reject the increase and prepay the mortgage—without any penalty.

The banks, for the most part, like the variable-rate mortgage because it does not lock them into a fixed rate of interest. But whether this mortgage is suitable for you is a more difficult question.

At first glance, it is seductive. Interest usually begins at a lower rate than on the conventional mortgage. Thereafter, however, you are speculating on the cost of money; and as an investment adviser once told me: "Don't try to outguess the money market. You'll lose. It's a game of who can outguess whom, you or the bank. And, in that game, the bank has to win."

Furthermore, if inflation has, in fact, become one of the certainties of life, you can expect that interest will, over the long term, go up rather than go down.

In order to avoid an endless upward spiral in the interest cost, you should, before you enter into one of these mortgages, negotiate a limit with the bank on how high the rate can go.

You should also ask the bank for a "side-by-side" comparison of the terms of the conventional versus the variable-rate

mortgage, showing the worst case—the maximum allowable
increases in the interest rate.

Roll-over, or renegotiable-rate, mortgages. The roll-over, or
renegotiable-rate, mortgage constitutes another approach to
avoiding fixed interest rates, and is a modification of the variable-rate mortgage. This mortgage provides for interest adjustments at periodic intervals—usually every three to five
years.

While the roll-over mortgage has been described as the
clone of the variable-rate mortgage, the fact is that it
predates the variable-rate mortgage by many years, having
been "alive and well" in Canada for several decades. It has,
up to now, been overlooked.

Recently, however, the roll-over mortgage has been "redis-
covered," and it may turn out to be the most promising alternative (or, depending upon your point of view, threat) to the
fixed-rate mortgage.

The name of this type of mortgage describes its process. It
is a short-term mortgage (having an original term of not
longer than five years) that can, at your option (and not the
bank's), be "rolled over," or extended, for additional periods
totaling up to 40 years.

If you had obtained, on January 1, 1982, a $60,000 roll-
over mortgage at 10% interest, with a 5-year initial term and
five optional terms of 5 years each (a total of 30 years), you
would have the right to extend the ultimate maturity date to
December 31, 2011. The successive terms would begin on
January 1 of 1987, 1992, 1997, 2002, and 2007. You could
not exercise all of the options on the same date, but only suc-
cessively, at each 5-year interval. And if you ever declined to
renew the mortgage, it would terminate; you would not have
the right to renew it at a later time.

Even though a roll-over mortgage might start with a 3-, 4-,
or 5-year term, the mortgage installment payments are calculated as if the mortgage had been fully extended. For example, if the mortgage had a 5-year initial term, with five 5-year
options, the installment payments will be based upon a 30-
year maturity.

At the end of each 5-year period, you and the bank will
have to renegotiate the interest to be paid during the next
period. If there is a change in the rate, the installment payments for the remaining term (including all the remaining

option periods) of the mortgage will have to be modified. A rise in the interest rate will increase these payments, and a decrease will lower them.

The provisions of the roll-over mortgage relating to an appropriate index for interest rate adjustments, notice requirements, and prepayment rights are comparable to those for the variable-rate mortgage.

I would advise you, as I did with the variable-rate mortgage, to select the conventional fixed-rate mortgage over the roll-over mortgage. When it comes to predicting the direction in which interest rates are going to go, you should assume that the bank is going to be better than you are. The trouble is, however, you may not have the luxury of choice. Banks are not usually required to give you the option of selecting between these two types of mortgage. They do not have to persuade you to take the roll-over mortgage; they can insist upon it—leaving you with the lone alternative of accepting or rejecting it.

This lack of choice has led to vigorous protests by consumer groups. Despite their concerns, however, the roll-over mortgage is not the "end of the world" for the homebuyer. There are certain factors that soften its supposed negative effects.

With interest rates as high as 15%, the roll-over mortgage may work to your advantage. If, as I predict, rates fall close to 10% within a year to 18 months, then the rate on the roll-over mortgage will also go down. Furthermore, I question whether banks will readily abandon the fixed-rate mortgage. With interest now at historically high rates, your bank may forget its "dire need" for a mortgage with interest fluctuations and instead delight in holding on to a certain rate of 15% for the next 25 or 30 years.

The roll-over mortgage is, moreover, part of a package of changes in the banking system. These changes, when taken together, may eventually result in a substantial increase in the supply of money available for investing by banks in home mortgages. And to the extent that classical economics holds sway, as the supply of money gets larger, the cost of mortgage money, as reflected by interest rates, will decline.

If you do obtain a roll-over mortgage, be certain you have the absolute right to roll it over for a specified number of terms. Make sure that the only item that can be renegotiated is the interest rate. Only you, and not the bank, should have the option to terminate the mortgage after any three-, four-, or five-year period. It should not be left to future negotiation; otherwise you may find that you are not simply bargaining with the bank over your rate of interest, but over whether you have a mortgage. Furthermore, the bank should not charge you any administrative or other fees if you do exercise any of the roll-over options.

You can expect that the forms and terms of the roll-over and variable-rate mortgages will continue to be modified; but eventually they should become more standardized as banks and regulatory authorities gain more experience in their use. But the essential purpose of these mortgages will continue to be the same—to allow periodic interest-rate adjustments in order to reflect current market conditions.

Graduated-payment mortgages. The graduated-payment mortgage is a response to the rapid increase in the costs of single-family homes. The combination of these escalating costs with high interest rates has resulted in installment payments on conventional mortgages that have, for many families, become prohibitively high.

The graduated-payment mortgage, by comparison, offers installment payments that are relatively low in the early years (usually for the first five to ten years). But they rise steadily each year until the payments reach a level that is higher than those on a conventional mortgage.

This has led to complaints that the graduated-payment mortgage "allows you to buy a house today that you will be unable to afford tomorrow. . . . It is applying the credit-card mentality to the purchase of a home." Nevertheless, this type of mortgage may, without encouraging profligacy, allow you to buy a home today, instead of having to wait or to abandon the purchase altogether.

Say that you want to buy a $75,000 home, with a $60,000 mortgage and $15,000 down payment. If it is a conventional, 30-year mortgage at 10% interest, the annual installment payments will be about $526.50 per month ($6,318.00 for the year). But, on your current salary, you can afford only about $5,500.00 a year for payments. You are, however, a man or woman "with prospects," and you expect to be able to pay $6,318.00 and more within the next few years. Under these circumstances, the graduated-payment mortgage may fit both your needs and expectations.

There are a variety of graduated-mortgage plans. A typical one, using the example of the $60,000, 30-year mortgage at 10%, might provide for monthly installment payments beginning at approximately $441 in the first year, which will increase at the annual rate of 3% through the tenth year. (The monthly payment would be approximately $454 in the second year, $468 in the third year, and would climb to about $575 in the tenth year.) In the eleventh year and continuing through the maturity of the mortgage, the amount would stabilize at approximately $592 per month. This would be about $65.50 per month higher than on the conventional mortgage.

This "climbing" obligation contained in the graduated-payment mortgage can, however, create a number of problems.

First, in the early years, the amount of the installment payments will not be sufficient to cover the interest due on the mortgage. At the end of the first year, in my example, there will be about $737 deficiency that has to be added to principal, so the unpaid mortgage amount beginning in the second year is $60,737. Since principal is going up instead of declining, you are diminishing rather than building up equity in your home. This can have the very practical effect of reducing or eliminating your profit when you sell your home.

Second, you will have to pay more in interest over the life of a graduated-payment mortgage than you would pay on a comparable conventional mortgage having the same interest rate and maturity.

Third, some banks may require that you make a larger down payment than on a conventional mortgage, because principal is going up on the graduated-payment mortgage during the first several years, instead of declining.

But the biggest problem is that you are transferring a great deal of the burden of the mortgage from the present to the future—to a time when you believe that burden can be borne more easily.

When I first heard of this type of mortgage, I was enthusiastic. (I tend to get excited over new mortgage ideas.) One of my partners looked at me soberly and said, "At forty-seven, Bob, you're too old." A discouraging remark—but true. This mortgage may suit the person who expects his income to grow with time—for example, the young professional or business executive. But for someone like me, whose earning curve has, I fear, flattened out, it can be hazardous.

The time may come when I will not have the money to pay the rising installment payments.

There are many variations of the graduated-payment mortgage I've described, and your bank can help you work out the plan that is best suited to your financial situation. There is also an FHA program that combines the graduated-payment and the low-down-payment mortgage.

At a recent meeting in my town to discuss housing for the elderly, a woman made an impassioned appeal on their behalf for financial assistance. She said: "We have short-changed our older citizens. They never, never, never get their fair share." And if the reverse-annuity mortgage is the best solution offered for the elderly home-owner, she is and will continue to be right.

For several years I lived near a woman in her seventies who, about two years ago, was forced to sell her home in Concord because she needed more money to live on. She moved to a rental apartment in another Boston suburb, where she died within a few months. "She was lonely," a neighbor told me.

Her Concord house had been a valuable but illiquid asset. She had fully paid off her mortgage, but the bank was not willing to give her a new mortgage because of her age. (Banks may be reluctant to give a conventional mortgage to a person over the age of sixty.) Thus, she was unable to convert her home into cash without selling it, a step she did not want to take for the most compelling of reasons—she loved her home and did not want to move.

Reverse-annuity mortgages. The reverse-annuity mortgage is intended to prevent such a situation. You borrow against the equity you have built up in your home, just as you might borrow against the cash surrender value of a life-insurance policy. The loan is secured by a mortgage on your home. However, instead of receiving the loan proceeds from the bank in a lump sum at the time you obtain the mortgage (as you would in the case of a conventional mortgage), you receive periodic payments, or an annuity, from the bank over the term of the mortgage. You or your estate do not repay the mortgage until it matures, which may be at the time of your death, at the time you sell your home, or after a specified number of years.

While banks and homeowners have had very little experience with this type of mortgage, one variation is as follows:

If you had paid off your conventional mortgage and had a $60,000 equity in your home, you might be able to borrow $45,000 from a bank. The $45,000 loan could be secured by a reverse-annuity mortgage on your home. The bank would not, however, give you the $45,000 in cash. It would take the $45,000 and purchase a lifetime annuity policy from an insurance company. The amount of the annuity payments would depend upon your age at the time you obtained the mortgage. (They would be larger the older you are, because you would have a shorter life expectancy.) The insurance company would pay part of each annuity payment to the bank to cover interest on the mortgage, and would give you the balance. For example, if the mortgage had a 9% interest rate and the annuity payments totaled $6,750 each year, $4,050 would be applied to interest—9% of $45,000—and $2,700 would be remitted to you. The annuity payments would continue until you die. Upon your death, the mortgage would mature, and your estate would have to pay the $45,000. It might be necessary, at that time, for your estate to sell your home in order to get the cash necessary to meet this obligation.

Another variation on this type of mortgage might be called a "term mortgage." The major difference is that, instead of a lifetime annuity, the bank would make periodic payments to you for a specified number of years. At the end of the period, the mortgage would be due whether you were dead or alive. For example, if the $45,000 mortgage were for ten years at a 9% interest rate, you would receive about $2,700 each year, or a total of $27,000. Interest would be accruing on these payments at the annual rate of 9%. At the end of the tenth year, the mortgage would mature and you would have to pay the $45,000—even if you had to sell your home in order to make the payment. This amount ($45,000) would enable the bank to recover the $27,000 paid to you, plus interest.

The problem with the reverse-annuity mortgage could not be more basic: it simply is not effective. First, the periodic annuity payments will be very small, both in relation to the value of your home and to your cash needs. Second, the total cost of the mortgage will be very high. And, finally, a reverse-annuity mortgage for a term of years does not give you the security it purports to provide. If you live beyond the maturity date, you may be forced to sell your home in order to pay for the mortgage. This will probably be at a time and age when you are most in need of the security and comfort of a home. (The bank may, however, be required by law to make financing available to you at the interest rate current at the time that payment is due on the term mortgage. However, there is a dearth of information and experience on the other terms of reverse-annuity financing, such as the maturity of the new mortgage.)

The mortgage with a lifetime annuity avoids this problem because it does not mature until your death; but, in return, this type of mortgage will, in most cases, be more expensive than a term mortgage.

The reverse-annuity mortgage may be an idea that is filled with good intentions. But while it may not put you on the road to hell, it is, at best, a detour from the path to heaven. Presently, this type of mortgage is not available in most states; and where it is available, very few banks offer it.

Two relatively new forms of alternative mortgage instruments are the shared-appreciation mortgage and the growth-equity mortgage.

Shared-appreciation mortgage. Typically, under the shared-appreciation mortgage, the lender gives you a below-market interest rate in exchange for the right to share in the increase in the value of the home when you sell. If you do not sell within a prescribed period of time, customarily 10 years, then the amount of the appreciation is determined by appraisal. In either case, upon the termination of the mortgage (whether due to a sale or the expiration of 10 years), the mortgage has to be repaid, along with the lender's share of the appreciation. If you accept this type of mortgage, you are giving away, at least in part, one of the more important benefits of owning a home—appreciation in value. I urge you to resist this mortgage unless there is no other way for you to afford the home or unless the lender offers you a very substantial interest rate concession.

Growth-equity mortgage. The growth-equity mortgage provides, initially, for the same periodic payments that would have to be made under a conventional fixed-rate mortgage. However, they grow progressively larger each year, with the increases being applied to the principal of—not interest on—the mortgage. As a result, a mortgage starting out with a 30-

year maturity might be paid off within 12 or 13 years because of these growing principal payments. I see little advantage to this type of mortgage from the homeowner's point of view, unless he or she gets a low interest rate from the bank. Otherwise, it is not much different from a 12- or 13-year mortgage, requiring excessively high periodic mortgage payments.

Second Mortgages

Up to now in this chapter I have been discussing alternatives to the conventional mortgage. In order to complete the discussion, I have to explain another type of mortgage, one that is better described as an addition to, rather than a variation of, the conventional mortgage. It is called the "second mortgage."

First and second mortgages. Understanding this kind of mortgage requires learning some law, but only the smallest amount. If you buy a $75,000 home and obtain a $60,000 mortgage from the bank, this mortgage is a "first mortgage." In order to complete the purchase, you will have to use your savings to make a down payment of $15,000—unless you can find someone who will lend you all or some part of the $15,-000. If you can borrow an additional $10,000 (thereby reducing the remaining down payment to $5,000), this loan can be secured by another mortgage on your home. It is, literally, a second mortgage.

In a competition among your creditors, the first mortgage gives the bank the highest possible claim against your home. The second mortgage is next in priority, with all your other creditors standing behind the bank and the person holding the second mortgage. It is as if your creditors were a crowd of flailing arms trying to grasp at your property. The one asset they would be prohibited from touching is your home—until the first and second mortgages are repaid.

Imagine the worst situation: You become insolvent and cannot pay your debts, including the first and second mortgages. You may be forced to sell your home in order to satisfy your obligations. The bank will get the first $60,000 of the sale proceeds (or an amount equal to the outstanding balance of the first mortgage, if less than $60,000). Only if your home can be sold for more than $60,000 will there be any money available to repay the second mortgage. If the sales proceeds are $65,000, $60,000 will go to the bank, $5,000 will go toward repaying the second mortgage, and there will be a $5,000 deficiency. Your home will have to be sold for at least $70,000 before the second mortgage can be paid in full; and unless the sale is for more than $70,000, your other creditors will get nothing.

Higher interest rates. Whoever gives you the second mortgage is, of course, taking a much greater risk than the bank, and may charge an inordinately high rate of interest in order to compensate for this risk—18% or more (assuming that state usury laws do not prohibit such high rates).

Banks infrequently give second mortgages, and in many cases are limited by law in their power to do so. But there is a trend toward expanding the right of banks to give these mortgages.

You may be able to obtain a second mortgage from a finance company or some other investor; but with interest at 18%, the cost may be prohibitive. There is, however, one person who may be willing to give you the second mortgage at a reasonable price: the person selling you the home.

Purchase-money second mortgages. If you cannot make a down payment of more than $5,000 on the $75,000 home, the seller may, if he wants to make the sale, give you a $10,-000 second mortgage. By doing so, he is getting his full $75,-000 asking price—$60,000 from the first mortgage, $5,000 from the down payment, and $10,000 from the second mortgage. This type of second mortgage is commonly referred to as a "purchase-money second mortgage." The seller does not actually lend you $10,000 in cash. Rather, he sells you the home for $75,000, accepts $65,000 upon purchase, and defers receipt of the $10,000 balance. You will have to make periodic payments (usually monthly) on this mortgage, just as you would on the first mortgage from the bank. The seller may, however, be more flexible than the bank as to the amount and composition of these payments; for example, he might require only the payment of interest during the term of the second mortgage, with the payment of the $10,000 principal being postponed until its maturity.

The obvious benefit to the seller is that he is getting what he asked for—$75,000 (although $10,000 is being deferred). Additionally, he will be earning interest on the $10,000 until it is paid.

From your point of view as buyer, the purchase-money second mortgage allows you to buy the home with a minimal down payment—$5,000. (Do not forget, however, that you are only deferring, not eliminating, the obligation to pay the $10,000.)

There are no standard terms for a purchase-money second mortgage. They will vary with the needs and the personality of the seller. They may depend upon matters as subjective as the fact that the seller likes you and wants you to have his home, particularly if he is remaining in the neighborhood.

Many years ago, a good friend of mine moved from New York to the Boston area to start his own business. He wanted to buy a $45,000 home in Newton, but since most of his money had to be invested in the business, he only had $5,000 for the down payment. He got a $30,000 first mortgage at 6% interest. (Those were the "good old days"—forever part of the nostalgia of the 1960s.) The person from whom he was buying the house gave him a 15-year, $10,000 purchase-money second mortgage at 5.5% interest.

"How did you ever get such a good deal?" I asked my friend.

"I'm surprised at you, Bob," he answered. "It's so obvious. It's my kids. You never realized how wonderful they are. They remind the seller of his children."

Because higher interest rates are making it more difficult to finance as large a percentage of the cost of a home through a bank as was the case a year or two ago, sellers have become more amenable to providing second mortgages. And faced with the realities of the current economic conditions, they may be willing to give you very liberal terms (labeled, in recent newspaper ads, as "creative second-mortgage financing" or "seller will assist financing") if they want to get their full asking price.

Caution: Check with the bank first. Before you take out a second mortgage, you must find out whether the bank that is giving you or that holds the first mortgage will permit it. Unless prohibited from doing so by law, the bank might not allow you to have a second mortgage, reasoning that it imposes too great a financial burden on you and increases the risk that you will default.

You should also compare the cost of taking out a second mortgage with that of an insured first mortgage. As I dis-

⌂ CHECKLIST

THE FIVE ALTERNATIVE
MORTGAGE INSTRUMENTS

The variable-rate mortgage   The interest rate is adjusted periodically (within specified limits) to reflect current market conditions. If you have a choice (and you usually do), don't choose it. Don't gamble against the bank on interest rates.

The roll-over mortgage   It usually has an initial term of three, four, five years. You (and not the bank) have the option to extend the mortgage for as many as five additional periods. My advice on this mortgage is the same as that for the variable-rate mortgage: Don't choose it. However, you are less likely to be given a choice.

The graduated-payment mortgage   It allows you to keep your installment payments low during the first few years. But eventually they will exceed the payments you would have to make on a comparable conventional mortgage. I would be careful about choosing this mortgage, unless it is the only way you can finance your home.

The reverse-annuity mortgage   It allows an elderly person who has built up substantial equity to keep his home and receive an annuity either for a specified number of years or for the balance of his life. This isn't an attractive or effective mortgage, however, because, among other reasons, the annuity will usually be very small in relation to the value of the home.

The shared-appreciation mortgage   The bank is entitled, under this type of mortgage, to share in any appreciation in the value of your home, usually within a 10-year period.

The growth-equity mortgage   A mortgage providing for progressively increasing principal payments each year, so that it will usually be paid off in 12 or 13 years.

The second mortgage   It supplements the first mortgage, in effect allowing you to finance part of your down payment. But unless you can get the second mortgage from the seller (known as a "purchase-money second mortgage"), the interest rate will probably be prohibitive.

cussed earlier, a bank may give you a first mortgage that covers as much as 90% to 95% of the purchase price if it is insured by the FHA, VA, or a private mortgage-insurance company. This may enable you to buy a home with a low down payment, at a cost that is less than that for a second mortgage.

The variations on the conventional mortgage discussed in this chapter demonstrate a housing market that is in ferment. They reflect many of the problems that have arisen of late and indicate the financial community's attempt to deal with some of them.

As imperfect as these various mortgages are, they demonstrate that traditional mortgage practices, alone, cannot adequately deal with today's conditions. There will have to be considerable modification and refinement of these newer instruments before they can have broad and effective use. And you can expect the introduction of still other forms of experimental mortgages.

All of this will make financing your home more complicated, and perhaps may create greater confusion. But it will also offer you a broader choice, if you are willing to learn something of the mechanics of the mortgage process.

Five

CONDOMINIUMS
AND COOPERATIVES—
A VERTICAL APPROACH
TO THE AMERICAN DREAM

MANY WRITERS OF NONFICTION BELIEVE THAT THEY GET A more intimate feeling for their subject if they read a novel on the period or theme they are writing about. For instance, there's no better study of the American entrepreneur of the late nineteenth and early twentieth centuries than in Theodore Dreiser's trilogy about Frank Cowperwood—*The Financier*, *The Titan*, and *The Stoic*. And John O'Hara's book *From the Terrace* (not the movie) is an entertaining and accurate account of the New York investment-banking community.

With this in mind, I picked up a best-seller called *Condominium*, hoping to gain some psychological, as well as technical, insight into life in a condominium—what might be called a three-dimensional view. This is what I learned:

A condominium is a tall building. It is legally owned by its occupants, but is controlled by an unscrupulous developer. The neighbors dislike each other, but find that their proximity provides them with remarkable opportunities to expand their sexual experiences. The cost of living in and maintaining the building are much higher than had been projected by the developer. And the building will probably collapse with the first passing hurricane.

It was difficult to reconcile this description with the growing popularity of condominium living; and it was clear that I needed to expand my research.

74

Ownership By the Occupants

Condominiums and cooperatives are usually apartment buildings, although in many cases condominiums are garden apartments, townhouses, and detached housing units within a real estate development. What makes condominiums and cooperatives unique as multiple-unit dwellings is that they are owned by the persons living in them rather than rented.

The condominium: direct ownership. The form of ownership differs for a condominium and a cooperative. In the case of a condominium, each person individually and directly owns the apartment unit in which he lives. He also owns, together with his neighbors, the areas that are used in common. Such common areas might include the land beneath and surrounding the building, the basement, the storage areas, the swimming pool and other recreational facilities, the central air-conditioning and heating facilities, the corridors, and the elevators.

The cooperative: indirect ownership. In the case of a cooperative, an occupant's ownership is indirect. The actual owner will typically be a corporation, which issues shares of stock to the persons who live in the building. It is these shares, and not the apartment units themselves, that are owned by the occupants. Each shareholder has the right to the use of his apartment unit, but it is a right granted to him by a lease from the corporation, known as a "proprietary lease." He has, then, a dual legal interest in the building—as a shareholder in the owning corporation and as a tenant.

As you shall see, these differences in ownership are more than a matter of form. They affect your rights and liabilities and how you finance the cost of buying into the building.

The Condominium vs. the Single-Family Home

My first experience with a condominium came when I went to visit an aunt and uncle of mine in Palm Beach, Florida. They had lived most of their lives in the Northeast and had grown tired not only of the impossible winters but also of the responsibility of keeping up a house. Since it was time to reap the reward of years of hard and diligent work, they had moved to a place in the Florida sun.

When I drove my family onto the condominium property,

I was assigned a "guest parking spot" and was promptly instructed to be sure, at all costs, that my tires stay within the painted diagonal lines—any encroachment being a serious violation of "house rules."

After our first day on the beach, we dutifully paraded, one after the other, under the outside shower, carefully dislodging the last particle of sand from our bodies. This was another "house rule." And then we proceeded barefoot into the building. An elderly man confronted my uncle and said sternly: "Doctor, you know the rules. No bare feet!" It seems that the fear of athlete's foot in Palm Beach is as real and as urgent as the fear of radiation poisoning near Three Mile Island, Pennsylvania.

For me, this experience with "group living" was claustrophobic. I felt that the condonimium complex had a life of its own, and that I was being impinged upon by its rules and concrete.

I was being unfair; but my uncle, being tolerant, intelligent, and, above all, balanced, was not offended. He suggested that I was failing to see the many benefits of his "home," as he insisted upon calling it.

"To begin with," he told me, "we enjoy life here—and you can't argue with that. It's a fact." Therefore, he said, we had to look at the condominium "from the point of view of whether it is a smart real estate investment."

He explained that he got much more for each dollar he put into the condominium than would have been the case if he had bought a single-family home.

"I have six rooms, including a large living room and master bedroom. I have a balcony, overlooking the ocean, where we can eat our meals if we want to. There are also around-the-clock security guards, a swimming pool, a tennis court, a billiards room, a beach-front, and guaranteed parking. And someone else worries about maintenance of the building.

"If we had tried to duplicate what we have here with a single-family home in Palm Beach, it would easily have cost us two or three hundred thousand dollars. My apartment, on the other hand, cost me considerably less than one hundred thousand dollars."

While any study of the comparative values of a condominium and a single-family home tells you more about "one man's meat" than it does about the economics, a solid claim can be made that you get (as they would say in the Pentagon) "more bang for the buck" in a condominium than in a detached, single-family house. This is because of the land costs and shared amenities. The cost of the land atributable to each apartment unit in a condominium will usually be less than that for a single-family home in the suburbs or for a townhouse in the city. And most people could probably not afford a swimming pool, tennis court, professional maintenance, and other such shared amenities if they had to pay the entire cost themselves.

Shared amenities mean, however, that you have to live with, and not merely beside, your neighbors; and I, perhaps, am emotionally handicapped when it comes to group living—having lived too long in Concord, where the refrain "Good fences make good neighbors" is acknowledged more as a rule of law than as poetry.

My inability or unwillingness to accept the condominium as a "home" is not, however, a view shared by my uncle, his bank, or the Internal Revenue Service.

Financing. One of the reasons for the emergence and growth of the condominium is the willingness of the banks to provide mortgage financing. The occupants mortgage is not on the entire building. Each owner gets his own mortgage, which covers only his apartment and his interest in the common areas. The terms of his mortgage are negotiated separately with the bank and may be different from those obtained by his neighbors.

When my uncle purchased his unit in 1975, he paid $60,-000. The bank gave him a $45,000 mortgage, requiring a $15,000 (or 25%) down payment. It was a mortgage on Apartment 3B and on his portion of the shared facilities. The terms of this mortgage, including the interest rate and maturity, were in most respects comparable to a mortgage that he might have obtained on a single-family house costing $60,-000. (The FHA, VA, and private mortgage-insurance companies will also insure condominium mortgages.)

Tax advantages. And if further confirmation is necessary that the mortgage is a mortgage and that the condominium unit is a home, the Internal Revenue Service has provided it. Interest paid on the mortgage is tax deductible, as are real estate taxes. Each owner can deduct the allocable real estate taxes on his apartment unit and on his share of the common areas.

Some mortgage drawbacks. The condominium owner may, however, find that some of the mortgage terms may be somewhat more severe than those on a single-family home. The interest rate may be slightly higher or a larger down payment may be required. Furthermore, he may not have flexibility in "shopping" for a mortgage. Very often, particularly in the case of a newly constructed condominium, one bank has a contractual right to provide the mortgages for all the apartments in the building. A bank may not be willing to give a mortgage on only one or two units, since the series of rights, obligations, and relationships involved in a condominium may not make it sufficiently profitable for the bank to make an isolated loan.

Rights and obligations. Buying into a condominium is not merely acquiring a measurable unit of space circumscribed by a floor, a ceiling, and four walls. You are also buying into a bundle of rights and obligations, which are defined in a series of legal documents.

When my uncle purchased his apartment in the Excelsior, as best I recall the name, he became a party to the "declaration and bylaws." If we perceive the condominium not only as a building but also as a community or a "minigovernment," such documents are the constitution and body of law that define his rights and responsibilities. They are documents to be studied carefully in order to know precisely what you own and, just as important, what you do not own. While I have to keep my dog on a leash in Concord, at the Excelsior my aunt and uncle are not even allowed to have a dog.

The declaration (or, as it is called in some states, the master deed) and the bylaws set forth your "percentage-interest" in the common areas; your share of the costs of maintaining and repairing these areas; the other costs that may be imposed on you, such as those for insurance and capital improvements; and any restrictions on your right to sell or lease your apartment. They might also cover matters as minor as the pets you are permitted and the draperies you may use on your windows.

Condominium government. These documents also establish the condominium "government." At the top of the organization there is a condominium association, composed of all the owners. Frequently, however, it is not "one man, one vote."

Each owner usually has a weighted vote, based upon his percentage-interest in the common areas. This interest is originally fixed in the declaration and is usually related to the initial value of each apartment. (It may also be based upon the size of each apartment; if it is, make certain that the voting interest bears a reasonable relation to value.) The relative weights of these percentage-interests cannot be changed without the consent of all the members of the condominium association even if, over time, there has been a change in actual apartment values. There may be exceptions to this in some condominiums, but you should be wary of entering into an arrangement that allows for a revaluation at a later date unless you retain veto power.

A large percentage-interest is not an undiluted benefit. The condominium organization may be the only extant form of government where responsibility is truly proportional with power. The greater your percentage-interest, the more of the common-area expenses you will probably have to pay. This can, perhaps, best be described as "taxation with representation."

Like any other corporation, the condominium association delegates most of its power to a board of directors, which is elected by the members of the association. The board enacts the "house rules" and regulations for the daily operation and use of the condominium. It can hire a managing agent and other personnel. Most important, it adopts a budget that allocates funds for insurance, repairs, maintenance of the common areas, and other operating expenses. The budget also covers real estate taxes and utility charges, unless they are billed directly to the unit owners. (The budget does not cover items such as mortgage payments, which relate specifically to an individual apartment unit and are billed separately to the owner.) The board then assesses each owner for his proportionate share of these common costs and expenses, which are usually payable monthly. Thus, often, in addition to a monthly mortgage payment, the condominium owner is responsible for a monthly maintenance fee (which is not tax deductible).

Condo advantages. Whether or not I would like living in a condominium is undoubtedly irrelevant to the question of whether the condominium is a sound investment. My preferences certainly did not move my uncle. He saw too many benefits:

- The wealth of physical amenities that would have been unobtainable if he had bought a single-family home.
- Mortgage financing that was comparable to that on a single-family home.
- The tax advantages of being able to deduct mortgage interest payments and real estate taxes, which he could not deduct if he rented. (He can also deduct, to the same extent as the owner of a single-family home, uninsured casualty losses—that is, losses caused by a fire or other damage and not covered by insurance.)
- Professional maintenance, which makes condominium ownership especially attractive to older persons.

In addition to these benefits, many people find the community life of a condominium very satisfying. "It's like living under a real democracy," I was told. "It's the communal life that America has lost."

It seemed to me more like living under a tyranny of neighbors. There are special concerns and problems you should be fully aware of and able to accommodate before you buy into a condominium.

The condominium is a government by neighbors. For example, the condominium association and its board of directors, by regulating how and when the common areas are to be used, is putting limits (whether reasonable or unreasonable) on your freedom to use your home.

Since these neighbors control the purse strings, they have the power to add to your expenses for such things as improvements, maintenance, and management. This power also carries with it—and this is often overlooked—the right of parsimony. A majority (and sometimes less) of your neighbors may, for example, be able to reject additional assessments and block needed improvements.

Furthermore, you may be faced with a recalcitrant or defaulting neighbor who refuses to or cannot pay his share of the condominium's obligations. The association can pursue its legal remedies against him, but such methods can be cumbersome and, above-all, they are not swift. In the meantime, the outstanding obligations have to be paid by someone—and that someone is going to be you and the other members of the association. In some states, if a unit is sold to the bank holding the mortgage or some other person because of a default under the mortgage, the new owner is not required to pay any unpaid assessments of the defaulting owner. Rather, they become common expenses of the association and, as such, are imposed upon all the owners.

Common liabilities. The common areas can result in common liability. If someone is injured in the lobby or in a hallway, all members of the condominium may be liable for resulting legal damages. It is essential, therefore, that adequate insurance be maintained by the association in order to protect the owners against this contingency.

Restrictions on your right to sell or lease. You may not have complete freedom to sell your apartment. In many cases, the board of directors of the condominium association has a "right of first refusal." This right may also extend to the leasing of your apartment.

Assume that my uncle decides to sell. Before he can complete the sale, he may be required, first, to offer his unit to the board. The board usually has about 30 to 45 days in which to exercise its right of first refusal and to purchase the unit or produce a purchaser. Only if it fails to do so can my uncle consummate the sale to an outside party. You should be sure before you buy in that the board would have to meet the same terms, including price, as those offered by a prospective purchaser; and that it does not have either an absolute veto power over the buyer you have selected or the right to purchase upon an arbitrary set of terms.

While it is unlikely that the board will exercise its first-refusal right, the possibility does, as one real estate agent explained, "create a problem. It's psychological. Usually a buyer makes a decision to buy in the flush of enthusiasm. Give him thirty days to think it over, and he'll find things to worry about. He may walk away from the deal, even if it means losing his deposit. It doesn't happen this way very often. But it happens."

The right of first refusal allows your neighbors in effect to veto a buyer who—using a benign phrase full of malignant meaning—may not be a "compatible person." If the association does buy my uncle's unit, then the remaining members are assessed a proportionate share of the cost, which will be recouped only when the unit is resold.

Difficult developers: some cautions. You may also have to contend with the developer. "The condominium can carry the developer on its back," I was told by a builder, "like King Kong wrapped around the Empire State Building."

The condominium was conceived and created by a real estate developer. Unlike certain other creations, it was not done for theological or aesthetic reasons. It was done for money—a perfectly acceptable motive in our society. But he may also want to continue to make money after the building has been built and sold—and this may be much less acceptable. My builder friend took the Bible as his authority: "He's entitled to what he can get during the first six days. But by the seventh day, he's had enough and should rest."

The ground lease: Who owns the land? While most states have enacted legislation that prohibits the more flagrant abuses of "self-dealing," the developer may, nevertheless, keep a financial connection with the condominium through a "ground lease," a "recreation lease," or a "management agreement." This will limit your control and may increase your expenses. Before you buy, you should know what rights have been retained by the developer.

First, the developer may not be selling the land underneath and surrounding your building. In this case, he continues to own the land, and leases it to the condominium association. The association pays rent under the lease—called a ground lease, or a land lease—and you are assessed for your proportionate share. When the term of the ground lease is over, the developer will own both the land and the building, unless you and your neighbors have discovered a way to remove the building from the land. Thus, you would be ill-advised to buy into a condominium that is subject to a short-term ground lease. Unless you are getting some unusual advantage (such as a bargain purchase price), the remaining term of the ground lease at the time you buy should probably be 75 years or longer.

The recreation lease. Under a recreation lease, which may be part of a ground lease, the developer may own the recreation areas or facilities, such as the swimming pool and tennis court, which he leases to the condominium association. Once again, you will have to pay your share of the rent under this lease. Some of these leases provide for an increase in rents if, for example, the cost of maintaining and operating these facilities goes up. The increase may even be tied to a less direct formula, such as a rise in the Consumer Price Index published by the U.S. Department of Labor. The developer may also have the right to allow outsiders, along with you, to use the recreational facilities for a fee; and that is going to interfere with your use and privacy. (Even if there is no recreation lease, and the condominium association owns these facilities, it could vote to open them up to outsiders in order to defray expenses.)

One contention often made by developers in defending their ownership of the land and recreation areas is that this will reduce the purchase price of the individual apartment units within the condominium. Even if this is the case—and the best way to find out is to do some comparison shopping among condominiums—you can reasonably assume that the developer is not going to give anything away. If he lowers the purchase price, you can expect that he will be well compensated for doing so by retaining ownership of these areas and charging for their use.

The developer as manager. The developer may also have retained, particularly in the case of a new condominium, the right to manage the complex, for which he will receive a management fee. Be sure that any such arrangement is of short duration and that the association has the absolute right to terminate the management agreement if it becomes dissatisfied with the developer's performance.

Condos under construction. You should be especially wary when you are buying into a condominium that is under construction. If you agree to buy your apartment before the building is completed (and you may get a lower price or a better choice of apartments if you do), you should be satisfied that the developer has the financial capacity to complete construction and fulfill his other obligations. And any deposit you make on your apartment unit should be escrowed (that is, set aside in a separate fund that cannot be used by the developer) until he has finished the building and you can move into your apartment. If he is unable to perform as promised, your deposit should be returned to you.

The developer as co-member. Even when the developer completes the building, he will own those units that he has not as yet sold (and he may have the right to lease them). This makes him a co-member of the condominium association, and his interest in these units may enable him to control the board of directors until most of the units are sold. In this situation, he should be required to appoint some individual owners to the board. He at least should not be allowed to alter or amend the declaration without your permission, particularly regarding such matters as your voting rights, your interest in the common areas, and your share of the assessments. Nor should he be able to modify his responsibilities to the condominium.

The Structure of the Cooperative

In a cooperative, each stockholder is entitled to the use of his apartment by right of a lease (called a proprietary lease) from the corporation. The rents payable under the lease cover each stockholder's share of the expenses of the cooperative (rents generally are based on the number of shares owned)—expenses that include common-area maintenance, repairs, management, real estate taxes, and debt-service payments on the "blanket mortgage," an instrument I shall discuss in a moment.

And the cooperative, like the condominium, has an internal government; the stockholders elect a board of directors who enact the rules and regulations and are responsible for the budget.

A longtime friend and business associate of mine who was born in New York City moved to Long Island after he was first married. He had made some money, so he bought a home that, he said later, "fitted my Jay Gatsby period." The house, standing alone, was charming, but the grounds were absolutely breathtaking—a swimming pool and acres and acres of manicured lawns and exquisite beds of flowers whose blooming was professionally orchestrated. During the weekend I spent with him, he told me—over and over again—how happy he was.

I saw him a few weeks later. He was selling his home and buying a cooperative apartment on Central Park West, right in the middle of Manhattan. I told him I was shocked that my weekend visit could bring about such an abrupt change. He reassured me: "I'm a New Yorker. I get vertigo on flat land—I need tall buildings. And I'm in the real estate business. Whenever I see a patch of green space, I want to build on it."

Cooperative advantages. My friend, like most converts, had also become a proselytizer—bursting with reasons why I and everyone else should live in a cooperative. The advantages are, for the most part, similar to those found in a condominium—more amenities than in a single-family house because of shared expenses; and professional management and maintenance.

The stockholders in a cooperative also have the federal tax benefits of ownership; each stockholder can deduct his share of the mortgage interest and real estate taxes on the building. (Unlike the owners of a single-family house, however, the stockholders are not allowed a deduction for an uninsured casualty loss. You should be sure, by the way—particularly if the cooperative leases out offices or other commercial space—that 80% or more of the gross income of the cooperative is derived from the tenant/stockholders. Otherwise, you may lose your tax benefits.)

The blanket mortgage. The differences between a cooperative and a condominium are not just organizational. While in the case of the condominium there are separate mortgages on each owner's apartment unit, in a cooperative there is a single mortgage covering, or "blanketing," the entire building; hence, its name, the "blanket mortgage."

When my friend bought into his cooperative there was a $3-million blanket mortgage on the building, and he had to assume the seller's share of that obligation. He also had to pay the seller $40,000 in cash, and he wanted to borrow as much of it as he could. But he quickly found out that this was not easy to do.

"I learned a lot of law," he told me, "when I tried to finance the apartment. More, I bet, than they taught you at Harvard." (He was right.) "I wanted to borrow at least thirty thousand of the forty thousand dollars. But the bank told me I didn't have enough security."

He could not use his apartment to secure a bank mortgage because he did not own it. Rather, the cooperative corporation owned it and had, years ago, placed the blanket mortgage on the entire building, including his unit.

"All I could do was pledge my shares of stock and my lease. The bank officer told me that if he granted me a loan and I defaulted on it, the bank's only recourse, other than suing me, would be to take over my rights to the stock and lease." If this happened, the bank itself would become subject to the blanket mortgage and to the rules and regulations of the cooperative—including some very restrictive rules on selling an interest in the cooperative. (Consequently, many banks will not make such a loan unless the cooperative agrees, in the bank's case, to waive or relax the restrictions on a sale.)

My friend finally did get a loan—for $20,000. It was, in reality, a personal loan based upon his credit, and not a real estate loan (even though it was secured by his shares of stock and his proprietary lease).

Tougher terms from banks. Over the past several years, some banks have begun to specialize in making loans to the individual stockholders in cooperatives; but the terms are usually more onerous than those involving a condominium or a single-family home. The loan is typically not more than 60% to 70% of the purchase price; and while the maturity can be as long as 30 years, it is usually less. And the interest rate will probably be about 0.25% to 0.50% higher than that charged for a mortgage on a single-family home. Complicating this problem, the cooperative may also limit the amount you can borrow.

The bank's position is understandable. It only holds, in effect, a second mortgage, which may not be adequate security for a large loan. But why would the cooperative have a borrowing limitation?

Defaulting neighbors. The stockholders of the cooperative (whom I will call the owners) each have a direct and legitimate stake in the solvency of the other owners. If my friend defaults on his loan, for instance, the bank can succeed to his interest in the cooperative—and the bank may not be an acceptable neighbor. Furthermore, if he becomes financially overextended, he may not be able to pay his share of the costs of operating the cooperative, which may, in turn, require the other owners to pay them. For example, if he cannot pay his share of the blanket mortgage, the other owners will have to pay it in order to avoid a default. They will have a claim against him, but they will still have to make the payment in order to protect their own investment in the cooperative. Thus, the owners want him to be a "man of means."

Cooperatives and "our own kind." The owners may also be

concerned with his financial condition because they equate it with social standing. The statement "We want to live with our own kind" refers today more to money than to ethnic background. This was made clear to my friend when he applied for membership in the cooperative. "We love the poor people," he was told, "but not in this building. This building is an 'exclusive neighborhood.' "

The owners of the cooperative have the power to maintain such exclusivity. They have almost unlimited discretion over who can move in, and, therefore, over whom you can sell to, so long as the laws against discrimination are not violated (although, as a practical matter, most cooperatives can also use their power to evade these laws).

My friend recalled how he was made painfully aware of these financial and social strictures when he and his wife were interviewed by a two-man admissions committee appointed by the board of directors of the cooperative corporation:

> One was a young man, in his early thirties, who I can't remember saying anything, but who took notes. The other was about sixty-five or seventy and had lived in the building for more than twenty years. It was like being cross-examined by a prospective father-in-law who was determined to be sure that I had enough money to support his daughter in the style she had been accustomed to.

> His first question took me completely by surprise—How much life insurance did I have? I explained that I didn't have much because I didn't believe in it. This was clearly the wrong answer, so I changed my tactics. I figured he was being fatherly, so I said: "I see what you mean. With a new wife [I was recently married], I have new responsibilities. I'll look into insurance right away."

> But he wasn't being fatherly. He probably wasn't happy about being anybody's father, particularly mine. And he didn't give a damn about my wife. He told me I should have insurance because if I died, my wife would need the money to meet the obligations of living in the building. He was not concerned about our well-being, but about his well-being.

> The inquisition continued along these lines for about an hour. When it was over, I felt I had been through an IRS

⌂ CHECKLIST

SEVEN MATTERS TO CONSIDER
BEFORE BUYING A CONDOMINIUM
OR COOPERATIVE

Government of neighbors   The condominium or cooperative is a government of neighbors. Fellow owners can encroach upon your privacy by establishing
rules and restrictions on how you use your apartment
unit and the common areas.

Percentage-interest   Your share in the common property will usually be based upon the original value or
the physical area of your apartment unit. Make sure
that your proportionate interest cannot be changed by
your neighbors without your consent.

Costs of operations and maintenance   Your share of
these costs will usually be based on your percentage-
interest in the condominium or cooperative. Your
neighbors will, in great part, be deciding how much
these costs will be.

Recalcitrant neighbors   Your share of the costs of
operations and maintenance may increase if you have
a recalcitrant neighbor who cannot or refuses to pay
his share. You have legal remedies against him, but
they can be cumbersome and time-consuming.

Financing   In the case of a condominium, you can
generally expect that the mortgage terms will be somewhat more severe than those for a single-family home.
    In the case of a cooperative, you may be able to ob-
tain individual bank financing, but generally on more
onerous terms than those for either a condominium or
a single-family home. You should also look into any
restrictions that the cooperative may impose on the
amount you can finance.

Limitations on sale   There will usually be restrictions on your right to sell or lease your apartment unit. These restrictions will generally be more harsh in the case of a cooperative.

Rights of the developer   Watch out for any rights and interests retained by the developer. He may, for example, own the recreation facilities and the underlying land; and, if he does, you may have to pay extra charges for their use.

audit. My wife was fuming. In the elevator on the way down, she said, "I don't know if I even want to live in a building with a son-of-a-bitch like that." But I told her: "Once we buy it, he becomes our son-of-a-bitch. Can you imagine anyone who would protect our investment better than he would?"

Financing limitations and tight control over who can live in the building are the most fundamental differences between the cooperative and the condominium. The scarcity of traditional mortgage financing makes buying into a cooperative an option that is generally open only to those who can afford to invest a large amount of capital in a home. A New York real estate agent puts it very bluntly to people who come to him: "Don't waste your time or my time looking for a co-op unless you're rich or going to be rich pretty damn soon."

This is not the case with a condominium, where the apartments can be financed, as you have seen, as if they were single-family homes.

The fact that you can obtain conventional mortgage financing for a condominium apartment, combined with the rising cost of single-family homes, accounts in great part for the spectacular increase in condominium living. Indeed, the condominium may be becoming a vertical solution to the American Dream. The condominium may enable thousands of people who could not otherwise afford to do so to own a home—particularly those who want to live in the city. Through this alternative, they will be able to enjoy the permanence and investment benefits of ownership, which would not be available through renting.

But in most cases a condominium or a cooperative, because of its physical structure, does not have the privacy of a single-family home. And, with this fact in mind, you would

⌂ CHECKLIST

THREE MAJOR DIFFERENCES BETWEEN A CONDOMINIUM AND A COOPERATIVE

Ownership   In a condominium, ownership is direct. Each occupant owns his apartment unit and a proportionate interest in the common areas.

In a cooperative, ownership by the occupant is indirect, since the owner is typically a corporation. Each occupant owns shares of stock in the corporation, and has the right to use his apartment unit pursuant to a proprietary lease from the corporation.

Financing   In a condominium, each owner can separately finance his apartment unit and his interest in the common areas with a first mortgage from a bank. The mortgage is comparable to that on a single-family home.

In a cooperative, there is usually a single mortgage covering, or "blanketing," the entire project. Individual financing by each occupant is, in effect, a second mortgage. While separate bank financing for each occupant may be available, the terms are usually more onerous than those for a condominium unit or a single-family home. The cooperative corporation may also limit the amount any occupant can borrow against his interest in the cooperative.

Sale   While there may be some limitations on the right of a condominium owner to sell his unit (such as a right of first refusal granted to the board of directors of the condominium association), a cooperative corporation has an almost unlimited right to reject a prospective buyer.

do well to remember the advice I was given in my college days by a professor of religion during one of his periods of skepticism: "The biblical injunction to 'love thy neighbor' was based upon an underlying assumption that you have first chosen him very carefully."

Six

INFLATION

MY DREAM HOUSE IS ON AN ISLAND, LOCATED IN THE middle of a ten-acre meadow where the grass, burned by the summer heat, has turned the color of hay. It overlooks a lagoon on one side and has a view of the ocean on the other. It is a sprawling farmhouse, paneled in weather-beaten shingles, with so many rooms in odd places that each time you walk through you feel like you're exploring. It is a house to make you look forward to staying indoors on a rainy day.

I rented this house during the summer of 1960. It was on Martha's Vineyard, the island about ten miles south of Cape Cod in Massachusetts. And I could have bought the house for $23,000, then.

With a unanimity rarely found in any family, I was urged by everyone—my father, my uncle, my wife, my brothers—to buy it. My eldest daughter was only two at the time, but I seem to remember that her first full sentence sounded something like, "Buy that house, you dope."

Well, I didn't. I held firm, showing a strength of character that has turned out to be my only reward. I was just beginning my professional career; and, intending to be the model Wall Street lawyer, I would tolerate no inclination toward improvidence in my fiscal affairs.

Today, two decades later, I could buy that same house for about $225,000, if it were being offered for sale.

For whatever solace it provides (and it provides precious little), most people I know could tell a story like mine. My uncle has never forgotten the twenty-room estate, with a gatehouse, he could have bought on Atlantic Avenue in Gloucester, Massachusetts, for $20,000 in the early 1950s. And there is the Victorian mansion with a gymnasium and running track on the third floor, on exclusive Fisher Hill in Brookline, Massachusetts, that my father could have bought for a small fraction of its market price today.

These missed opportunities have been called "the curse of the American middle class." Whatever their sociological significance, such stories tell us something about the recent history of housing costs in the United States.

The average purchase price of a new single-family home was about $23,100 in 1963, $35,500 in 1970, and around $90,000 in 1982. For an existing home it was about $19,700 in 1963, $30,000 in 1970, and approximately $70,500 in 1982. Very few people doubt that these figures will continue to climb during the next ten years—there being a general perception of rising prices as a permanent reality, as if they were an immutable law of nature.

What is behind this perception? It derives, in great part, from a "certainty" about inflation—not merely an awareness of its presence, but a belief in its permanence and persistence. Such faith in inflation has been described as "the closest we have come in the twentieth century to a universal religion." And i tapplies not only to homes but to almost every type of real estate (as you'll see when I discuss commercial properties in Part Two). It is a faith that tells you that you can afford to buy now—indeed, that you had better buy now—because prices are going to keep rising higher and even higher.

This view of inflation seems to be supported by experience. But statistics such as those I have just quoted do more than give historical perspective. They create a passion for investing; and homes are looked at as not merely shelter from the wind and the rain, but as the "growth stock" of the future.

Such numbers also seem to have encouraged a creative urge. There has, over the past year, been a spate of books, magazine articles, and newspaper columns telling how to "beat inflation" by buying a home, on the theory that home values will go up faster than the inflation rate. One financial writer said to me, somewhat skeptically, that "more words are being written these days about the inevitability of inflation in home prices than about sex; and that's dangerous. No matter how much you read about increasing your potency, down deep you know there are physical limitations. You just have to stop. But inflation is something else. It's like a perpetual-motion machine. Once people accept as a fact that prices are not going to come down, they seem compelled to spend more and more money on homes—which only adds to inflation."

This feeling of inevitability may be only an illusion, but the sound of the figures generated by inflation is seductive—a modern man's Siren call. And I have not always been immune. When one of my real estate partners suggested in 1977 that we invest in single-family homes, I was enthusiastic. We could buy an inventory of about five houses, rent them out for two or three years, and then sell them for a substantial profit.

A year went by without our doing anything. My partner repeated his suggestion at a dinner party at my home. When I again responded positively, he turned to my wife and said: "You know what's going to happen? We're going to sit here next year, and we'll have the same conversation. But all we will do is console each other about not having acted sooner. Your husband is one of the great real estate voyeurs of all time. He loves to look, but he's afraid to touch."

He was right, of course. I enjoyed talking about the idea, but I would not act on it. Nevertheless, I had legitimate reasons for avoiding the business of buying and selling houses.

I was unwilling to gamble on inflation. And my partner was looking to inflation as our guarantee of a profit. A home can be an excellent investment (as you'll see in the next chapter), but it is foolhardy to rely only upon inflation for its success.

"Investing in inflation" is speculating—a form of speculating for which most people are unsuited. I have become increasingly concerned about how frequently investors are taking this risk. An example of this occurred a few years ago, when a neighbor asked me whether I thought her mother should buy an apartment in a Florida condominium. "She is a very nervous woman," I was told, "and hates to make a decision. She's sure that once she buys, prices will drop. What do you think?"

I responded that prices were high, but that I doubted whether they would come down in the near future; so if her mother really wanted to live down south, she should buy without delay.

The mother wavered for several months, and the apartment that she could have bought for $60,000 finally cost her $65,000. I wondered how she felt, having waited so long before taking my advice.

"She's ecstatic," my neighbor told me. "Prices are still going up. Now she's looking for another apartment to buy as an investment. She'll lease it out for a year, then sell it for a profit."

I tried to explain that her mother was becoming a real estate speculator—a hazardous business even for someone who is not "very nervous." But neither my neighbor nor her mother was listening. They had joined the expanding ranks of the "believers."

This is not an isolated example. In California, I am told, acting on the "inevitability" of rising prices is almost a way of life. It is called "trading up."

Trading up: how it works. A graduate of the Harvard Business School with whom I had some dealings on the West Coast made a separate business out of trading up. He started soon after he was married. He and his wife took the money they had received as wedding gifts and bought an $80,000 home outside of San Francisco.

"We paid $15,000 down and borrowed the rest," he explained. "We did some cosmetic work on the house, like painting and refinishing the floor. We sold the house two years later for $100,000. This gave us $35,000 to work with, since we got back our down payment and made a $20,000 profit. So we then bought another house, for $180,000—this time using the $35,000 for the down payment. We'll do a little fixing up again, and sell it next year or the year after. This time we expect to clear a $40,000 or $50,000 profit. Then we'll move onward and upward to the next house." (Furthermore, he will avoid having to pay federal taxes on his profit if, each time he sells, he buys another home within 24 months for a purchase price that equals or exceeds his selling price.)

He told me his plan with an air of certainty that, at one time, I thought was limited to graduates of the Harvard Business School; but his faith in trading up seems to have spread to all homeowners. A real estate consultant summed up the attitude for me: "It's true that most people have no business speculating on inflation. They don't have the capital and, in the long run, they don't have the courage. But they feel that they have found a loophole in the law of gravity—as if everything that goes up has to come down, except the price of houses."

No one can, with certainty, predict the movement of home

prices. What's involved is not an exact science. But prices can and do go down, as they did during the Depression and, as they are doing now in some parts of the country.

Reaching the peak: the pyramid law. Homes, like all other investments, are subject to what is known as the "pyramid law." At some point, an investor who depends upon inflation finds himself at the top. He cannot build any higher without the whole structure toppling down. You rarely know when this point will be reached until you actually get there. But with the price of the average home having increased by more than three times from 1963 to the end of 1982, you can be reasonably concerned that if the peak has not been reached, it is perilously close. Indeed, higher and higher interest rates seem to have slowed down the rise in the price of homes and to have accelerated the emergence of a "buyer's market."

Inflation vs. real value. Even if home prices do continue to go up, you have to ask the next question: Is this the result of inflation or of a rise in real value? It is not an easy distinction to make, and the difficulty of distinguishing between value and inflation was the second reason (besides the pyramid law) that inhibited me from acting on my partner's proposal.

I remembered the experience of a Cambridge, Massachusetts, couple who had owned a $25,000 home on Brattle Street since 1948 and were offered $175,000 for it in 1978. They had not, until they received this unsolicited offer, given any thought to moving. But they felt that they could not refuse. This price was seven times their original investment.

After weeks of searching for a house in a comparable neighborhood, they were stunned to find that they would have to spend at least $175,000 in order to duplicate their Cambridge home. As a result, they did not sell. "I am not an economist," the husband told me, "but I now know as much about inflation as any of them. Having to pay $175,000 for a $25,000 home is inflation. It's that simple."

It is probably not quite that simple, but it is close. What had happened was that the market price of their home had increased sevenfold, but the value (based upon what they could buy with the $175,000) had remained stable.

The experience of the Cambridge couple is not typical. Statistics show that in most cases the rate of growth in home prices has, over the past several years, exceeded that of inflation, and in some cases the differential has been dramatic. This should provide a measure of comfort for anyone who invests in a home. Nevertheless, I continue to have a healthy disrespect for the statistics. They vary too often according to the person doing the compiling. Moreover, they are based upon an imperfect sampling.

While the statistics may tell you something about the price of homes in general, they do not tell you about your home in particular. Yours may turn out to be the home that brings down the average. In this respect, such figures are like the actuarial tables used by insurance companies. In theory, the tables tell you how much longer you can expect to live, but they won't prevent a fatal coronary attack from striking you before your allotted time. Like actuarial tables, housing statistics can't determine the future; they can only tell you about the past.

Furthermore, statistics do not tell you how long it will take to sell your home. You may eventually get your asking price, but any delay in making the sale will reduce your net return. Until you sell, you have to continue making any remaining mortgage payments and meeting the other financial obligations on your home.

Profit may be an illusion. But most important, in a period of rapid increases in prices, the line between value and inflation (notwithstanding the statistics) becomes blurred. To the extent that price increases are the result of inflation, there is no real profit because there is no buildup in value. A morass of statistics showing that home prices have doubled, tripled, or quadrupled will be of little solace to you if you sell your home and find that to buy a comparable house you have to use all the proceeds. As I explained to my partner, I was not just worried about whether prices would continue to go up; I was worried whether we would be getting anything out of our investment, even if they did. We had to contend not only with the pyramid law of investing. "There is also," I told him, "the 'balloon factor': It doesn't matter how much air we blow into it. It still ends up being the same balloon—it only looks bigger."

What I've said in this chapter up to now can be looked at as a warning; and, as such, it may be the best advice you will ever receive about dealing with inflation. It is not a warning against buying a home—but against buying a home for the purpose of profiting from inflation. Inflation is an unstable source of return—vulnerable to factors and events over which you have no control, ranging from oil prices and overbuilding to government policies and general economic conditions.

In a world that is growing more sophisticated in the use of money, people sometimes forget the fundamental reason for buying a home: It is a place to live—ideally, the place where you want to live. There are, of course, other benefits, but they are subsidiary. Among these are the protection a home can afford you against inflation. And, in certain cases, a home may allow you to profit from inflation. Clearly, you should take these possible benefits into account when you buy a home. But this is far different from buying a home to make a fortune, whether large or small, because of inflation. It is within this context that I want to discuss some of the advantages of owning a home during a sustained period of inflation.

How inflation can help you. Inflation can, if you sell in time, turn a bad deal into a good one. You may have overpaid for a house, but you may be able "to ride with the flow" of the statistical averages. Inflation will, at times, pull the price of a house up to a level that is far above its worth. This may add proof to the adage that "it is better to be lucky than smart," but it is not evidence that inflation will necessarily cure your mistakes. It should be seen as aberration in the marketplace, one upon which you should not rely.

You may also benefit from inflation if you "trade down." If the Cambridge couple had sold their home for $175,000 and were willing, for example, to purchase a $50,000 condominium unit, they would have made $125,000. But they would have had to be willing to accept a more modest home. The ultimate trade-down occurs, of course, when you die, and it can provide your heirs with a substantial cash estate.

A home: a hedge against inflation. A home can be a hedge against inflation. My home in Concord, which cost me $125,-000, can be sold today (ten years later) for about $270,000. If a comparable house would also cost $270,000, I would not have gained anything in value, but I would not have lost anything either. If, for some reason, I had to move, I would at least have the funds to replace my home. This may be an example of running in order to stay in the same place. But it is preferable to running and falling behind, which might have been the case if, during the past decade, I had rented my home.

Inflation and refinancing. Finally, you may be able to take advantage of inflation by refinancing your mortgage. Assume, for instance, that you bought a house several years ago for $50,000, with a $40,000 (80%) mortgage. If the market price has gone up to $100,000, you might be able to obtain a new mortgage for $80,000 (80% of the $100,000 market price) by refinancing—that is, by prepaying your original mortgage and getting a new one. You would take the $80,000 from the new mortgage and use it to pay the entire amount you owe on the old mortgage. This would give you at least $40,000 in cash without having to sell your home; and you would not have to pay a tax on this money. Actually, depending on the rate of equity buildup, the amount would probably be greater than $40,000. For example, if the principal balance of your current mortgage has been reduced to $30,000 and you refinance for $80,000, your cash proceeds will be $50,000.

You should, however, consider the additional costs of refinancing. You may have to pay a higher rate of interest, as well as a prepayment premium. And your periodic mortgage payments may go up, depending upon both the interest rate and the maturity of the new mortgage.

Whether or not you should refinance will depend, in great part, upon the use you can make of the cash proceeds. (See chapter 2 for a discussion of the alternative use of money.) If you can invest these proceeds for a return greater than the additional mortgage costs, you should seriously think about refinancing.

How inflation can hurt. Inflation can also be painful. It profoundly affects mortgage financing. If I were buying a house today and trying to arrange a mortgage, I think I would feel like a Lilliputian standing before Gulliver. Inflation magnifies every aspect of the buying process: the purchase price, the down payment, the mortgage amount, and the periodic mortgage payments and other carrying costs.

Inflation and financing your home. If you had purchased a home in 1968 for $50,000, today you might have to pay $100,000 for the same house. Of course, $50,000 is not a small number, but $100,000 is even more intimidating. The impact is not merely psychological; it also effects your approach to the financing of a home.

To begin with, certain facts are obvious: If a $100,000 home cost $50,000 ten years ago, the amount of the down payment and mortgage will probably have doubled also. Since 1968, the maximum ratio of the conventional mortgage amount to the down payment has remained at about 80% :20%. Despite the stability of these percentages, they have to be applied to much higher figures. Ordinarily, the minimum down payment on a $100,000 home will have to be $20,000 (with a $80,000 mortgage), as compared with a $10,000 down payment (and a $40,00 mortgage) on a $50,-000 house. Thus, while the mortgage and down payment have remained in balance, the dollar burden of both has severely increased.

Interest rises with inflation. Interest rates, as has been brutally demonstrated, also rise during inflation. In the first half of 1982 the average effective rate of interest on a conventionally financed single-family home was above 14% and in some places hovered around 16%. Whatever we think about the virtue or good sense of bank and government policies regarding interest, we cannot expect that these rates will fall below 10% so long as inflation continues at a rapid pace. The bank will want higher rates in order to compensate for inflation. The government, on the other hand, may, as it has before, increase rates in order to combat inflation, on the theory that high interest rates discourage borrowing and curtail economic expansion.

Furthermore, real estate taxes and the premiums on homeowner's insurance will be higher if inflation continues. They usually go up with the market price of a home, although not necessarily in direct proportion. (You should look into the tax policy of the town or city in which you are buying in order to find out whether there is a trend toward higher real estate taxes.)

Faced with these facts, how much of the cost of a home should be financed and on what terms during a period of inflation? For the most part, you can apply the principles of mortgage financing discussed in chapters 2 and 3. Inflation does, however, add a dimension that has to be considered separately.

What to do if your savings are modest. Because of inflation, your biggest stumbling block may be coming up with the increased down payment. Therefore, if you have modest savings, I would advise you to get as large a mortgage with as long a maturity as possible, so long as you have sufficient income to meet the mortgage payments. You should not, remember, use all of your savings in making a down payment. This would leave you without money for emergencies or other investment opportunities.

But trying to get your bank to agree to a down payment of less than 20% ($20,000 on a $100,000 home) on an uninsured, conventional mortgage would be about as fruitful as Oliver Twist asking for "more."

Among the solutions, as I discussed in chapter 4, is the low-down-payment, insured mortgage, guaranteed either by a private mortgage-insurance company, the Federal Housing Administration, or the Veterans Administration.

If your situation is different and you can easily afford a 20% down payment ($20,000, in my example), there are two additional considerations.

If by using private mortgage insurance your down payment only has to be $10,000, what can you do with the extra $10,-000? Applying the principle of the alternative use of money (chapter 2), you should probably invest it elsewhere—and not use it for the down payment on a conventional mortgage—if you can safely get a return greater than the mortgage cost on the $10,000.

"Cheaper dollars." If inflation continues, you will be repaying the mortgage with "cheaper dollars" in the future. While the value of each dollar loaned to you by the bank is fixed as of the time the bank makes the loan, the value of each dollar you have to repay to the bank will be declining. Inflation causes a "devaluation" of the dollar or, put more somberly, "debases the currency." This should encourage you (subject to the qualifications discussed below) to borrow as much of the cost of your home as you can. There may, however, be another side to this "coin" you are investing. If you later sell your home, you, like the bank, may also be paid in cheaper dollars, thereby losing much of the advantage you expected from taking out a large mortgage.

If you can solve the down payment problem during inflationary times by getting a larger mortgage, you then will have to face the problem of higher mortgage installment payments. Financing a home is like balancing an equation—if you lower the burdens on one side, you add to them on the other.

If on a $100,000 home you obtain a $90,000 (90%) mortgage instead of a $80,000 (80%) mortgage, your installment payments would have to be larger (assuming the same interest rate and maturity date). You have more to repay. On a 25-year, $90,000 mortgage at 10% interest, your monthly mortgage installment payments would be about $826 as compared with $734 on a comparable $80,000 mortgage—a $92 difference ($1,104 annually). You would also have to insure the $90,000 mortgage, and the premium payable on the insurance would increase this differential.

There are also the other carrying costs, such as real estate taxes and the premiums for the insurance on your home. These costs, as I discussed earlier, can be expected to increase as long as inflation continues.

Longer maturity can ease the burden. One way to lower the larger mortgage payments brought on by inflation is to get a longer-maturity mortgage. If the maturity on a $80,000 mortgage at 10% interest were 30 years, your monthly payments would be about $707 instead of $734 on a 25-year mortgage. Your total cost over 30 years would be greater (because you would have more interest to pay), but your immediate cash obligation would be reduced by $27 each month and $324 each year.

As I said before, interest is not quite as awesome as it might appear. Interest rates during an inflationary period can keep a manic-depressive in a state of constant depression. However, interest is tax deductible, which does lower your actual cost (as explained in chapter 3). Inflation may also cause your salary and other income to rise—moving you into a higher tax bracket. While this is hardly the cloud with a silver lining, remember: the higher your tax bracket, the more your interest deduction will reduce your taxes. (For example, in the 50% tax bracket a $1,000 interest deduction will reduce your taxes by $500, whereas in the 40% bracket the reduction will only be $400.)

Furthermore, interest rates may go down if inflation abates. Given this possibility, it is urgent that you keep the right to prepay your mortgage. This will allow you to take advantage of a decline in rates.

The bank also shares your concern with the soaring interest rates that accompany inflation. Since high interest rates will increase your carrying costs, the bank will be scrutinizing your financial ability to meet these greater costs; and one result of this investigation may be to require that you make a larger down payment (30% or more) than you would have to make in more normal times.

Don't gamble against the bank. You can also expect your bank to encourage you to take out a roll-over or variable-rate mortgage. If you are tempted to accept because of the possibility of a future reduction in the interest rate, try hard to resist. The bank is betting on the probability that interest will go up—not down. And, repeating some earlier advice: Don't gamble against the bank on interest rates. The banker is a professional. You are not. Even if there is a significant decline in rates, you'll be protected if you've guarded your right to prepay a conventional, fixed-rate mortgage.

Inflation and the graduated-payment mortgage. Another alternative mortgage instrument that has grown popular as inflation continues is the graduated-payment mortgage. Its attraction, as discussed in chapter 4, is that you may be able to make relatively low mortgage payments during the early years (up to five to ten years, depending upon the length of the graduated-payment plan). However, don't forget that the mortgage payments will rise each year until they reach a level that is higher than that payable on a traditional mortgage; and you run the risk that you may not be able to make these enlarged payments. The graduated-payment mortgage is truly a child of inflation and is greatly dependent upon it. This type of mortgage may be an appropriate alternative for you, but in accepting it, you should be aware that you may be relying upon a fragile assumption—namely, that inflation will increase your income sufficiently to enable you to meet your future obligations.

One other point you should consider: The old rules of thumb—those myths about the limits you should place on the cost of a home and the size of the mortgage payments—become even less valid when inflation runs high. Among the realities forced upon us by inflation is that a single-family home will cost more to buy and to operate than in the past. This does not simply mean that your individual standards of prudence guiding how much you should spend on a home have to be adjusted upward along with the price of housing. It also means that you have to reevaluate what I've called the trade-offs in determining what constitutes a satisfactory standard of living. One indication of how inflation is affecting trade-offs is the increase in the number of people who are buying condominiums instead of purchasing single-family homes, since the "shared facilities" within a condominium can reduce the cost of ownership.

Myth: Buy today to beat inflation. It has been said that inflation is one of those subjects no one is neutral about. It's like politics—everyone thinks he's an expert. Despite the disparate points of view on inflation, they seem to have converged into still another myth: *Buy that house today; inflation will make it cost more tomorrow.*

There are many "facts" given in support of this myth. Two of the most popular are that building costs have to rise and that demand for houses has to grow.

As to building costs rising—not necessarily. As unlikely as it may appear today, building costs could be reduced if, for example, new construction techniques were used. And many home-builders will tell you that the necessary technology (such as factory-built housing) is available. Only the implementation is missing.

Much of the anticipated demand for housing is based upon the so-called post-World War II baby boom. The children born between 1947 and 1961 are supposedly flooding the market and will for years to come. Well, the "babies" may have swelled the number of potential buyers, but the demand won't affect everyone: the home buyers may not want to move to your town or live in your house. Furthermore, a great deal of the demand could be absorbed by condominiums, which might lessen it for single-family homes. Besides, there could always be a natural disaster, like Mount St. Helens erupting, which would dissipate demand. And looking at it from a historical perspective, a periodic plague is probably more certain than a constant inflation.

None of this is to suggest that prices will significantly go down. The greater likelihood is that they will go up. But the fact is that there are no certainties, only competing predictions. And for those of you who persist in relying upon continuing inflation and acting on the myth, I commend to you the wisdom of one of the more philosophic home-builders I know: "Inflation is accepted as predestined fact. But there is nothing predestined in inflation or in real estate. The real truth is: No one knows what's going to happen in this business until it happens."

Seven

YOUR RETURN
ON INVESTMENT

BY NOW YOU HAVE HAD ENOUGH FACTS, FIGURES, AND OPIN-
IONS and want to make a rather critical judgment: Should
you put your money into a home or into something else?

Just how good an investment is a home?

Opinions on this tend to go to extremes, ranging from "the
best investment you will ever make" to "your financial ruin."
Whatever its position between these two poles, a home is for
most people an enormous financial and emotional commitment. Is it worth it?

The answer to the financial half of this question depends
upon the return on your investment—what you get back for
what you put out. In order to evaluate this return, you have
to know how much you actually pay for a home and what
you sell it for. You also have to calculate the effects of time,
inflation, taxes, and mortgage financing. And, finally, you
have to compare investing in a home with other investment
options.

The Cost of Purchasing

The starting point is the cost of buying your home and the
amount for which you sell it.

Closing costs. Assume that you buy a $100,000 home. You
obtain an $80,000, 20-year mortgage, and have to make a
$20,000 down payment. There will be other incidental ex-
penses, referred to as closing costs (they "close the deal"),
which will ordinarily be between 1% to 3% of the purchase

price, or $1,000 to $3,000 on a $100,000 home. (There can, however, be significant variations in closing-cost amounts, depending upon where the home is located.) Among the most important closing costs are:

- *Attorney's fees.* These include the fees of the bank's lawyer and your lawyer. Frequently, a buyer relies upon the bank's attorney. I would advise against this, despite the additional cost of having your own lawyer.
- *Title insurance.* This insurance assures both you and the bank that you have legal title to your home. It guarantees that you actually own the home you have bought and that you have not purchased (and the bank has not made a loan secured by) the equivalent of the Brooklyn Bridge. In many states the practice is for the bank's lawyer to investigate and certify title, and in these cases title insurance may not be required.
- *Survey (or plot plan).* This is a drawing of the legal boundaries of your property and the location of your house within these boundaries. It provides graphic proof that your home has been built on your land and not on your neighbor's.
- *Recording fees and taxes.* These are the costs of filing your deed and mortgage on the public record.
- *Appraisal.* The bank may require an independent appraisal of your home in order to confirm that the price you are paying does not exceed its market value.
- *Inspection.* The bank may want a contractor or engineer to inspect your home in order to determine if it is structurally sound and free from termites and other pests. Even if the bank doesn't require an inspection, you should have one made before you buy the home. The inspector can also give you an estimate of the cost of needed repairs or any remodeling you may want done.
- *Application fee.* The bank may require such a fee before it will consider your request for a mortgage. If they do not give you the mortgage, they will probably refund the fee.

Additionally, you may have to pay a fee to the bank for other costs of processing your loan, such as the cost of a credit review and other administrative expenses.

If the total of these expenses was $2,000, then the actual cost of your home would be $102,000, requiring an initial cash investment of $22,000—$2,000 plus the $20,000 down payment. (Note that I am not including as part of the investment the continuing expenses of owning a home—installment payments on the mortgage, real estate taxes, and the cost of utilities, repairs, maintenance, and insurance. For the moment, I'm assuming that they would be equivalent to what you would have to pay if you leased a comparable home, and hence not significant for the purpose of evaluating the cash investment. Nor have I included "points," which I consider another form of interest on the mortgage. Also, in some situations you may have to pay a fee to the broker who has arranged the sale, but this fee is customarily paid by the seller.)

Time and your investment. The next step is to find out how time affects the return on your cash investment. I have been told many times that anyone smart enough or lucky enough to have bought a house in 1968 would have more than doubled or tripled his money by now. This vision of bathing in cash is almost erotic, but is it real? The statement suggests that if you buy a house for $102,000 (including the $2,000 in closing costs) and sell it for $204,000, your return is 100%. But in reality it will be below 100% because of the time lapse between buying and selling.

If you buy a $102,000 home at noon today and simultaneously sell it for $204,000, your return really is 100%. If you sell it tomorrow, it will be slightly less than 100%, since one day has gone by during which you couldn't invest the money elsewhere. And if you sell ten years from now, your return will be considerably less than 100%. The investment principle involved is simple: One dollar received today is worth more than a dollar received tomorrow, and it's worth much more than a dollar received in ten years.

"If you have any doubt about the relationship between time and money," I was told by a man whose affection for his eighty-year-old father was wearing desperately thin, "try waiting for an inheritance." Time affects return; and the extent to which it does becomes clearer when you examine equity buildup and capital appreciation. Equity buildup and capital appreciation have one thing in common: before you can realize any return from either, time must elapse and you must sell or refinance your house.

Equity buildup as return. Equity buildup, as you remember, occurs as you repay the principal of the mortgage. If 20 years from now you sell your home for $102,000 (after the

$80,000 mortgage has been repaid in full), both your equity buildup and your cash return will be $80,000: the $102,000 selling price minus your $22,000 initial outlay. But you would not have been receiving any of the $80,000 for 20 years (and in fact would have been making monthly payments to the bank). And $80,000 20 years from now is not the same as $80,000 today.

In order to determine the effect of time—getting the $80,000 after 20 years instead of today—you must find the interest rate at which $22,000 has to be invested over a 20-year period in order to reach $102,000. The rate would be approximately 8%. This becomes clearer if you assume that, instead of buying the house, you deposited the $22,000 in a savings account on which you earned 8% per year (compounded annually). You would have made $1,760 in the first year—8% of $22,000—and your $22,000 would have increased to $23,760. In the second year, the bank would have had to pay you 8% on $23,760, or $1,901. At the end of that year, the total amount of your savings would have risen to $25,661 ($23,760 plus $1,901), on which the bank would, again, have to pay 8% during the next year. This process would have continued for 20 years, by which time you would have accumulated approximately $102,000. With $22,000 as your initial investment, the $80,000 balance would have been your profit. But since you had to wait 20 years for this profit, your rate of return would have been 8%, the same as on your investment in your house.

Capital appreciation as return. You would make a similar calculation in order to find your return when there's capital appreciation. Capital appreciation is the actual increase in the market value of your home over the price (including the down payment and mortgage) you originally paid for it. If, for example, you could have sold your home after 20 years for more than the $102,000 you paid for it, some of your return would have been the result of capital appreciation above and beyond the equity buildup. Assuming you could have sold your home for $204,000, your cash return would have been $182,000 (the $204,000 selling price minus the $22,000 cash investment). As you have just seen, $80,000 of this $182,000 cash return would have been equity buildup; the remaining $102,000 would have been capital appreciation. Once again, you have to take into account the passage of time. In this situation, it has taken 20 years for $22,000 to increase to $204,-000. And the rate at which $22,000 would have to be invested to grow to $204,000 over 20 years is approximately 11.75%. This time it's as if you had invested the $22,000 elsewhere at 11.75% and at the end of 20 years had accumulated approximately $204,000 ($22,000 at 11.75% would become $24,585 after one year; $27,474 after two years; $66,819 after ten years; and about $204,000 after twenty years).

Having considered your profit and the effect of time on your return, there are some other factors you have to analyze: the cost of selling your home, taxes, inflation, and the mortgage.

Let me first look at the performance of homes as an investment for the years from 1972 through 1982.

The year 1972 is a reasonable point at which to begin because it is recent enough to be relevant still and far enough in the past to provide some historical perspective. It also has intense personal meaning for me. It was the beginning of Watergate. Vietnam seemed an endless commitment. The economy was beginning to show deep and fundamental strains. And I bought a house for $125,000. Before I had a chance to let the trend in national and international events develop into an excuse not to buy, a friend, who knew me well, told me not to "start looking for rational reasons for making an irrational decision. Buy the house. It's terrific, and you've gotten a great deal."

I did buy it, and it has been a "terrrific" house. And, based upon available statistics, it has also been a "great deal." The average price of an existing home was about $33,400 in 1972 and $70,500 in 1982. This is roughly a 111% increase. In my case, the increase has been even greater. Based upon several unsolicited offers, the market value of my home today would be closer to $270,000—a 116% increase. This is more than a number: it is euphoria. I do, however, have to make some adjustments.

My down payment was $35,000 and my closing costs were about $2,000, making my initial investment $37,000. I obtained a $90,000 mortgage, maturing in 25 years and bearing interest at 10%. The balance on my mortgage at the end of 1982 was approximately $75,500, which I would have had to pay if I sold my home. If I sold for $270,000, I would have cleared $194,500 ($270,000 minus $75,500).

Had I used a real estate agent to sell my home, I would

have had to pay a brokerage fee—usually about 6% of the selling price, or about $16,000. In addition, there would have been other selling expenses, such as attorney's fees and recording costs, of about $750. I would have been left with $177,750—$194,500 minus $16,000 minus $750.

(Real estate agents generally are not eager to negotiate their fees; but they may be forced to do so in order to avoid violating antitrust laws. You may also be able to reduce the brokerage fee by limiting the services you require of the agent. Another way to avoid such a fee is to try to sell your home without a real estate agent. But this may not be easy or wise to do. The agent will have an inventory of potential buyers and, unless you know someone who wants your house, the agent will probably be able to make the sale more quickly than you.)

Then there are taxes. If I were in the 40% tax bracket, I would have had to pay $20,200 in federal income taxes in connection with the sale. This would have reduced the $177,-750 to $157,550—$177,750 minus $20,200. (I will, later in this chapter, discuss the federal tax treatment of the sale of a home, including certain exemptions and how I arrived at the tax figure of $20,200.)

Thus, on the original investment of $37,000, my net proceeds would have been $157,550. My profit, or gain, would be $120,550—the net proceeds of $157,550 minus my cash investment of $37,000. Table 8 (page 111) is a summary of these calculations.

I now have to account for the ten years that elapsed (1972 to 1982) since I bought my home. Since my net proceeds were $157,550, my return rate would have been equivalent to the interest rate at which I would have had to invest $37,000 (my initial cash investment) in order to accumulate $157,550 over ten years. The annual rate would have to have been about 15.6%—$37,000 invested in 1972 at 15.6% would have grown to approximately $157,550 by 1982. (In arriving at this figure, I have not adjusted for inflation. Such adjustment would, of course, have reduced this return percentage, but in the same proportion as on any other investment I might have made with my $37,000.)

My return could have been greater if I had borrowed more than $90,000—say $100,000. My initial investment—my down payment plus incidental expenses—would have been only $27,000 (instead of $37,000), and my profit would have

remained the same. Thus, I would have made the same dollar
profit on a smaller investment, which would have increased
my return to about 19.3%. This illustrates the advantage of
leverage—the use of someone else's money (the bank's, in
this case) in order to buy a home.

TABLE 8

Calculating Profit on the Sale of a Home

Original cost of investment		$ 37,000
Down payment	$ 35,000	
PLUS		
Closing costs	2,000	
Total	$ 37,000	
Gross proceeds (assumed selling price at the end of 1982)		$270,000
Costs and expenses of sale		$112,450
Mortgage balance	$ 75,500	
PLUS		
Brokerage fee	$ 16,000	
PLUS		
Other selling costs	$ 750	
PLUS		
Federal income taxes	$ 20,200	
Total	$112,450	
Net proceeds		$157,550
Gross proceeds	$270,000	
MINUS		
Costs and expenses	$112,450	
Result	$157,550	
Profit		$120,550
Net proceeds	$157,550	
MINUS		
Cost of investment	$ 37,000	
Result	$120,550	

Perhaps leverage can be better understood by thinking
about what is happening in terms of distances instead of dollars or percentages. In measuring your return, if you buy a

$125,000 home without investing *any* of your own money (borrowing the full cost) and sell it for $270,000, you have arrived at infinity. But for every $1 you invest, you are moving away from infinity. And you are farther away when you invest $37,000 than when you invest $27,000.

Leverage is a cardinal principle of real estate investing, but is not an unqualified benefit. It is diluted by risk. For example, a large mortgage means higher installment payments, which increase the economic pressure on you. In Part Two, I'll expand upon the advantages and disadvantages of using leverage.

I could not, obviously, have obtained a 15.6% return rate if I had invested my $37,000 in a conventional savings account. And I would have had to been a shrewd, clever, or lucky investor (and, more likely, a combination of all three) to reach or exceed this level by investing in stocks or bonds.

Liquidity vs. your home investment. However, savings accounts, bonds, stocks, and similar investments do have one major advantage—they are liquid. Unlike a home, they can be turned into cash almost immediately. On the other hand, it takes time to sell a house—to find the buyer, complete the sale, and make the physical preparations for moving.

Liquidity clearly compensates for some of the difference in the rate of return between a home and these other investments. It allows you to have cash readily available not only for an emergency, but also for other investment opportunities as soon as they arise.

The loss of liquidity that occurs when you buy a home may be a reasonable argument in favor of borrowing as much as you can—and limiting the amount of your down payment. But liquidity is not a sufficient reason to rent a house instead of buying. The return on the investment in a home is just too compelling.

Buying vs. renting. Perhaps one advantage of renting over owning is that renting has the allure of nomadic life. The American Dream, in this sense, would not be a home, but mobility. Renting allows you to move quickly and frequently— the luxury of impermanence not available to the homeowner.

But this is a question of taste and not of economics. Unless you are forced to rent because you do not have the money for a down payment, or unless you have an urgent need for liquidity, the economic advantages of owning rather than renting are overwhelming.

As soon as you pay rent, you have consumed your money. You own nothing. You have not built up any equity, nor can you benefit from capital appreciation. These advantages belong to your landlord, even though your rent will ordinarily cover all of his carrying charges—the mortgage payments, real estate taxes, utilities, insurance, and a reserve for repairs and maintenance. And unless he is carried away by some charitable impulse, he will also charge you enough to make at least a small profit. (There may be situations in which the carrying costs on a home you own would be more than the rent you would have to pay for a comparable house. In that case the return on investment would be lower than I have indicated in this chapter. This would most likely occur if you borrow more than a conventional amount—for example, if you obtain a 90% instead of an 80% mortgage, thereby increasing your periodic installment payments.)

Furthermore, the landlord will have certain income tax advantages that are not availalbe to you as a renter—the right to deduct real estate taxes and interest on his mortgage. He will also be entitled to a tax deduction for the depreciation— the "wear and tear"—of his house, so long as he is renting it to you (as I'll discuss in chapter 9). He may pass his tax savings along to you in the form of lower rents, but only if he is compelled to do so by his competition and not because of any legal requirements.

Renting may, in your case, be an economic necessity, but it rarely carries an economic benefit. What you are buying with your rent is a certain amount of freedom from responsibility. This may appeal to you because you prefer the "life of the open road" to staying in one place. If you do, I urge you to buy a trailer instead of renting. At least a trailer may have some trade-in value.

In an age in which relative values seem to be displacing absolute truths, one exception is a 15.6% investment return. I expect that this return is the closest that I, as an investor, will ever get to a feeling of absolute joy. But even here I have to intrude a few words of caution. My analysis of the return on my home is, and has to be, imperfect, because it is based, in part, upon a series of assumptions. And while I believe that my assumptions are both justified and reasonable, they may not apply to you.

The most important of these assumptions is the time period—1972 through 1982. If I had used the 10 years beginning with 1962, my calculated return would have been much less, since in that period the average price increase of an existing home was much smaller. I could also have gone back 20 or 30 years rather than 10 years and come up with different results in each case.

Furthermore, the experience of the past several years is not a guarantee of the future. The years 1972 through 1982 were good ones for homes. While estimates for the next ten years—1982 to 1992—range from optimistic to spectacular, the last two decades should have taught you to be prepared for uncertainties. And even if the cost of homes continue to escalate at the present rate, and the market value of my $270,000 home grows to $583,200 by 1992 (another 116% increase), there may be more cause for concern than unremitting happiness. As a local real estate lawyer put it: "It sounds wonderful. But it will mean that everything has gone to hell. Dollars will have to be moved in wheelbarrows, like in Germany in the 1920s."

Another assumption was my use of statistical averages to determine the market value of my home. Complete statistics on home prices are probably impossible to compile and must, of necessity, be imperfect. Even if they could be compiled, just as nobody fits precisely into any statistical model of the average person, there is probably no average home. My home will undoubtedly be better, or worse, than any such average.

And in using averages to compare the return on a home with investment alternatives, you exclude the possibility that you might have been able to make some extraordinary investment that would have made the return on a home look, if not puny, at least anemic.

Finally, I assumed that my carrying costs would be the same as the rent for a comparable home. But the extent to which the carrying costs are greater or less than the rent can have a material effect on the actual return.

This is not an exhaustive list of the assumptions involved in calculating return on investment, but they are the most decisive ones. They also illustrate another investment principle: *Be careful of the assumptions used in any investment analysis.* They are critical to the result. Assumptions are not facts, only reference points. As assumptions change, so will your calculated return.

There is a story that has turned into a parable for real estate investors. A broker walked into his partner's office and saw him looking forlornly over a column of figures. When he asked what was wrong, he was told that the numbers did not add up to the return he needed in order to sell a particular investment to a client. "Stop worrying," his partner told him. "Tell me the return you're looking for and I'll get it for you. I'll just change some assumptions."

Taxes on Sale of Your Home

Whenever there's talk about money, the subject inevitably turns to taxes. This can be an intimidating subject. But the homeowner, because of special dispensations granted to him when he sells his home, has less reason to be concerned than other taxpayers.

My accountant once told me that "taxation either frightens or angers most people, because taxes take away what we think we own." This fear and anger is also inspired by the legislation that spawns taxes. It is close to incomprehensible—the thousands of pages of turgid prose contained in the Internal Revenue Code having been described by former President Carter as "a disgrace to the human race." The Code, with volumes of rules and regulations encrusted upon it, has become so complex and convoluted that those specializing in it might, in earlier days, have been accused of having mastered some art of black magic and, perhaps, have been burned for practicing witchcraft.

You can, nevertheless, understand how you are taxed by the federal government on the sale of your home by proceeding, step by step, through a series of questions:

- What is it that is being taxed?
- How much is the tax?
- Are there any exceptions to or exemptions from the tax?

What is taxed: the net profit. First, what is it that is being taxed? It is your net profit, or net gain—not the sale's proceeds. If I had sold my $125,000 home for $270,000, my gross profit would have been $145,000 ($270,000 minus $125,000). But this is only the starting point. In order to find

my net profit, it is necessary to make some additions and sub-
tractions.

I paid $2,000 in closing costs when I bought my home.
This raised my cost from $125,000 to $127,000. In most
cases, my cost would also have gone up by the amount of
any capital expenditures made for alterations, additions, or
replacements that would have increased the value of my
home or extended its life. For example, if I had repaved my
driveway for another $2,000, my cost would have risen to
$129,000. (You should maintain records of any such expendi-
tures in order to prove to the Internal Revenue Service that
the improvements have actually been made.)

When I sold my home, I could have subtracted the $16,000
brokerage fee and the $750 of other selling expenses. This
would have reduced the total selling price to a net (or adjusted) selling price of $253,250 ($270,000 minus $16,000
minus $750).

Therefore, my net profit would have amounted to $126,-
250—the $253,250 net selling price minus the total cost of
$127,000. This is the amount—$126,250—upon which my
tax will be calculated, as is summarized in table 9.

You should note that in calculating my taxable gain I ig-
nored the mortgage—the fact that I borrowed $90,000 and
that there is an outstanding balance of $75,500 at the time of
sale. In making these calculations, you can assume that the
mortgage does not exist. For tax purposes, it neither adds to
nor reduces the cost of the home or the amount of the sale's
proceeds. The federal government does not care how you pay
for a home, whether you borrow the funds or pay for it with
your own money.

How much tax? Now that I've found that my taxable gain
would have been $126,250, the second step is to find out the
amount of the tax.

Earlier, I assumed that I was in the 40% tax bracket. Ordinarily, this would mean that 40% of my taxable gain would
have been taxed. But this is not the case with a home. So
long as I have owned my home for more than 12 months,
60% of my gain—whatever my tax bracket—would have es-
caped (would have been "excluded" from) taxation. On a
$126,250 gain, $75,750 (60% of $126,250) would not have
been taxed. I would have been taxed only on the remaining
$50,500—$126,260 minue $75,750. Since I was in the 40%

tax bracket, the amount of my tax, as table 10 on this page shows, would have been $20,200—40% of $50,500. If I were in the 50% or 30% bracket, I would still only have been taxed on $50,500, but the amount of tax would have been $25,250 and $15,150, respectively, in these brackets.

Exceptions to capital-gain tax. There are exceptions to the tax on the gain from the sale of a home; and I might not have had to pay the $20,200 tax at the time I sold the house.

TABLE 9

Calculating Taxable Gain on the Sale of a Home

Total cost		**$127,000**
Purchase price	$125,000	
PLUS		
Closing costs	2,000	
Total	$127,000	
Net selling price		**$253,250**
Total selling price	$270,000	
MINUS		
Brokerage fee	16,000	
MINUS		
Other selling expenses	750	
Result	$253,250	
Taxable gain		**$126,250**
Net selling price	$253,250	
MINUS		
Total cost	127,000	
Result	**$126,250**	

TABLE 10

Calculating Tax on the Sale of a Home

Amount to be taxed		**$50,500**
Taxable gain	$126,250	
MINUS		
60% exclusion (60% of $126,250)	75,750	
Result	$ 50,500	
Tax in 40% bracket (40% of $50,500)		**$20,200**

A lawyer specializing in the Internal Revenue Code once explained: "Our tax laws begin with a simple rule, which usually requires nothing more than the multiplication of one number by another number. The rule is followed by an exception which, in turn, breeds other exceptions and then there are exceptions within these exceptions. When I'm working late at night and getting tired, I sometimes feel, as I go through the Code, that I'm watching a monster mutating."

While these exceptions are the source of most of the complications, they also contain the provisions (or, as they are sometimes unkindly called, the "loopholes") that cut down the amount of taxes you have to pay.

In the case of a gain on the sale of a home, there are two exceptions. First, if you purchase another home within 24 months before or after the sale, all or some part of the tax will be deferred or postponed. Second, if you are fifty-five or over when you sell your home, up to $125,000 of the gain can be excluded forever (not merely deferred) from taxation.

Buy another home and defer tax payment. With respect to the deferral: If I had sold my home for $270,000, the net selling price (as shown in table 9) would have been $253,250. But I could have postponed paying the capital-gain tax if I had bought and used as my principal residence another home for $253,250 or more within 24 months before or after the sale.

What if the second home costs less? If I had paid less than $253,250 for my next home, I would not have been able to postpone all of the tax. I would have been taxed on the difference between the net selling price of my first home and the purchase price of my second home.

For example, since my net selling price was $253,250, if I had purchased the second home for $233,250 (a $20,000 difference), I would have been taxed on $20,000. This means that instead of a deferrable tax-gain of $126,250, only $106,250 ($126,250 minus $20,000) would have been deferred.

However, the amount of the gain to be deferred could have been increased by expenses incurred in fixing up my house for sale. Using the example above, if I had painted my house for $1,000 within 90 days before I had entered into an agreement to sell and had paid the $1,000 within 30 days after the sale, the deferred gain would have been $107,250—

$106,250 plus $1,000. In this case only $19,000—$126,250 minus $107,250—of my gain would have been taxed.

Deferral is not optional. The deferral is mandatory. You cannot elect to pay the tax. Only one transaction in any 24-month period qualifies for the deferral (unless you have to move for reasons of employment); and both the house I sell and the house I buy must be my principal residence (not, for example, a vacation home).

The deferral does not, however, eliminate the tax. It merely postpones it. I may live to pay it another day because the Internal Revenue Code keeps a hold on the $126,250 gain. It does this by the way it defines the cost of my new home.

If I pay $270,000 for the new home, it costs me $270,000. Despite my impeccable logic, the Code disagrees—it says that my cost is less than $270,000. If this sounds confusing, it's because, once again, a fiction is involved. Under the Code, my $270,000 cost has to be reduced by the amount of my untaxed gain from the sale of my first home—in this case by $126,250. Thus, even though the actual cost of my new home is $270,000, my "imputed cost" is $143,750 ($270,000 minus $126,250 in untaxed gain). If I sell the new home at a later date for a net price of $270,000, my taxable gain will be $126,250—the $270,000 sale price minus the imputed cost of $143,750. This is illustrated in table 11 below.

One way to visualize the concept of imputed cost is to imagine the $126,250 of untaxed gain hovering somewhere in

TABLE 11

Calculating Taxable Gain on the Sale of a Second Home		
Imputed cost of new home		**$143,750**
Purchase price of new home	$270,000	
MINUS		
Untaxed gain on old home	126,250	
Result	$143,750	
Taxable gain on new home		**$126,250**
Net selling price of new home	$270,000	
MINUS		
Imputed cost of new home	143,750	
Result	$126,250	

space until I sell my new home. At that point it is pulled down to earth by the tax. (Actually, I can keep the $126,250 in this state of suspension indefinitely by successively purchasing and selling homes. There is no limit to the number of transactions to which this deferral applies, subject to the 24-month qualification.)

In addition to this deferral, the Code may allow you to escape the capital-gains tax on the sale of your home. If you are fifty-five or over when you sell your home, you can elect not to be taxed on up to $125,000 of your gain. (The home must have been owned by you and used as your principal residence for at least three years during the five-year period ending on the date of the sale.)

This is a once-in-a-lifetime exclusion and should be used carefully. If, for example, I qualified and had exercised this right when I sold my home, I could never use it again—even if my taxable gain had been less than $125,000.

Even if I do use this exclusion, the deferral provisions of the Code continue to apply to later purchases and sales. In addition, both the exclusion and the deferral can be used in the same transaction. For example, if the net selling price of my first home had been $378,250 (instead of $253,250), my taxable gain would have been $251,250. If I had purchased another home for $378,250, $125,000 of this gain could have qualified for the exclusion, and the remaining $126,250 of this gain would have been deferred.

While the foregoing describes the most pertinent Code provisions relating to the sale of a home, there can be many variations. For example, your marital status, the manner in which you and your spouse hold title, your age, and what you have done in the past can affect the amount of taxes you have to pay. There may also be state and other local taxes that will differ from place to place. Unfortunately, tax planning is not a do-it-yourself project, and you should consult your lawyer or accountant for specific advice and guidance. For example, the method in which you and your spouse decide to hold title should be dictated more by estate-planning considerations than by love.

Each time I bought a home it was

as clear to me as sunshine . . . that the greatest possible stumbling blocks in the path of human happiness and improvement are these heaps of bricks and stone, consolidated with mortar, or hewn timber, fastened together with spikenails, which men painfully contrive for their own torment, and call them house and home! [*The House of the Seven Gables*]

Despite Hawthorne's lament, the truth is that I have never regretted, after making the purchase, any of my homes. Buying a home must, I suspect, be something like childbirth. I am told that you forget the pain after the event. Nor do I have any reason for regrets. My homes have been among the few pleasures I have experienced that have never lost me money.

I expect the growth in market values will continue into the future, although probably not at the stunning pace of the past several years. Even if this rate of growth should decline, it would have to be a precipitous drop before the words "Home, Sweet Home" become more an expression of sentiment than advice on where to invest your money.

Two

BEYOND THE HOME— INVESTING IN COMMERCIAL PROPERTY

CREDIT AND NONCREDIT
REAL ESTATE—
THE ESSENTIAL DISTINCTION

AFTER THE DIRECTORS' MEETING OF A NEW YORK-BASED company, I shared a taxi to La Guardia Airport with another member of the board. As we were driving through Manhattan, going toward the Triborough Bridge, he kept looking around. Finally he said, "Do you know what New York City is?"

It had been a long and tiring day, but I was sufficiently alert to know that whatever answer I gave was going to be wrong or at least irrelevant. And, since he was really conversing with himself, I said nothing.

"It's real estate," he answered, "and that's where the fortunes are made. Did I ever tell you about the time my father took me out on a Sunday for a drive through Trenton? I was fourteen, and he pointed out all the buildings he could have bought into, but didn't. He told me that if he had taken advantage of the opportunities, he would have been a rich man; and he never wanted me to go through life like him, regretting that I had missed the main chance.

"I've never forgotten that experience," he went on. "My father was right—it's where the action is. Now that I've saved some money, I'm going to put it into real estate. I don't intend to miss my opportunity."

My first reaction was: What a strange childhood. It was certainly in sharp contrast to my own; my father decided that I had "arrived" the moment he no longer had to support me.

More to the point, I was surprised at my colleague's outlook toward real estate. He was, at the time, a partner in an investment-banking firm and was supposed to be sophisticated in financial matters. Yet, he was being incredibly naive about real estate investing. It is not a get-rich-quick scheme. Unless he was willing to quit his job and spend all of his time and money in the real estate business, or unless he was astonishingly lucky, this was not where he was going to make his fortune.

Real estate can be a sound investment, but the part-time investor should not expect to become a millionaire. (It rarely happens even to the full-time investor.) Nor can I tell you how to make a fortune in real estate. The only person who gets rich from a book on how to become financially transcendent by investing in real estate is the author. As a successful developer put it: "Anyone who has found the formula of how to make a million dollars in real estate is not going to write about it. He'll be afraid of the competition."

What I *can* do is describe the opportunities; how to approach them; what you can and should expect from your investment; and, most important, what to watch out for and be afraid of. If you use this information, along with the advice and counsel of your lawyer and accountant, you should be able to make a respectable return on your money, with a minimum of risk.

I have already discussed most of the investment principles to be applied. It might surprise you, but *the same or similar principles that apply to the home also apply to commercial real estate*. The major difference is that with a home you will be investing both your money and your emotions. With commercial property, you will be wise, despite the passions aroused by money, to keep your emotions out of the investment decision.

In this chapter and those that follow I will be discussing properties costing $1 million or more. Don't stop reading. I recognize that very few people (including me) have anywhere near that amount to invest. However, by joining with others, you will have the opportunity to invest in such expensive properties. In chapter 14, you will see that you can, by investing through a limited partnership or a real estate investment trust, participate with as little as $1,000 or $2,000.

Before taking up specific types of property, I want to discuss my general approach to analyzing commercial real estate. Let me take a look at another mistake made by my fellow board member.

On our ride to the airport, he spoke of real estate as if it were a single generic investment. He should have known better. *Real estate comes in many different forms. It is not an undifferentiated mass.*

While any property may consist of land, wood, bricks, and mortar, this is where the similarities end. The mix of these materials differs from property to property—they come together in different configurations, they are in different locations, and they have different uses.

If there is anything intimidating about real estate, it is not that it is monolithic; rather, it is the fact that there is an endless variety of possibilities, each of which is a separate venture—from raw, undeveloped land to office towers to be leased for decades to multinational corporations. The options include every conceivable use of land, whether for single-family homes, apartment houses, office buildings, shopping centers, industrial facilities, motels, racquetball clubs, or massage parlors.

Credit vs. Noncredit Real Estate

Real estate can, however, be simplified. I start by dividing it into two general categories—credit and noncredit real estate—since any particular property is closer to one than to the other.

Whether a property is categorized as credit or noncredit real estate depends primarily upon the financial strength and stability of the tenant leasing it. The higher the credit standing of the tenant, the more likely it is that the property will be credit real estate.

When I speak of a property as a productive investment, I mean that it can be leased to someone who will pay a reasonable rent in return for its temporary use. The property is being "loaned" to a tenant for use as a store, warehouse, factory, office, home, or for some other purpose; and the rent is the "cost of borrowing." Therefore, before you invest, you must know who this tenant is, and whether he can afford to pay the rent.

A real estate broker telephoned me about a property under lease to K mart. He wanted me to buy it. Since K mart is a very successful retailing operation, I was interested, and I asked the broker to arrange for an inspection of the property.

"Why the hell do you have to see it?" he asked. "It's like

all the other K marts. It's got sixty thousand square feet, and K mart pays the rent for twenty-five years. What else do you need to know?"

I persisted, explaining that "Rembrandts are great paintings, but before I buy one I want to look at it so I can be sure it's really a Rembrandt. I don't pay for anything until I can see it and touch it."

He ended this rather ineloquent exchange with: "What are you, an amateur? No one has to see a K mart. Do us both a favor and do business with someone else."

The explanation for his fit of impatience (besides a touch of psychosis) was that he was selling me a credit property. It was leased to one of the largest retailing corporations in the United States. Under the lease, K mart agreed to pay a fixed rent for 25 years, as well as all the expenses of operating the property, such as utilities, real estate taxes, insurance, maintenance, and repairs. I would have no responsibility for the property during the term of the lease; and if the store turned out to be unprofitable, K mart would still have to pay the rent.

Credit Real Estate

As a result, the broker could not understand why I had to see the property. It had all the elements of credit real estate: a strong tenant; a net lease—one that's long-term, with a fixed rent, and free of operating expenses; and no management or maintenance responsibilities for the owner. In short, K mart was taking all of the real estate risks. I was being asked to take only the risk of K mart.

Under these circumstances, it does become less important whether the property is located on Fifth Avenue in New York City or in the swamps of Georgia or Florida. But this does not mean that the real estate itself is irrelevant.

I was entirely correct in insisting that I inspect it before buying. At the very least, I should have made certain that there really was property—remembering the millions of dollars that have been lost over the years by some of the most sophisticated financial institutions, which invested in salad oil and in tank cars that existed only in someone's imagination. But whether or not I should have invested was, in this case, more a credit than a real estate decision: the crucial fact was the financial strength of K mart.

Noncredit Real Estate

By contrast, noncredit real estate shifts the emphasis from the tenant to the property—its location, quality of construction, management, and cost of operation. A residential apartment building fits within this category, and illustrates most of the differences from the K mart store.

The apartment building will usually have several tenants instead of one; and the leases will be for a short term—not more than 1 to 3 years, as compared with the 25-year K mart lease. This allows the tenants to "take another look" at the property at least every 2 or 3 years and to decide whether to stay or leave. (The owner, as you shall see, also has the opportunity to reconsider the tenants.)

The owner of the apartment house, not the tenants, will be responsible for managing and maintaining the building. The rent he receives will not ordinarily be net of all operating expenses. Unlike the K mart lease, if these expenses rise, the owner may have difficulty in passing the increases along to the tenants either directly or in the form of higher rents. This means that he will have to pay them, and thereby reduce his profit.

The key difference, however, lies in the economic reliability of the tenants. They may, in the case of the apartment building, be respectable and civic-minded, and they may believe fervently in the sanctity of paying their bills on time. But whether they do or not, these tenants do have one thing in common: They are not K mart or Sears or General Motors, which come as close to perpetual existence as any landlord could hope. Tenants in an apartment building die and have to be replaced. They are more likely than large corporations to go bankrupt and be unable to pay their rent. Or they may move out, if they can obtain better terms elsewhere.

Noncredit problems. Thus, noncredit real estate lacks the stability of tenancy found in credit real estate. It also makes an owner vulnerable to competing projects, to changes in traffic patterns, to changing neighborhoods, to increased operating costs, and to general declines in business conditions—risks that are assumed by K mart. Without K mart on a long-term lease, it is the real estate itself that becomes decisive. Together with management and operation, it is the key to attracting, retaining, and replacing tenants.

A real estate developer has explained the difference between credit and noncredit real estate this way: "K mart isn't the real estate business. It's the investment business. If you want to be in real estate and make money at it, you've got to buy a property you can worry and work into success."

The distinction is not, however, always so clear. The dividing line is often blurred, with a particular property combining the elements of both categories. Shopping centers and office buildings, which have several tenants, are examples of this combination. Nevertheless, *any real estate project will be oriented more in one direction—credit or noncredit—than another*. You are, as often as not, dealing with points along a spectrum.

Assume that, instead of being the sole tenant, K mart were part of a 100,000-square-foot shopping center that also included a variety store, a beauty parlor, and several other stores. If K mart were the dominant tenant, leasing 60,000 to 70,000 square feet, the center would be closer to a credit property. If K mart had only a small store in the center (say, 10,000 to 20,000 square feet), with smaller, locally based tenants occupying the remaining 80,000 to 90,000 square feet, the complex would be closer to a noncredit property. Even in the case of the apartment building, if it were leased in its entirety to the Rockefeller brothers it would (unhappily) be more of a credit transaction than if the apartment units were leased to the Nessen brothers.

How to Evaluate a Property as Credit or Noncredit

The basic tests that determine the characterization of a property are as follows.

The first is, of course: *Who is the tenant?*

Second: *Is there more than one tenant?* A property leased to a single tenant is more likely to be credit real estate than one leased to several tenants. When there are a number of tenants, there is usually a range of quality, as in the case of a shopping center.

Third: *How long are the leases?* In credit transactions, the leases are usually for a period of 15 years or more, while in a noncredit transaction, the duration of each lease is ordinarily less than 15 years and, commonly between 1 and 5 years.

Fourth: *How "net" are the leases?* Or, expressing it another way: *Who pays the expenses of operating the property?* They are usually paid directly by the tenant in the credit transaction; and the lease is referred to as a "net lease" because the rent is net of these expenses. With a noncredit property, most of the operating expenses are paid by the owner. (There may be variations; for example, the tenants might pay utilities or real estate taxes and the owner pay the other expenses.)

Fifth: *Who has to manage and maintain the property?* When it snows, who shovels? The tenant will under the lease of a credit property; in the case of a noncredit property, this will usually be the owner's responsibility.

Generally speaking, a freestanding retail store net-leased to K mart or Sears, a warehouse net-leased to General Motors, or a fast-food restaurant net-leased to McDonald's will be credit real estate. Apartment buildings and vacant land are examples of non-credit real estate. And shopping centers and office buildings leased to more than one person will be somewhere in the middle. (I will take a closer look at each of these types of property beginning with chapter 10.)

Having made the distinction between credit and noncredit real estate, where should you invest your money? This is a troublesome choice, because no matter what you decide, you will be giving something up.

Credit Problems

When you invest in a property that is net-leased to K mart for 25 years, you are buying safety and freedom from responsibility. But in so doing, you will have to accept a low and fixed cash return. (The cash return is often called "cash flow.") This return generally relates to what K mart has to pay on its long-term (20 years or more) bonds. For example, if K mart has to make annual payments of 10% to the holders of its 25-year bonds ($100,000 on each $1 million of these bonds), your return would be a function of this payment—typically about 1% or 2% less than K mart's bond rate, or 8% or 9%.

There are a number of reasons for this low return. There is an extraordinary demand for credit real estate, which has driven up the price of these properties; and a company of the financial strength of a K mart is fully aware of this demand. It does not underestimate its desirability, and will insist upon low rents in return for becoming your tenant. Investors have been described as "carrying on a love affair with K mart" and similar companies. But it is a one-sided love affair, with K mart exacting a heavy price for its affections.

A credit tenant also pays low rents because it assumes most of the real estate risks. And one of the natural laws of investing is that your reward will, with rare exception, correspond to your risk.

A far more serious problem than a low cash return on credit property is the inflexibility of the rents during inflationary periods. Rents are, in a credit transaction, usually fixed for the duration of the lease, which may be as long as 25 years. If you purchase the K mart property, the relative certainty of, for example, a 9% return may be comforting. But it may not allow you to keep up with inflation. If the inflation rate exceeds 9%, then the rents will fall behind. Thus, fixed rents transfer the burden of inflation from the tenant to the owner.

· The contrast between credit and noncredit real estate was articulated by the owner of a small Concord office building, a noncredit property leased to several locally owned businesses. "This is not an investment for the fainthearted or the lazy," he explained. "I have to make more housecalls than anyone I know without a medical degree. And every time the roof leaks (and it does occasionally—it's an old building), my 'loyal' tenants threaten not to pay the rent or, worse, to move out. It can be very upsetting. I'm a decent guy, and I don't like to see anyone get cold or wet. But this doesn't seem to matter to them. If you're a landlord, you rank third in the hierarchy of villains, just behind moneylenders and oil companies."

"Why," I asked, "don't you sell the building?"

"Because, so long as I own it, I'm not stuck with a fixed return. And I won't put my money into anything that doesn't have some 'upside'—not in this economy."

Inflation has added a new, and unfortunate, dimension to real estate investing. Whether or not expectations of continuing inflation are warranted, they have greatly increased the demand for noncredit real estate. There are two reasons. First, you can usually charge higher initial rents for noncredit property and receive more cash flow. (How much more your return will be will depend upon the specific property and the quality of tenants.) And second, as the owner of the Concord office building recognized, you can adjust the rents. Since noncredit-property leases are "short-term," they can be renegotiated at least every few years, or you can find new tenants. The opportunity to make rent adjustments may afford you protection against inflation, and may even allow you to take advantage of it in your rent structure. There is, of course, the possibility that rents will decline, but this may be a more tolerable risk than having your return ravaged by inflation.

Thus far, I have been engaged in what might be called a "balancing of the aggravations." The K mart property may be safe, and it may be a passive investment (similar to a highly rated corporate bond); but there is the frustration of being forced to watch the value of your money being eaten away if there is no abatement in the rate of inflation.

The Concord office building, with the opportunity to adjust and increase the rents, can be a defense against inflation. But it is volatile. Tenants may leave; and operating expenses may rise, absorbing an increasing amount of the rents. The property will require supervision and will be very susceptible to conditions in the marketplace.

Equity Buildup and Tax Benefits

However, before you can choose between these two properties, you have to consider some of the other reasons for investing—namely, equity buildup, tax benefits, and capital appreciation.

The return from equity buildup and tax benefits will, ordinarily, be greater for credit than noncredit real estate. Equity buildup and tax benefits bear a direct relationship to the amount you can borrow. You could, as a general rule, obtain a mortgage of between 75% and 100% of the cost of purchasing the K mart property, but rarely more than 70% to 80% of the cost of the Concord office building.

In order to understand the relationship between borrowing and equity buildup, you should recognize that the capital structure of commercial real estate is similar to that of a home. Whether you buy a retail store, office building, or shopping center, you will probably pay only a small portion of the purchase price with your own money. Most of the cost will be borrowed; and the cash you invest is the equivalent of the down payment on your home. And, as with a home, equity buildup will increase with the size of the mortgage. Equity buildup is, as already discussed, simply the process of paying off (or, as it is frequently called, amortizing) the mortgage.

Assume you bought the K mart property for $1 million and obtained a $900,000 mortgage (90% financing). You would have to invest only $100,000 (10%). By the maturity date of the mortgage, you would have increased your equity by $900,000—the original amount of the mortgage. Thus, your return from equity buildup would have been nine times your cash investment (assuming the value of the property had not declined but had remained at $1 million).

By comparison, you probably could not borrow more than about 75% of the cost of the Concord office building. The reason is that the major tenant is an independent drugstore. The local pharmacist may be the backbone of our free-enterprise system, which earns him the respect and honor of his community; but he is not a strong, credit tenant, and his reputation seems to dissipate the closer he gets to the bank. Therefore, if you also had to pay $1 million for this building, the bank would be unlikely to give you more than a $750,000 mortgage. You would have to invest $250,000, and equity buildup could not exceed $750,000, or three times your cash investment.

(Equity buildup can, in the case of either type of property, be a substantial source of return. But you have to keep it in perspective. As with the home, it is a future, or "long-term," benefit that will not materialize until you sell or refinance.)

The mortgage affects tax benefits as well as equity buildup. In brief, the tax benefits come from the interest payable on the mortgage and the depreciation of the property, both of which are deductible expenses under the Internal Revenue Code. As I'll explain in the next chapter, a larger mortgage (in relation to your cash investment) will increase your return from these deductions. This confirms, once more, the importance of the credit/noncredit distinction, since the mortgage amount and thus the size of your deduction will depend, in great part, upon the tenants who are leasing your property.

The "Nonrecourse" Mortgage

There is another fact about the commercial-property mortgage that adds to the importance of equity buildup and tax benefits, and that reinforces the bank's preference for credit real estate: the mortgage is "nonrecourse."

Unlike a home mortgage, it is not a personal obligation, and you will not be personally liable if there is a default. The bank will have a claim only against the property and the rents. It is relying upon the rents for repayment. Thus, the quality of the tenants is as crucial to the bank as it is to you, and influences both the amount and the other terms of the mortgage.

Occasionally, the bank may request that you assume personal liability for the mortgage. You should, without exception, decline, even if your refusal means that you will be unable to purchase the property. The risk is too great. (Whether or not you are personally liable, the bank may also want the mortgage to be repaid if you sell the property before the maturity date. You should try to resist having this requirement put in the mortgage, because it may be easier to make a sale if your purchaser can take over, or assume, your mortgage.)

You, as well as the bank, are relying upon the tenants to repay the nonrecourse mortgage. Their rents are building up your equity. One banker, in trying to justify the outrageous interest rates being charged on real estate loans, described the nonrecourse mortgage as, from the owner's standpoint, "closing in on perfection—using our money to buy the property and someone else's money to pay us off."

Capital Appreciation

Perhaps the most seductive appeal of real estate is the possibility of capital appreciation—the chance that the property will go up in value. While the words "Yeah, but does it have potential" may lack the lush quality and inspirational effect of "blood, toil, tears, and sweat," they became the rallying cry of real estate brokers and investors in the 1970s. Translated, this phrase about potential means that as bad as a property may be today, it will get better with age—it will appreciate in value.

When I last heard this statement, my firm was being offered a warehouse net-leased to a company that has been quivering on the edge of bankruptcy for several years. The cash return being proposed was less than 6%. Fortunately, I have a partner who saves time by being far less reticent than I in expressing his feelings.

"You're right," he said. "It does have potential. In fact, with a six percent cash flow from a miserable credit, and no right to increase the rents, that's all its got. It has to have potential—it can't get any worse."

Capital appreciation is contingent upon the future and is, therefore, uncertain. Yet, because of inflation, its attraction is growing. Investors seem to believe that real estate is intimately bound to inflation.

This reliance upon inflation can be misplaced. If, however, you can make frequent rent adjustments, you may be able to increase your cash flow and, as a result, the price at which you can sell a property. Based solely upon this possibility, the Concord office building would be a better investment than the K mart.

But no property carries with it a guarantee of capital appreciation. The upward trend of rents is a statistic that does not insure the performance of any particular property. As I emphasized early in this chapter, real estate takes many different forms. It is not a commodity, like potatoes, wheat, or automobiles, and price changes do not have a uniform effect.

There is also a real danger that operating expenses will rise more rapidly than rents. Inflation strikes unevenly. It does not abide by any mathematical rules requiring that rents and operating expenses move in tandem. Moreover, you should not become so conditioned to inflation that you overlook the possibility of a decline in rents. Indeed, this is one of the goals of a government-induced recession. And, of course, it is doubtful that a poorly located or constructed property, or one that is badly managed, can be saved by the "miracle of inflation."

Capital appreciation is a valid goal; and your best chance of achieving it will come from investing in noncredit real estate. Nevertheless, the opportunity is filled with risks and uncertainties. Perhaps it is true that faith will move mountains; if so, the statement "Real estate has to go up in value" might be reasonable. However, unless this statement comes from some authority (theological, scientific, or otherwise) of which I am unaware, it should be recognized as part of the mythology of real estate and promptly forgotten.

I come back to the question: Where should you invest? The answer depends upon your needs and the price, in terms of money and effort, you are prepared to pay in order to satisfy these needs.

If you are already rich, and not trying to amass another fortune, you should seriously consider a credit property. It will help to preserve your income from taxes (as chapter 9 explains) and promises the long-term benefits of equity build-up, which may counteract some of the effects of inflation.

If you are willing to take some risks with your money and to engage actively in the real estate business, you should purchase a noncredit property—an office building, an apartment project, or even a three-family house. Such a property has the potential of capital appreciation, which is the key to riches in real estate. But investing for the sake of capital appreciation can also be the unmaking of fortunes. Noncredit real estate is not the place for the casual investor; it is a business that takes time and requires supervision.

If your financial position is similar to mine, with a moderate amount of money to invest—about $5,000 to $25,000— your choice lies somewhere in between the two extremes, but nearer to the credit side of the line. My preference would be a medium-sized shopping center (about 100,000 to 150,000 square feet) with two credit tenants and several "local" ones. The credit tenants provide stability and minimize the management responsibilities, while the local tenants make capital appreciation a realistic possibility. I have been told that watching me invest has "all the excitement of the saga of Goldilocks choosing a bed." But unless some anonymous person leaves me an inheritance or unless I am able to spend more time than I can now afford in overseeing my investment, this middle position is an appropriate compromise.

This chapter has raised many pertinent issues and problems about investing in commercial properties. It is not, of course, a definitive exposition on how to invest. The purpose has been to begin to find an approach that untangles the multiplicity of alternatives.

I have raised several questions that remain to be answered, such as: What are the specific investment possibilities? Where do you find them? What are their tax and other benefits? How should you finance them? How do you calculate your return? and, In what legal form should you own a property? In the coming chapters, I will try to answer these and related questions.

Nine

TAX BENEFITS

EVERY COMMERCIAL PROPERTY CONTAINS SOME MEASURE of tax benefits. Sometimes these benefits are so predominant as to be the basic, if not the only, reason to invest. A real estate investment fitting this description is referred to as a "tax shelter."

Tax Shelters

The concept "tax shelter" has, in the past, been enshrouded in mystery, as if it were part of the world of the occult. There was a feeling that you needed special qualities, setting you apart from ordinary men and women, before you could be initiated into its secrets—qualities like being very rich.

But the obscurity of "tax shelter" has dissolved as people have become more knowledgeable about our tax system, and have come to understand that a tax shelter is simply an investment that generates large tax deductions. These deductions reduce your taxable income, enabling you to save, or "shelter," money you would otherwise have to pay in taxes. In real estate, interest and depreciation deductions produce most of these tax savings.

In the late 1950s as a young lawyer, I was introduced to the tax shelter. I had been practicing law for about six months when I was sent by my law firm to Las Vegas to represent a very wealthy client. He was buying a building leased to a department store similar in credit standing to Sears, Roebuck. The terms of the transaction were as follows.

The purchase price was $1 million. My client was able to finance the entire cost with a 25-year nonrecourse mortgage of $1 million, bearing interest at the rate of 10%. He did not have to make a down payment. (At that time, interest was actually much lower than 10%, but I am using this rate here in order to simplify the mathematics of the example.) The annual installment payments required on the mortgage (covering both interest and principal) were approximately $110,-000. The net rent payable by the company under the lease, after the payment of all operating expenses, was also $110,-000.

Since the incoming rent was the same as the outgoing interest and principal on the mortgage—$110,000—there was no money left over for my client; he did not have any cash flow. "Then why," I asked myself, "does he want to own the building?"

Of course, there was the possibility of equity buildup and capital appreciation, but these were benefits arising in the future. They seemed too ephemeral to justify paying what he had described as the "immorally high" fees of my law firm and the real estate broker.

Since I was new to the legal profession, I was afraid to admit that I had no idea about what was going on. Besides, I was already conspicuous enough—being, I believe, the only man in Las Vegas wearing, publicly at least, a Brooks Brothers three-piece suit. But I finally decided to risk a show of ignorance, and I quietly put the question to my client's accountant.

"My boy," he said, "Uncle Sam works in strange, devious, and wonderful ways. He is going to let our client save money, lots of money, in taxes by investing in this building."

How a shelter works. Then he explained how the magic worked. First, the $110,000 in rent had to be considered an addition to my client's taxable income, even though all of this rent was used to pay the mortgage. Second, interest on the mortgage and a depreciation allowance were deducted from this income.

In the first year of his investment, interest was $100,000—10% of $1 million. Since it was tax deductible, the rental income was, in effect, reduced from $110,000 to $10,000—$110,000 in rents minus $100,000 interest. (As with a home mortgage, the interest deduction would decrease in each succeeding year as the principal of the mortgage was repaid. I will explain the tax effect later in this chapter.)

Next, he deducted depreciation. In the theology of real estate, there is nothing more revered than depreciation. In searching for an analogy, the closest I can come is the Holy Spirit. You can feel its presence, although you can neither see nor touch it.

Depreciation arises out of an anthropomorphic concept contained in the Internal Revenue Code. Under the Code, a commercial building is presumed to have a life—a useful, or, as it is sometimes called, an economic life. The structure is useful for a certain number of years and then dies, or fades away, or does whatever buildings do when their lives are over. As the years go by, the usefulness supposedly declines steadily. This theoretical decline is known as depreciation, and it is an "expense" that is deductible from income.

Before 1981 the useful life of any building would vary depending upon, among other factors, its use, size, location, type of construction, wear and tear, natural physical deterioration, and the possibility of technological obsolescence and change. But in 1981, the Economic Recovery Tax Act declared arbitrary and specific lives (known as "recovery periods") for all types of real estate. Now, you can elect to depreciate real estate over either 15, 35, or 45 years. (There are some exceptions. In the case of certain public utility properties and residential manufactured homes, for example, the depreciable period is 10 years. Moreover, the pre-1981 rules for depreciation apply to any property which you owned in 1980, or which you buy and lease back to someone who owned it in 1980.) Ordinarily, you would select the 15-year option, since it would enable you to get your deductions sooner than with the 35 or 45-year options.

Based upon the 1981 tax act, my client could have depreciated the Las Vegas department store over 15 years at the rate of $66,667 each year. (In preparing my calculations below, I shall assume that the 1981 tax act was in effect when he purchased the building.) I arrived at this figure by dividing the cost of the building, $1 million, by 15 years. This method of depreciation, where an equal amount is deducted each year ($66,667 in the case of the Las Vegas building) is known as straight-line depreciation.

The $66,667 deduction further reduces the aftertax rental income from $66,667 to "minus $56,667." This is shown in table 12.

The significance of depreciation lies in the fact that it is not an expense in any ordinary sense. It is not a real loss;

TABLE 12

Calculating Aftertax Rental Income on Las Vegas Tax Shelter

Rental income before deductions	$110,000
MINUS	
Interest on the mortgage	100,000
MINUS	
Depreciation	66,667
Result—rental income after deductions	**—$ 56,667**

and my client was not paying out $66,667 in cash. It is, rather, a "paper" or "accounting" expense. Furthermore, it would not be necessary to prove that the building was actually depreciating or wearing out. My client would be entitled to the deduction whether its value had gone up, gone down, or stayed the same.

Thus, despite all the mystery and obscurity, the calculation of tax benefits is this simple: The rent you receive from a property becomes part of your income. You then deduct interest and depreciation. In the example of the Las Vegas building, the result was minus $56,667. The question you might ask next is: "What on earth can anyone do with minus $56,667?" Or, "How can you win by losing?"

Most of us have been taught that "gains are good, and losses are bad." The truth of that advice is incontrovertible in a world confined to physical phenomena. For example, when you have to pay out more money than you take in on a property, this is a real cash loss—a loss to be avoided. But when you move from the physical world into the world of taxes, you come up with an exception—a world where losses can be gains.

My client would have ended up with a "loss" of $56,667. (The $56,667 is, as I said earlier, based upon the 1981 tax act. Since he invested prior to 1981, his actual loss was less than $56,667 because his depreciation deductions were less under the old law.) Yet he paid nothing out-of-pocket. He received $110,000 in cash from the tenant, and he paid $110,-000 in cash to the holder of the mortgage. However, because of interest and depreciation, he "lost" $56,667. One of the few blessings of the Internal Revenue Code is that it allowed him to subtract this "loss" from his other income.

My client had taxable income of about $200,000 a year from various business ventures. Assuming that he had to pay 50% of the $200,000 in taxes, he would have been left with only $100,000. (Actually, as I discussed earlier, not all of his income would have been taxed at the 50% rate, but I am applying the 50% rate to all of his income in order to simplify this discussion.)

Since he could subtract the $56,667 "loss," his income was reduced to $143,333—$200,000 minus $56,667. The tax on $143,333 at 50% was $71,666.50. He saved, therefore, $28,333.50 in taxes in the first year of his investment—the difference between a $71,666.50 tax on $143,333 and a $100,000 tax on $200,000. Another way of calculating his tax savings is to multiply his loss by his tax bracket. In the 50% tax bracket, his tax savings were 50% of his $56,667 loss, or $28,333.50. (If he had been in the 40% bracket, his savings would have been 40% of $56,667, or $22,666.80). Table 13 below shows how my client's tax savings were calculated.

Such calculations have been described as "entering into the world of make believe," but you will soon find out that there is reality in this "world of make believe." There was nothing illusory about the money my client was saving. While these savings did not put new cash into his pocket, they allowed him to keep $28,333.50 of the cash already there.

There was one other fact about this transaction that was

TABLE 13

Calculating Tax Saving on Las Vegas Tax Shelter (100% Financing)

Income from business ventures (exclusive of Las Vegas transaction)	$200,000
MINUS	
"Loss" from Las Vegas transaction	56,667
Result—total income	143,333
Tax before Las Vegas transaction (50% of $200,000)	$100,000
MINUS	
Tax after Las Vegas transaction (50% of 143,333)	71,666.50
Result—tax saving (50% of $56,667 "loss")	$ 28,333.50

even more startling to me than the turning of losses into gains. My client was entitled to the $28,333.50 in tax savings even though he did not use any of his own money to buy the building (other than to pay legal and brokerage fees and some incidental costs). He borrowed 100% of the purchase price with a nonrecourse mortgage. Nevertheless, he could still deduct interest and depreciation. The right to these deductions without risking any cash is unique to real estate. To some, this is a loophole that constitutes a massive welfare grant to the real estate industry. But, as I was told, "it takes a brave man to question the rightness of these deductions. You will be called a traitor. It's almost as if the real estate industry looks upon itself as a separate nation, with its motto being 'Interest and depreciation forever.' "

Whatever the virtue or vice of our nation's tax policy, it shows, once again, the importance of leverage. The more you borrow, the higher your return from tax benefits. If you can make $28,333.50 without investing anything, you have an infinite rate of return. Another way of putting it: you reduce your return with every dollar you invest.

Now assume that the tenant paid $88,000 in rent, and that my client could borrow only $800,000 (80% of the cost of the building). He would have to make a $200,000 cash investment as a down payment. If the interest rate on the mortgage remained at 10%, the annual payments (including both the 10% interest and principal) would be about $88,000. In the first year, his rental income would be $88,000; and he could deduct $80,000 interest (10% of $800,000) and $66,667 depreciation. (Depreciation is based upon the $1 million cost of the building, whether all or none of the cost is borrowed.) His loss would be $58,667 ($88,000 in rent minus $80,000 interest minus $66,667 depreciation), for a tax saving of $29,333.50 (50% of $32,000). But this time he would have to invest $200,000 for this saving, as summarized in table 14.

Generally speaking, a credit property will provide the maximum tax benefits because you can borrow up to 100% of the purchase price. And, as you might expect by comparing tables 13 and 14, you will have a greater return on each dollar you invest the closer you get to 100% financing.

Straight-line vs. accelerated depreciation. You will also have greater tax benefits in the early years of a real estate transaction, if you exercise another option made available in the

TABLE 14

Calculating Tax Saving on Las Vegas Tax Shelter (80% Financing)

Income from business ventures (exclusive of Las Vegas transaction)	$200,000
MINUS	
"Loss" from Las Vegas transaction	58,667
Result—total income	$141,333
Tax before Las Vegas transaction (50% of $200,000)	$100,000
MINUS	
Tax after Las Vegas transaction (50% of $141,333)	70,666.50
Result—tax saving (50% of the $58,667 "loss")	$ 29,333.50

1981 tax act—the option to use the accelerated method of depreciation. "Accelerated depreciation" would not have allowed my client to deduct, over the 15-year "life" of the building, more than he could have deducted using the straight-line method, but it would have allowed him to speed up the time over which he could have taken the deductions.

TABLE 15

Calculating First-Year Tax Saving on Las Vegas Tax Shelter Using Straight-Line vs. Accelerated Depreciation

	Using Straight-Line Depreciation	Using Accelerated Depreciation
Rental income before deductions	$110,000	$110,000
MINUS		
Interest on the mortgage	100,000	100,000
MINUS		
Depreciation	66,667	120,000
Result—rental income after deductions	— $56,667	—$110,000
Tax Savings	$28,333.50 (50% of $56,667)	$ 55,000 (50% of $110,000)

Under the accelerated method, 12% of the 1 million cost of the Las Vegas building—or $120,000 (instead of $66,667 using straight-line)—could have been depreciated in the first year. That would have made his "loss" $110,000 instead of $56,667, as you can see.

There are, however, disadvantages to accelerated depreciation.

First, unlike straight-line, the depreciable amount will decline each year. In the example of the Las Vegas building, the second-year deduction will be $100,000, and in the third year it will be about $90,000. By the tenth year, it will drop to $50,000. (See Table 16.)

But a far more serious disadvantage to accelerated depreciation is that you will suffer a penalty, known as "recapture," when you sell the property. This penalty makes it highly unlikely that you will choose the accelerated option, as I will explain in detail later in this chapter.

As with most other things, the law of compensation also governs the tax shelter. If you want to maximize tax savings, you have to be prepared to give up something.

Tax savings vs. other benefits. Tax savings usually conflict

TABLE 16

Accelerated vs. Straight-Line
Depreciation Deductions on Las Vegas Tax Shelter

Year	Deduction Using Accelerated Depreciation	Deduction Using Straight-Line Depreciation	Difference
1	$120,000	$66,667	$53,333
2	100,000	66,667	33,333
3	90,000	66,667	23,333
4	80,000	66,667	13,333
5	70,000	66,667	3,333
6	60,000	66,667	—6,667
7	60,000	66,667	—6,667
8	60,000	66,667	—6,667
9	60,000	66,667	—6,667
10	50,000	66,667	—16,667
11	50,000	66,667	—16,667
12	50,000	66,667	—16,667
13	50,000	66,667	—16,667

with other economic benefits, as evidenced by their effect upon cash flow and equity buildup.

When you use any of the rents you receive from a property to pay interest on the mortgage, you increase both your deductions and your tax savings. But when these rents are applied to interest they cannot be retained by you as cash flow, nor are they available to pay principal on the mortgage.

In the case of the Las Vegas building $100,000 of the $110,000 in rents was applied to interest in the first year. If you had to pay interest of 11%, instead of 10%, on the $1 million mortgage, you would have had to apply all of the $110,000 in rents to interest (with nothing being paid to principal). In this case, both your deductions and "losses" would have been increased by $10,000—since interest would have been $110,000, and not $100,000. But there would have been nothing left over for cash flow; nor would there have been any equity buildup, since no principal was being repaid.

If, on the other hand, only $90,000 of the $110,000 of rents had to be used for interest in the first year, the extra $10,000 would have gone in one of two directions—either to cash flow or to principal and equity buildup. But the "losses" would have been reduced by $10,000.

Another example of the inconsistency between tax and economic benefits is found in the treatment of land. For tax purposes, land does not "wear out." It is immortal, nondepreciable, and nondeductible.

Up to now, I have been assuming that the Las Vegas building had a $1 million cost, with no value being ascribed to the land on which it was located. The entire $1 million of cost was, therefore, depreciable at the annual rate of $66,667 using straight-line depreciation. But if the land had constituted 25% ($250,000) of the cost, then only $750,000 of the building cost could have been depreciated. The annual depreciation deduction would have been $50,000 ($750,000 in building costs divided by 15 years) instead of $66,667—a difference of $16,667 each year.

Many "tax shelter" investors try to avoid buying real estate with a large land component because they can't depreciate the land. It has been argued, and with considerable merit, that this is not simply an anomaly. It is a monstrosity—a perversion of values. When you invest in a property, its greatest potential can be in the land. Unlike the building, the land does not wear out. But Congress, through the tax laws, actually penalizes you for owning land.

Is a tax shelter suitable? It may be worth it to trade economic benefits for tax savings. Before you do, however, you should be sure that a real estate tax shelter is suitable for you.

The standard test of suitability is whether you are in at least the 40% tax bracket or higher; all of the income being "sheltered" by your investment should be money that would otherwise have been taxed at least at the 40% rate (and closer to 50% when you take state and local taxes into account). Furthermore, you should reasonably expect to remain in this bracket for at least the next several years.

Ordinarily, you will have to purchase a tax shelter from a real estate broker or promoter. (In chapter 14, I'll look at the role of the real estate promoter and how you find one.) The amount you pay will be based upon the projected "losses" from the property. Typically, these losses should be 3.5 times your cost. At a 3.5-to-1 ratio, if you pay $25,000, your losses should be $87,500, and, applying the suitability test, they should save you $35,000 in taxes—40% of $87,500.

If your tax bracket is below 40%, you will be overpaying for the losses. In the 30% bracket, for example, $87,500 of losses will be worth only $26,250 (30% of $87,500)—hardly a fair or sensible return on a $25,000 investment.

Another test is the timing of your return. You should receive losses of two times your investment in not less than five or six years. If you pay $25,000, your losses should, over this period, be $50,000.

Don't use tax savings for consumption. Even if these tests are met, you should not buy a tax shelter if you are going to use the money you save in taxes to increase your consumption. These tax savings are the equivalent of cash, but you should invest in a tax shelter only if you intend to use most of them to earn more money—that is, if you intend to reinvest them.

This is more than advice. It is an admonishment. In any transaction, there is only a limited amount of "losses." Eventually they will be used up. *At some point, the losses will stop, and you will have to start paying taxes.* This occurs because the interest payments get smaller each year, as the principal of the mortgage is being paid off, and depreciation ends after 15 years.

Try to imagine yourself in the position of my client. The

best year of his Las Vegas investment was the first. During that year his deductions, including interest of $100,000, exceeded pretax rental income by $56,667 (see table 12); and he had tax savings of $28,333.50 (table 13). In the second year, however, both interest and the "losses" dropped by $1,000. And by the sixteenth year, there will be no more losses. You can see this in table 17 (page 149).

When shelters stop sheltering. The rental income stays at $110,000, while the interest deductions decline. By the sixteenth year, there will be no more depreciation, and interest will be only $68,200. As a result, the rents will exceed the total deductions by $41,800. And now you are in for a shock. He will have to pay a tax of $20,900 on this excess income (50% of $41,800)—and there will be no cash flow from the building to fund the payment. All of the rent is being applied to interest and principal on the mortgage. As with a home, the amount of each installment payment remains constant ($110,000 annually, in the Las Vegas example); but as less interest is being paid, the principal payments are becoming larger. My client is, of course, building up equity—but equity buildup is not cash. He will have to use his own money to pay the $20,900 tax.

This may prompt you to complain, as another of my clients did, that "with all these phantom losses and phantom income, I feel like I am being dragged down in a metaphysical swirl. I get losses without losing money, and taxable income without receiving any money."

However, just as the "losses" result in real cash savings, there is nothing hypothetical about the taxes you are eventually going to pay. And after the sixteenth year, in my example, the situation will get even worse. In the twentieth year, the taxable income will be $61,200, requiring the payment of a $30,600 tax (50% of $61,200); and by the twenty-fifth year, my client will have to pay $49,250 on taxable income of $98,500 from his "tax shelter."

Experienced real estate investors use a mix of metaphors to explain what is happening: "The lines are crossing, and you have to pay the piper." That means that when the rent exceeds deductions, you will have a tax liability even though there is no cash flow from the property with which to pay it. That will usually occur in any transaction after the fifteenth year, when there are no more depreciation deductions.

There is no way to prevent this "crossing of the lines;" nor

TABLE 17
Breakdown of Tax Loss and Saving on Las Vegas Tax Shelter Using Straight-Line Depreciation

Year	Rental Income	Interest	Depreciation	Total Deductions	Tax Loss*	Tax Saving (50% Bracket)
1	$110,000	$100,000	$66,667	$166,667	$56,667	$28,333.50
2	110,000	99,000	66,667	165,667	55,667	27,833.50
3	110,000	97,900	66,667	164,567	54,567	27,283.50
4	110,000	96,700	66,667	163,367	53,367	26,683.50
5	110,000	95,400	66,667	162,067	52,067	26,033.50
6	110,000	93,900	66,667	160,567	50,567	25,283.50
7	110,000	92,300	66,667	158,967	48,967	24,483.50
8	110,000	90,500	66,667	157,167	47,167	23,583.50
9	110,000	88,600	66,667	155,267	45,267	22,633.50
10	110,000	86,400	66,667	153,067	43,067	21,533.50
11	110,000	84,100	66,667	150,767	40,767	20,383.50
12	110,000	81,500	66,667	148,167	38,167	19,083.50
13	110,000	78,600	66,667	145,267	35,267	17,633.50
14	110,000	75,500	66,667	142,167	32,167	16,083.50
15	110,000	72,000	66,667	138,667	28,667	14,333.50
16	110,000	68,200	0	68,200	— 41,800	— 20,900.00
20	110,000	48,800	0	48,800	— 61,200	— 30,600.00
25	110,000	11,500	0	11,500	— 98,500	— 49,250.00

NOTE Interest figures are rounded to the nearest $100.
* Rental income less total deductions.

is it intended that there should be. The government allows you to avoid taxes for several years, and then it wants some of the money back.

I tried to explain this process to a friend who has become a well-known doctor. He invited me out on his new thirty-foot sailboat. "I work too hard and worry too much about my patients," he told me. "So I bought this boat, to relax on weekends. And the government paid for it. Instead of paying half of what I make in taxes, I got into a 'real estate shelter' deal. What I don't pay in taxes, I put into the boat."

But he had been caught in a trap. The government had not paid for the boat. It had only loaned him the money with which to buy it. His tax savings were more an interest-free loan from the government than an outright grant. And when there were no more "losses," he was going to have to start paying the government back. After 15 years, he would probably have to sell the boat and start working weekends in order to meet this accruing tax liability.

Although this is a problem without a perfect solution, there are a number of ways to ease the pain.

Shelter Advice

First, as I suggested, you should take most if not all of the money you are saving each year in taxes and invest it elsewhere. The real advantage of a tax shelter is that it allows you an alternative use of your money—instead of paying it currently in taxes, you can invest it in stocks, in bonds, or in other real estate. While you will eventually have to repay at least some part of your tax savings, you will be able to keep the money you have made in the meantime from these other investments. (Part of your return from these other investments may, of course, be taxed.)

Capital gains treatment. Second, you can sell the tax shelter when the tax benefits have been fully exhausted. You will have to pay a tax on any gain from the sale, but in most cases, you will not be taxed at ordinary income-tax rates. So long as you own the property for more than 12 months, your gain will usually be treated as capital gain, rather than ordinary income. As a result, only 40% of the gain will be subject to taxation and 60% will be excluded. Therefore, it you sold the property and your gain was $100,000, you would be taxed on $40,000 (40% of $100,000). The tax on $40,000, if you are in the 50% bracket, would be $20,000.

The 60% exclusion of the gain from taxation is known as a "tax preference." You are being given preferred treatment under the tax laws. However, in 1982 Congress passed an alternative minimum tax which will be payable if it exceeds your regular tax in any year. The purported purpose of the minimum tax is to prevent you from sheltering all or most of your income through real estate and other tax shelters. The more tax preferences you have, the more likely it is that you will have to pay the alternative minimum tax. Obviously, you will have to check with your accountant to find out, given your personal tax situation, whether you will be subject to this new tax.

How to Figure Your Gain on a Tax Shelter Sale

In determining your gain on the sale of a tax shelter, you will find that once again the tax universe has its own internal logic that, at times, confounds your expectations. The gain from the sale of any commercial property has, under the tax laws, nothing to do with the money that ends up in your pocket. Taxable gain is the amount for which you sell the property—including both cash and the mortgage balance—minus its undepreciated cost. This can best be understood by looking again at the Las Vegas building.

If you sell the building for $10,000 in cash plus the mortgage at the end of the fifteenth year, this is how your gain and your tax on this gain are arrived at:

First, you begin with the sales price. It is not $10,000. It is $10,000 plus the outstanding principal of the mortgage at the time of the sale—even though you will be receiving only $10,000 in cash. At the close of the fifteenth year, the mortgage balance is approximately $682,300, so the sales price is $692,300—$682,300 plus $10,000.

Then, you find the undepreciated cost of the building. Your original cost was $1 million, even though you had financed the entire amount through a mortgage. This cost is reduced each year by the depreciation deductions. Over a period of 15 years, they total $1 million—15 years times $66,667. Therefore, your undepreciated cost when you sell is zero—$1 million minus $1 million.

Finally, you calculate your gain by subtracting your undepreciated cost—zero—from your sales price of $692,300. The result is $692,300. Since there is a 60% capital-gain exclusion,

40% of the $692,300 gain, or $276,920, is subject to taxes. Your tax on $276,920 in the 50% bracket is $138,460.

These steps are summarized in table 18.

TABLE 18

Calculating Capital-Gain Tax on Sale of Las Vegas Tax Shelter

Sales price		**$692,300**
Cash received	$ 10,000	
PLUS		
Outstanding mortgage balance (at end of fifteenth year)	682,300	
Total	$ 692,300	
Undepreciated cost		**$ 0**
Original cost	$1,000,000	
MINUS		
Depreciation deductions	1,000,000	
Result	$ 0	
Gain		**$692,300**
Sales price	$ 692,300	
MINUS		
Undepreciated cost	0	
Result	$ 692,300	
Amount to be taxed (40% of $692,300)		**$276,920**
Tax on gain (50% of $276,920)		**$138,460**

Since you received only $10,000 in cash, you will have to pay $128,460 of the $138,460 tax from your own funds. If you received more than $10,000, your taxable gain would be larger but you would have more cash with which to pay the tax.

Alternatives to Selling

There are some other possibilities that, under certain circumstances, may also be effective when a tax shelter begins "to turn" on you.

Refinancing. You may be able to refinance. This will allow you to start the mortgage process over again. If, for example, at the end of the fifteenth year you could obtain a new 25-

year mortgage in the amount of $1 million and bearing interest at 10%, your interest deduction would be $100,000 in the first year of the new mortgage (10% of $1 million), whereas on the old mortgage interest would have been only $72,000 (see table 17, year 15). Furthermore, there is no tax on the money you receive from a refinancing. The potential for refinancing varies, depending upon the type of property; however, you should assume, for the moment, that it will be difficult to accomplish a refinancing in a transaction that was originally put together as a tax shelter investment.

Exchanging the property. Instead of selling, you may be able to exchange the building for another property, and temporarily avoid paying tax. If the exchange is properly arranged, you can defer your tax liability. An exchange is, however, not easy to find; and it involves a complicated procedure requiring careful professional planning. You should consult with your lawyer and accountant before you entertain this alternative.

Dying. If all else fails, you can die; and in the words of a somewhat overzealous tax counselor, "the optimum moment will be when the 'lines cross.'" Despite its apparent disadvantage, dying may be the most effective solution, because your heirs will be allowed to redepreciate your property. Your death, according to the Internal Revenue Code, gives the building a new life. And the amount that can be redepreciated is not your undepreciated cost. It is the fair market value of the building at the time of your death. If the value has appreciated to $1.5 million, depreciation will be based upon this figure.

Other Shelter Problems

Although your options are limited when there are no more tax losses, at least you know it is going to happen and you can be prepared for it. There are, however, other problems with a real estate tax shelter that are difficult or impossible to prepare for. There are the risks that your tax bracket will change, or that Congress will amend the tax laws. In either case, you may lose some of your expected benefits.

There is always the chance that you will make less money in the future and change tax brackets. This can happen if you suffer a financial reverse, which may be difficult to predict or to protect against. But too many investors fail to consider another possibility, that they may, at some later time, voluntarily accept a reduction in their income. They may want to retire or just slow down. Whatever the reason, a decline in your income can reduce your tax bracket and the value of the "losses." (A change in your tax bracket can, of course, work in your favor, particularly during a period of inflation. Inflation may, without increasing your purchasing power, raise both your income and tax bracket. In this unhappy situation, at least your "losses" will be worth more, with the tax shelter providing you some protection against the artificial expansion of your income. However, after 1984, the federal tax rate schedules will be indexed for inflation, with annual adjustments to reflect changes in the Department of Labor's Consumer Price Index.)

Members of Congress are sporadically inspired, by pressure, conscience, or the desire to be reelected, to reform the Internal Revenue Code. And there is very little you can do about it other than write threatening letters to your representative. "Reform" has not, in the past, seriously impaired the tax advantages of real estate. In fact, the 1981 tax act significantly improved upon these advantages. But you are in an area that favors the rich and is, thus, continually vulnerable to the whims of political sentiment, which may be manifested by changes in the tax laws.

Both depreciation and interest deductions have been favorite targets of "reform." For example, you may not be allowed to take the full deduction for interest paid on a mortgage on a net-leased property. (I'll discuss this problem in chapter 13.)

Problems with accelerated depreciation. Under the tax laws, accelerated depreciation can also have serious negative consequences. If my client had elected the accelerated method, he would have been able to deduct $120,000 in the first year instead of $66,667 (see table 16). By making this choice, however, he would have been penalized when he sold the building. All of his gain up to the full amount of the depreciation deductions he had taken would have been taxed as ordinary income, and not as capital gain. (There are exceptions for housing projects, which I will tell you about in chapter 13.)

While this treatment of the gain (recapture) should, in most cases, discourage you from using accelerated depreciation, ask your accountant before you decide.

Moreover, the excess of accelerated depreciation deducted each year over straight-line is, under the tax code, a "tax preference," and may make you vulnerable to the alternative minimum tax, which I mentioned earlier.

Default disaster. The use of accelerated depreciation can turn into an undiluted disaster, if the tenant is unable to pay the rent, market conditions have turned against you, or the real estate is unsound. Whatever the reason, you may forfeit the property because of the failure to meet your mortgage obligations. While you may think that this is enough to suffer, it is the mild part of the punishment. When you lose the property under these circumstances, it is, for tax purposes, considered a sale.

The sales price will probably be the same as the unpaid balance of the mortgage, since it is unlikely that you would have defaulted if the property had appreciated in value. Your taxable gain is calculated in the same manner as the gain on a voluntary sale—the difference between the sales price (in this case, the mortgage balance alone) and the undepreciated cost. If default occurs in the fifteenth year, in the example of the Las Vegas property, your mortgage balance will be about $682,000 and your undepreciated cost will be zero. Your gain will be $682,000—and the tax, in the 50% bracket (after taking into account the 60% exclusion), will be $136,400 if you have used straight-line depreciation.

But if you elected the accelerated method, your tax will be higher because your gain will be taxed as ordinary income (50% of $682,000, or $341,000). And making matters worse than they probably should be, your tax bracket, and therefore your tax, may be increased (although not beyond 50%) by your having to take all of this gain in a single year—even though you have not received any cash from the property.

(There was a recent federal court decision holding that the amount realized from the disposition of real estate subject to a nonrecourse mortgage would not exceed its fair market value, even if that value was less than the mortgage balance. However, I would be surprised if the Supreme Court did not reverse that decision during its current session.)

The possibility of a mortgage default should not inhibit you from investing in real estate. It should, however, make you very careful about how you select a property. Frequently, people who invest primarily for tax benefits seem to

⌂ CHECKLIST

NINE POINTS YOU SHOULD KEEP
IN MIND WHEN INVESTING IN A TAX SHELTER

Conflict between tax benefits and economic benefits
You will, for example, have less tax savings the faster
you pay off the mortgage principal.

Your tax bracket   You should be in at least the
40% federal tax bracket (preferably closer to the
50% bracket). Your tax bracket may decline over
the years, making your investment less valuable.

Amount of "losses"   They should be about $3.50 for
each $1.00 of your investment. (Putting it another
way, if you invest $1,000, your losses should be
about $3,500.)

Timing of receipt of tax benefits   You should receive
$2.00 of losses for each $1.00 you invest within at
least five or six years.

Exhaustion of tax benefits   When the taxable income
from the property exceeds the deductions, the benefits disappear.

Future changes in the tax laws   Reforms may limit
or eliminate your tax benefits.

Recapture   If you use accelerated depreciation, all
or most of your gain from a sale of a property may
be taxed at ordinary income-tax rates rather than at
capital-gain rates.

Promoters' projections   Be wary of such projections,
particularly those dealing with the source and timing of tax benefits.

forget about the actual real estate. The numbers become too enticing.

Tax Shelter Cautions

The danger of the numbers is not only that they lull you into forgetting that you are buying real estate and not simply a string of tax losses. The numbers are also a "tool" of promoters who will be selling your real estate; and promoters can be extraordinarily inventive in generating these numbers.

For example, they may claim deductions that will be open to challenge by the IRS. And they may do this knowingly, having made the judgment that their profit is worth your risk. Any projections made by a real estate promoter, and the assumptions underlying them, should be thoroughly evaluated by professional advisers in order to be certain that optimism is matched by accuracy, particularly in view of the severe penalties imposed by the tax acts of 1981 and 1982 for the underpayment of your taxes. It is not that promoters are less honest than other people. They are just more exuberant—being in a business where "puffing" is an accepted and acceptable part of the practice.

When I was in law school, my tax professor told us that anyone who paid half of his income in taxes, even if he was in the 50% bracket, deserved to have his money taken away from him. From this I concluded that there was nothing illegal about a tax shelter. It is a way of avoiding taxes. And, as he also explained: "Tax avoidance is perfectly legitimate. It's only when you evade taxes that you go to jail."

Nor is investing in a tax shelter unpatriotic. You are not violating your duty to God or country. Deductions for mortgage interest and depreciation are incentives provided by Congress to encourage you to invest.

Although these deductions are available to every investor, the rich man will enjoy them more than the poor man. Life may, as you have been told repeatedly, be unfair; but a tax shelter is not a poorman's investment, nor one for a person of moderate means. And it is not an investment that rewards innocence. You may be able to make a great deal of money from a tax shelter, but not without the help (usually the very high-priced help) and protection of a tax lawyer or accountant.

Ten

RAW LAND

THERE MAY BE THOUSANDS OF PEOPLE WHO HAVE MADE millions of dollars by investing in raw land—but I have not met one of them. This is less an admission of my ignorance or limited experience than a recognition of the fact that buying land for future development is not an investment. It is a business—a tough business; one that properly belongs to the real estate professionals.

No advice, however, seems to curb the enthusiasm of investors for land. The sight of raw, undeveloped, empty land evokes an almost uncontainable optimism, despite endless examples of flawed expectations.

Most people can tell elaborate and chilling stories about the man who bought a large swath of land because of the never-to-be-built highway that was going to pass along the front of his property; or about the man who was forced, by federal and state regulations, to abandon his development plans and to become an unwilling environmentalist because his land came within a wildlife region. But these and similar tales do not appear to deflate hopes. If there is, as some politicians are claiming, a crisis of confidence in the American spirit, it is not to be found in the prevalent attitude toward land—which continues to arouse dreams of fortunes, like the search for gold and oil.

Raw-Land Problems

When you see a piece of land lying fallow and waiting to be developed with an apartment house, shopping center, or office building, you may be similarly enticed. But you would do well to exercise some restraint.

Tied-up money. This piece of land can tie up your money for several years until it can be cleared, graded, paved, built upon, and rented. While this is happening, you will have no return. And it may never get developed at all.

Inadequate financing. The possibility of failure accompanies every step in the process. You may not be able to obtain adequate financing; you may run out of money; or you may be worn down and finally defeated by ever-expanding zoning and environmental restrictions.

Legal restrictions. Even if the land does get developed, you may have difficulty in renting or selling it. Economic conditions or the desirability of the location may change during the building period, and the change may not be for the better.

Notwithstanding this inventory of potential disasters, thoroughly unqualified investors (which means most people) continue to be drawn to land; and I have been among them.

My infatuation began in the early 1950s, when I became friendly with the owner of a real estate agency in Massachusetts. He had a globe painted on the front door of his office, with these words printed beneath it: IF YOU LIVE ON THIS EARTH, OWN A PIECE OF IT! This was not mere advertising. In my case, at least, it was proselytizing; and I became an eager convert.

For $12,000, I bought two acres of land plus these words of reasurance: "Even if you decide not to build on it, you will be able to sell for a profit. No one ever loses on land."

Perhaps I confounded the wisdom of the ages; but when it became apparent two years later that I could not afford to develop the land, I sold it for $12,000 and lost money. This is how I did it:

I had to pay $7,200 of the purchase price (60% of $12,-000) with my own money, since I could obtain a two-year, $4,800 (40%) mortgage from a local bank at an interest rate of 8%. My experience was not atypical. A bank will probably not lend more than 40% to 66.6% of the land value; and the maturity can be as short as two or three years.

Over the two-year period, my $7,200, as well as the land, lay fallow. I had given up the use of my money. If I had, instead, deposited it in a savings account then paying 5% (compounded annually), I would have made $738.

Interest on the loan was $384 each year (8% of $4,800), for a total of $768. (I did not have to repay any principal until maturity, and therefore interest did not decline in the second year.) I also had to pay for liability insurance and real estate taxes—a total of $500 over two years.

Thus, my total cost for the land (without adjusting for income taxes) was $14,006, as shown in table 19. By selling for $12,000, I lost $2,006.

TABLE 19

Calculating Cost of Massachusetts Land

Initial purchase price	$12,000
PLUS	
Loss of earnings on $7,200 investment	738
PLUS	
Interest on mortgage loan	768
PLUS	
Real estate taxes and insurance	500
Total	**$14,006**

My experience illustrates several of the problems you might encounter when you purchase land, whether as an investment or for the purpose of building your home on it someday. The most apparent of these is that your money will not be earning money.

Raw land, fallow money. Raw land does not produce any current income unless it is farmed or sits on oil. Until it is developed or sold, it absorbs money. "It's like a baby," I have been told. "It requires lots of care and feeding. And like a baby, your big hope is that it will grow up at least fast enough to take care of you by the time you reach old age."

Bank problems. This absence of current income will also discourage a bank from lending you money, except upon the severest of terms. Furthermore, the bank may be unwilling to give you a nonrecourse mortgage, which means that the security, or collateral, for the loan will not be limited to the land. You will be personally obligated to repay the mortgage in the event of a default. Under these circumstances, you will be losing two of the main advantages customarily associated with the financing of commercial real estate—the use of the bank's money to pay 75% or more of your cost, and a loan upon which you are not personally liable.

Moreover, you will be giving up some tax benefits. First, there is no deduction for depreciation, because land is not depreciable.

Also, you may lose the benefit of being taxed at the capital-gain rate if you subdivide the land and sell off lots or parcels. Subdividing is a common practice. Many developers buy a large tract of undeveloped land (such as a farm), clear it of trees and underbrush, and divide it into separate parcels. They then sell these parcels to buyers, who build homes or other facilities on them.

Gain on subdividing may be ordinary income. Subdividing may be profitable, but your gain from the sale of the parcels may be taxed as ordinary income. Accordingly, you will be taxed on 100% of your gain, while on commercial real estate in general, as I explained in chapter 9, you are taxed on only 40% of your capital gain. There are exceptions to this tax treatment, but it may be difficult to fit within them. In such a complex area of taxation, you'll need the guidance of a professional tax planner. Without such help, what you make in the marketplace, you may lose in taxes.

The investment interest limitation. There may also be a limit on the amount of mortgage interest you can deduct if you buy land for speculation. You may not be allowed, under the Internal Revenue Code, to deduct in any one year more than $10,000 of the interest you pay on the mortgage. While this gets into the vague area of your intentions, if you acquire raw land without any specific plan for development, it may be difficult to persuade the Internal Revenue Service that you are not holding it for speculation. If you indeed intend to sell it (instead of developing it) at some time in the future when it has gone up in value, you are undoubtedly speculating, and the IRS restriction will probably apply.

This ceiling on the interest deduction is known as the "investment interest limitation" and is another of those areas in the tax laws that is both complicated and unclear. Whether, and to what extent, the limitation applies to you are questions you should ask your lawyer before you invest. (Even if you are subject to the limitation, there may be other factors in your tax situation, such as the nature or source of your income, that will enable you to deduct more than $10,000.)

How do you value land? There is another problem with raw land that is more fundamental, but less specific, than those discussed so far: the problem of valuation. When you invest in commercial property, you have tenants who are paying rents. These rents are a measure of value. They give you a basis upon which to decide how much to pay for the real estate. There are, of course, many other variables, such as the quality of the tenants, the other lease provisions, operating costs, and location. But if the rents total $100,000, you have a starting point: You can determine how much you should be paying for the $100,000.

Fixing value has always been difficult in real estate. There is no central marketplace, as with stocks and bonds, where prices are quoted from minute to minute. But with most commercial real estate, you begin with a known factor—the rents. In the case of raw land, however, the only approach you can follow in determining value is to make comparisons. What are similar tracts of land selling for? The trouble is, of course, that it will be hard and sometimes impossible to find comparable sales. Similar parcels of land in the same geographic area are not readily bought and sold. A lawyer who consulted me about some land his client owned on Cape Cod reduced the problem to its simplest terms: "My client has about thirty acres, and I can't get a handle on it. It's not just that we don't know what to do with the land. We don't even know what it's worth or how to find out."

Land continues to cast a spell over investors who are otherwise sober and prudent in how they spend their money. Among the reasons I have heard are "pride of ownership" and "I want something I can see and touch." I think, however, that this spell arises out of a central myth in real estate investing: *Real estate, and land in particular, must always rise in value because it is a resource that is in limited supply and is confronted by a steadily increasing demand.*

Whatever value this macroeconomic theory may have (and it has very little), it is both misleading and irrelevant when applied to a specific parcel of land. There may be overall population growth, but the demographics of any particular geographic region do not necessarily follow general population trends. Areas may grow, but they may also stabilize or decline both in terms of population and the ability of that population to afford the cost of land.

⌂ CHECKLIST

SEVEN THINGS TO WORRY ABOUT WHEN INVESTING IN LAND

Difficulties of development   Environmental and zoning restrictions.

Actual cost of investment   You will not only have to invest cash to cover the down payment and the carrying costs (such as mortgage interest and real estate taxes), you will also not be getting any return on your investment until the land is developed and sold.

Depreciation   Land is not depreciable, so you will not be able to take any depreciation deductions.

Subdividing   If you subdivide the land and sell off separate lots or parcels, your gain may be taxed at ordinary income-tax rates rather than at capital-gain rates.

Interest deduction   You may be limited in the amount of mortgage interest you can deduct.

Financing   You cannot usually finance a high percentage of the purchase price, and you may be personally liable on the mortgage.

Valuation   It may be difficult to measure value. There are no tenants paying rents and there may not be similar properties for making comparisons.

Like others who have spent most of their lives in New England, I have seen a plummeting in land values in areas where industry has moved out. And while no one can accurately forecast how sensitive land in the suburbs will be to rising energy costs, I have an unsettling feeling that in any given spot there is an inverse relationship between the cost of gasoline and land prices.

Furthermore, you cannot be sure that land is actually finite or, if it is, what its limits are. The modern skyscraper, for example, has expanded the use of available land far beyond bounds dreamed of one hundred years ago. I was also told recently of the feasibility, in view of the high fuel costs, of building factories underground, where, apparently, the temperature will remain constant. Whatever the practicalities of vertical building—whether above or below ground—the limits of expanding available space in the future through technology can only be guessed at.

But if you are not deterred by anything I have written, or if you already own some land, the next question you have to deal with is: *What should I do with the land?* There are an almost infinite number of possibilities. But this is a doubtful advantage—one that will probably add confusion rather than dispel it.

Find an experienced partner. My advice is quick and simple: Find a partner or joint venturer who is experienced in land planning and development. You will need one. You cannot underestimate the bureaucratic entanglements and other problems involved in land development. The land may have to be rezoned in order to be developd; and this can be a time-consuming political process. Even if the rezoning is accomplished, you may then be confronted with environmental restrictions on the use of the land that can test the patience of the most tranquil of men, and that can make the development so expensive as to be impractical.

The land developer has been called the closest we have come in three or four centuries to the Renaissance man. He has to know something about almost everything—from architecture, construction, and management, to the handling of a constant barrage of legal and tax problems. He will not be inexpensive. He will want a generous share of the profits; but he will know, far better than you, what is feasible, what it will cost, and how to raise the money. He will assume the burden of getting the development completed; and he can also be the focus of the inevitable complaints from "environmentalists" and other civic groups. If there has to be a devil, and there usually does when land is being developed, let it be the land developer.

I would prefer, however, that you take some better advice.

Put aside your courage. Conserve it and your money and use them in some other kind of real estate venture. As another friend of mine in the development business once said, "Land is a great place to be buried under—but only after you're dead."

RENTAL HOUSING

I KNOW A STOCKBROKER WHO MADE A SMALL FORTUNE IN the so-called go-go market of the 1960s. He took part of this fortune and bought an apartment building in Manhattan. He quickly learned that Wall Street clients, as difficult as they can be, were easier to deal with than tenants.

He thought he was becoming immune to the abuse of his tenants until he received a telephone call at 4:00 A.M. one morning. It was from a fifth-floor resident, complaining that a light bulb in the corridor had burned out.

"I don't believe this," the broker said. "It's four o'clock in the morning."

"I don't care what you believe. You own this building, and you have a responsibility to change the bulb."

"Not anymore, I don't," the broker answered.

"What do you mean? Of course you do."

"No, I don't. Tomorrow I'm going to sell the goddamned building."

He kept his promise and sold the building. He now lives happily a few blocks away in a cooperative apartment, his only real estate holding.

Apartments take work. This story illustrates the threshold problem of owning an apartment building: It takes work. Your tenants will demand service. Burned-out light bulbs have to be replaced, and leaks in the roof have to be repaired—not at 4:00 A.M. perhaps, but as soon after sunrise as possible. In short, the building may, from your perspective, be an investment; but as far as the tenants are concerned, it is their home. There will be many other factors determining whether or not you should buy an apartment building, but

166

unless you are willing to accept responsibility for its management, you should be looking elsewhere for a place to invest your money.

If you are prepared for an active investment, apartments can be profitable. They provide a wide range of opportunity. An apartment project can be as small as a two-family house; and it can be as large as a complex of several buildings, each containing 100 or more units. Whatever its size or configuration, the investment principles are substantially the same, as you will see from the description of the 55-unit project that I bought into in 1968.

This project was my first experience, as an investor, with rental housing. It consisted of 55 new apartment units located in Texas. I purchased it with some business associates as construction was being completed. The price was $1 million, with $750,000 coming from a nonrecourse mortgage bearing interest at 8.75% and maturing in 25 years. There were ten of us, and we each invested $25,000 of our own money, for a total down payment of $250,000.

Since the project had not yet been rented, we could only estimate our return. We assumed that each apartment could be leased for an average monthly rent of $220 ($2,640 per year), so the total annual rents on the 55 units would be approximately $145,000. Operating expenses (including real estate taxes and the costs of repairs, insurance, and utilities) were expected to be $50,000. Interest and principal on the mortgage would be about $75,000 each year. This would give us a cash flow of $20,000, or 8% return on our $250,000 investment, as summarized in table 20.

TABLE 20

Calculating Cash Flow and Pretax Return on Apartment House Investment

Gross annual rents	$145,000
MINUS	
Operating expenses	50,000
MINUS	
Interest and principal on mortgage	75,000
Result—cash flow	$ 20,000
Pretax return on investment ($20,000 divided by $250,000)	8%

A return of 8% might not be much to get excited about; but if our projections were accurate, it would be a good beginning. With proper management, the investment held the promise of growth. Moreover, we could look forward to sizable tax benefits.

Tax benefits and depreciation. In the first year, our net rental income, after paying operating expenses, would be $95,000 ($145,000 in gross rents minus $50,000 in operating expenses). For tax purposes, we could deduct interest of approximately $65,600 (8.75% on the $750,000 mortgage), reducing our taxable income from the property to $29,400— $95,000 minus $65,600. We would also be able to deduct depreciation.

The land, which was not depreciable, was valued at $100,-000. The balance of the purchase price was attributable to the apartments. That meant we would be able to depreciate a total of $900,000 (the total price of $1 million minus $100,-000 for the land).

At the time we purchased the project, we had to calculate our depreciation deductions based upon the real, useful life of the project. Since the enactment of the Economic Recovery Tax Act of 1981, the period over which depreciation deductions may be taken has been arbitrarily set at 15, 35, or 45 years. Therefore, assuming we had bought the building in 1981, we would have been able to deduct $60,000 each year, using the 15-year, straight-line method.

However, this was residential real estate, and we probably would have elected to use accelerated depreciation, because the recapture penalty I referred to in chapter 9 is much less severe for housing than for nonresidential commercial property. Under the 1981 tax act, when you sell a housing project, the amount of gain that will be recaptured will be only the excess of accelerated over straight-line deductions. If you hold the project for the full 15-year depreciable period, there will be no excess, with the deductions totalling $900,-000 under either method. In that case, all of your gain will be subject to capital gains treatment, with none of the gain being recaptured. (However, the excess of accelerated over straight-line depreciation each year will be a tax preference.)

I have set out in table 21 the amount of accelerated depreciation we would have been entitled to each year under the new tax act, based on a $900,000 cost of the projects (exclusive of the land).

TABLE 21

Calculation of Accelerated Depreciation on $900,000 Building*

Year	Percentage of $900,000 Cost	Amount
1	12%	$108,000
2	10	90,000
3	9	81,000
4	8	72,000
5	7	63,000
6	6	54,000
7	6	54,000
8	6	54,000
9	6	54,000
10	5	45,000
11	5	45,000
12	5	45,000
13	5	45,000
14	5	45,000
15	5	45,000

* This table assumes the purchase of the building in January. If you purchase after January, the amount of depreciation must be appropriately prorated.

If we had used accelerated depreciation, our taxable income in the first year (under the 1981 act) would have been "minus $78,600," as summarized in table 22.

TABLE 22

Calculating First-Year Taxable Income on Apartment House Investment

Gross annual rental income	$145,000
MINUS	
Operating expenses	50,000
MINUS	
Interest on mortgage	65,600
MINUS	
Depreciation	108,000
Result—taxable income	— $78,600

TABLE 23

Breakdown of Tax Loss and Saving on Apartment House Investment

Year	Gross Rents	Operating Expenses	Mortgage Interest*	Accelerated Depreciation	Tax Loss	Tax Saving (50% bracket)
1	$145,000	$50,000	$65,600	$108,000	$78,600	$39,300
2	145,000	50,000	64,800	90,000	59,800	29,900
3	145,000	50,000	63,900	81,000	49,900	24,950
4	145,000	50,000	63,000	72,000	40,000	20,000
5	145,000	50,000	62,000	63,000	30,000	15,000
6	145,000	50,000	60,800	54,000	19,800	9,900
7	145,000	50,000	59,600	54,000	18,600	9,300
8	145,000	50,000	58,300	54,000	17,300	8,650
9	145,000	50,000	56,800	54,000	15,800	7,900
10	145,000	50,000	55,300	45,000	5,300	2,650
11	145,000	50,000	53,600	45,000	3,600	1,800
12	145,000	50,000	51,700	45,000	1,700	850
13	145,000	50,000	49,700	45,000	300	150
14	145,000	50,000	47,500	45,000	— 2,500	— 1,250
15	145,000	50,000	45,100	45,000	— 4,900	— 2,450

* Rounded to the nearest $100.

Assuming that we were all in the 50% tax bracket, this "loss" would have been worth $39,300 (50% of $78,600), making the total return in the first year of our investment $59,300—$20,000 cash flow (see table 20) plus $39,300 in tax savings. If everything else remained the same (with no change in the rents or operating expenses), this amount would go down in each succeeding year because the interest and depreciation deductions (and, as a result, our tax savings) would be declining. By the thirteenth year we would run out of tax savings and would have taxable income from the venture. This is shown in table 23, which covers the fifteen-year period.

In making separate calculations for cash flow and taxable income (as in tables 20 and 24, respectively), you should visualize cash flow as a physical event, while taxable income should be understood as an accounting concept.

Cash flow, as the term suggests, involves the actual movement of money. We were to receive $145,000 in gross rents and had to pay out $50,000 in operating expenses and $75,000 for interest and principal on the mortgage. Thus, $20,000 would have been left over—"flowing" into our pockets.

Unlike cash flow, the physical movement of money is often irrelevant in calculating taxable income. We could not, for example, deduct the principal payments on the mortgage, even though there was an actual transfer of cash from us to the bank. We could, on the other hand, deduct depreciation, despite the fact that no money changed hands.

Table 24 shows our projected composite return from cash flow and tax savings for the first fifteen years.

Equity buildup as a return. Still another potential source of return was equity buildup resulting from the repayment of principal on the mortgage. By the end of the fifteenth year, we would have made about $265,000 in principal payments, and there would have been a corresponding increase in the size of our equity in the project. If the value of the project had remained at $1 million, we should have been able to turn this built-up equity into cash through a sale or a refinancing of the mortgage. If, for example, we had sold the project for $1 million (the original purchase price) at the end of the fifteenth year, we would have recovered an amount equal to the principal payments of $265,000 plus our original $250,000 cash investment—a total of $515,000. We would, however,

TABLE 24

Breakdown of Total Return from Cash Flow and Tax Saving on Apartment House Investment

Year	Cash Flow	Tax Saving (50% Bracket)	Total
1	$ 20,000	$ 39,300	$ 59,300
2	20,000	29,900	49,900
3	20,000	24,950	44,950
4	20,000	20,000	40,000
5	20,000	15,000	35,000
6	20,000	9,900	29,900
7	20,000	9,300	29,300
8	20,000	8,650	28,650
9	20,000	7,900	27,900
10	20,000	2,650	22,650
11	20,000	1,800	21,800
12	20,000	850	20,850
13	20,000	— 150	19,850
14	20,000	— 1,250	18,750
15	20,000	— 2,450	17,550
Fifteen-year Total	$300,000	$166,350	$466,350

have had a taxable gain, and would have had to pay a tax of about $180,000 on this gain. Therefore, our net profit after taxes would have been $515,000 minus the $180,000 of taxes, or $335,000.

Adding up the fifteen years of cash flow ($300,000), tax savings ($166,350), and aftertax sales proceeds ($335,000), we would have received a total of $801,350. However, this would have been spread out over fifteen years. In order to get a more accurate picture of our return, we would have to figure in the effect of time, recognizing that each dollar received in the first year is worth much more than each one received in the fifteenth year.

Our actual return would have been equivalent to the interest rate at which we would have had to invest the $250,000 in order to recoup our investment and to earn $59,300 in the first year (see table 24), $49,900 in the second year, $44,950 in the third, and so forth through the fifteenth year.

The overall rate, and therefore our aftertax return, would have been approximately 15%; and a 15% return after paying taxes would have been the equivalent of 30% before taxes if we had been in the 50% tax bracket. (This is the same procedure I went through in chapter 7 in finding the return on the sale of a home. Your accountant or investment adviser can easily make this computation for you with the help of a calculator. You would be unwise to try to do it yourself; it will take you too much time.)

While this is an accurate approach for calculating the aftertax return on a real estate investment—combining cash flow, tax savings, and the proceeds of a sale (or refinancing), and then factoring in the element of time—it is based (as it has to be) upon a series of assumptions about the future. And these assumptions, no matter how well reasoned or conservative, can never be more than predictions.

In the case of our apartment house investment, many of the predictions turned out to be inaccurate or incomplete. It was not that we had made any extravagant estimates. We had projected that cash flow would remain fixed at $20,000 and that there would be no change in the value of the property. Nevertheless, there were intervening events that we did not and, in some instances, could not anticipate.

Caution: the distance factor. To begin with, we did not take the problem of distance seriously enough. The project was in Texas, and we were in Massachusetts.

We hired a Texas management firm and promptly forgot about our investment. And once hired, the firm promptly forgot about the project. Because of vacancies, tenant turnovers, and erratic rent collection, our operating and mortgage costs during the first 18 months totaled $20,000 more than the gross rents. This gave us an additional $20,000 tax loss, which was worth $10,000 (50% of $20,000). It was, however, a real loss—one that had to be paid in cash if we were to keep the project. Whatever ironies may be contained in the tax laws, none of them, as yet, has made the payment of $20,000 in order to save $10,000 a good investment.

We hired a new management firm and, this time, carefully monitored its performance. Within a year, the project began to show a cash profit; but before we could become too accustomed to success, we fell victim, at the end of 1973, to the "energy crisis." We were able, eventually, to pass the increased fuel costs along to our tenants as their leases expired and new ones were entered into; but we never recouped the profits we lost during this transition period.

To say that our investment was, up to this point, a disappointment would be a mild translation of the expletives we used to describe the project. We were perplexed by events that seemed to be beyond our control.

But in 1976, conditions began to change. The price of housing started its unprecedented climb; the rents went up; and in 1979—ten years after we had made the investment— we were able to sell the project for a handsome profit of about $200,000. Most of us felt compensated for the grief we had experienced over the previous ten years—proving, once again, that "there are very few problems in life that can't be cured with a little more money."

We were, no doubt, lucky. In fairness, nevertheless, we had shown patience and perseverance. And, above everything else, we had learned to be resilient—to expect and to adjust to the unexpected. But there were other, more concrete lessons I can pass along to you.

Success requires good management. If I had to pick a single factor of overriding importance to the success of an apartment project, I would choose management. Good management may not save a bad project—but without it a sound project can, as we found out, quickly turn sour.

Since you probably do not have the time or experience to operate apartments, you need someone to act on your behalf. This should be a professional management firm located close to your property and familiar with the neighborhood. The management firm should, among its primary duties, take care of maintenance and repairs, collect the rents from the tenants, find tenants for vacant apartment units, and be responsible for keeping the books and other records of the project and for making sure the bills are paid on time. The firm should also employ a full-time agent—preferably a person who will live on the site—who can anticipate and promptly respond to the needs, real and imagined, of your tenants.

You should not, however, abandon all your responsibilities to a management firm. You have to supervise its performance by making periodic visits to the project and by setting up a reporting system that will alert you to problems before they can escalate into a crisis.

Management cannot, obviously, solve everything. It cannot

stop OPEC from raising oil prices. Nor can it correct shoddy construction, change a bad location, or prevent the government from imposing controls over the rents you can charge. Nevertheless, you can safeguard against many of these contingencies with some foresight and advance planning.

Who pays the operating expenses? In addition to making it more expensive to keep warm in the winter and cool in the summer, OPEC policies have made investors focus more closely on who is paying for operating expenses. Before inflation became an entrenched part of the economics of real estate, many apartment owners preferred to charge higher rents and pay these expenses themselves. They believed that they could achieve savings more easily than their tenants (for example, by making bulk purchases of fuel), thereby increasing their profits.

There has been a radical change in this point of view. Today, most owners would gladly forgo these potential savings and lower the rents if their tenants would agree to pay operating expenses. This is not, of course, a sign of any emerging benevolence on the part of the landlord class. It is a recognition that the security of a net lease is preferable to gambling on any future reduction in oil or other prices.

While you will not be able to transfer all of the operating expenses to your tenants, they should, at least, pay their own utility costs. You should also try to get them to pay any increases in operating expenses that occur during the term of their leases, particularly real estate taxes, which continue to rise despite the apparent popularity of "Proposition 13" and other similar proposals to put a ceiling on such taxes.

Expect operating expenses of at least between 35% and 45% of gross rents. Whatever success you have in allocating expenses to your tenants, you will probably still have to pay a large portion of them yourself, including insurance, repairs, maintenance, management, and appropriate reserves. Operating costs vary widely throughout the country. They are, for example, higher in the Northeast, because of the price of fuel and the high tax rates, than in Alabama or Louisiana. You can anticipate, nonetheless, that operating costs will, in most cases, be at least between 35% and 45% of the gross rents, wherever the project is located. While we used 35% in our projections, you would be safer in using at least 40%. If you are offered a project with operating expenses estimated at less than 35%, you are either being lied to or being invited to become a slumlord.

Vacancy factor. An honest estimate of performance will also include a vacancy factor and a "reserve" (to be funded out of gross rents) for future replacements and repairs.

You will often hear it said that there are no apartment vacancies in a certain town or city. While this may be true as of a particular moment, it is not possible to sustain full occupancy indefinitely. Even in the most robust market, when one family moves out of a building, their apartment has to be repaired and redecorated before another family can move in; and during this hiatus, no one is paying the rent. Moreover, market conditions can change abruptly. Builders have, throughout the years, shown a remarkable tendency to respond to a strong demand for rental housing by overbuilding.

So, you should assume that, over the life of any medium-sized to large project, an average of at least 4% to 5% of the apartment units will be vacant. We made the mistake, in planning for our Texas project, of overlooking potential vacancies. During the first three years, they averaged about 10%; and thereafter they were around 3%.

The reserve factor. Another way to be hurt by unexpected costs is to forget to set up, as part of the expense of operating the project, a reserve for replacements and repairs. Failing to plan for upkeep is nothing short of self-deception and will, eventually, make things worse than they have to be.

Repairs and replacements will have to be made. Refrigerators, carpeting, furnaces, and plumbing will wear out; roofs will have to be reshingled; and the buildings will have to be repainted. You can add to this list the unimagined emergencies that will possibly arise, such as storm, flooding, and even molten lava. In order to cover the costs of these repairs and replacements, you should be setting aside some of the rents each year. This is, literally, saving for a rainy day—one with hurricane-force winds that can cause expensive damage. The amount of the reserve (which can be invested until it is needed) will depend upon where the property is located and how well it is constructed. For instance, if it is in the South, the reserve for expected wear and tear can probably be smaller than if it is located in the Northeast, where the day-to-day weather will take a heavier toll. If construction is of the best quality, there will be a less frequent need to make repairs. (You should be aware that moneys put into such a reserve are not deductible until after they are spent on the project.)

Caution: poor construction. There is no reserve large enough to protect you against poor construction; and defects may not be readily apparent. A new building can be seductive. It is like a new car—so clean and sleek that it is hard to conceive that anything can ever go wrong. But things do go wrong, and unless you are an expert, you will not know what to look for in advance. You should hire an engineer, architect, or contractor to inspect the building and evaluate its structural soundness before you invest.

Your best defense, however, is to invest in a project built by an experienced and responsible developer, one with the financial strength to meet his obligations. You should carefully examine his financial statements and the performance of his other projects. Most developers have been born with thick skins or have grown them, and their feelings will not be hurt if you insist upon independently veryifying their qualifications.

Risk: investing during construction. You should also wait at least until the project has been substantially completed before you invest. You add a considerable risk by investing during construction. The developer can run into environmental, structural, labor, and other problems that he did not anticipate. These will cause delays that will increase costs or even prevent the project from being built.

Even after you have acquired the project, the developer should have continuing responsibilities. He should be required to repair any structural defects. These may not appear for several years—until, for instance, the foundation of the building has finally settled.

He should also protect you against operating deficits in the early years. A new apartment building is a new venture, and it will probably not be fully rented the day you open for business. In the initial months, the rents may not be sufficient to cover all the costs. The developer should, for at least the first 12 to 18 months, agree to pay any of these deficits. Another approach that is frequently followed is to postpone making the full amount of your investment until the rents are at least equal to the mortgage payments and the operating expenses.

While the developer may resist assuming these risks, you should think twice about investing unless he does. He should be (and frequently is) willing to stand behind the project by accepting these responsibilities.

Then, there is location. I have often been criticized for not giving a high enough priority to location. While I do not question the value of a good location, I do have trouble with the old real estate, refrain that tells you: *The three most important things about any property are location, location, location.*

If you know a potential buyer who believes this, he may be your pot of gold at the end of the rainbow. He will invariably overpay you for your property.

Obviously, location is important; and if it is true that there are "three most important things" about any property, location clearly ranks a place in the trinity, along with good management and sound construction. But locations are fickle. They can be vulnerable to events and circumstances that are beyond your control. A curtailment of commuter transportation service, combined with rising gasoline prices, can turn a desirable suburb into a ghost town of vacant apartments. By comparison, apartments in the inner cities were, until a few years ago, diligently avoided by investors, and are now being more eagerly sought after.

There is also the problem of overbuilding. As one real estate analyst said to me: "I have never doubted for a moment the capacity of my real estate brethren to overreact to demand. The minute they hear of someplace where there are no more available apartments, they will saturate that market with new buildings until everyone goes broke." His response may be as extreme as that of the developers he is describing, but real estate (and apartments, in particular) is one of the few remaining areas in our economy where there is a sensitive balance between supply and demand.

Investigate your market. Despite these vagaries of location, you can protect yourself, at least initially, by thoroughly investigating the market in which you intend to invest. There are many real estate consulting firms willing to make a "feasibility study," which will evaluate the current strength of the location, the possibility of overbuilding in the near future, and the accuracy of your projections about rents and operating costs. These studies can be expensive, however, frequently running as high as $1,000 to $5,000. Often the developer will, at his expense, provide you with such a study. If he does, make sure that it has been prepared by an independent consultant or appraiser, as opposed to one who depends upon the developer for business.

An existing property cuts your risk. Many of the mistakes in estimating the cost of operations, the quality of construction, and the desirability of the location can be avoided, or at least minimized, by investing in an existing project rather than a new one. Such a property has a history, and any promises that are made by the seller as to future performance can be tested against what has already happened.

Risks Today: Rent Control

There are some risks that are common to both existing and new projects. Rent control is one impediment that helps to account for the steady conversion of apartments into condominiums and the decline in the number of rental housing units. While government restrictions on your right to raise rents may offend your spirit of free enterprise and your common sense, no law has ever been passed that requires political expediency to converge with sensible economics.

Rising costs. You may also have difficulty in raising rents in order to cover increasing operating costs. Sellers often make projections that show rents going up at least as fast as these costs. This may describe things as they should be, but not always as they are. In fact, a serious defect in rental housing as an investment has been the failure of rents to move in relation to operating expenses. Even if leases give you the right to raise rents, tenants are notorious for their resistance. As I said earlier, they look at an apartment as their home, and often perceive rent increases as an invasion of their sanctuary.

Apartments as Sound Investments

Despite the uncertainties of operations and rent collections and the vagaries of locations, apartments can be a sound investment for the individual investor. They not only can produce a reasonable cash return, but also can become an investment that grows—providing capital appreciation as well as a hedge against inflation. Not long ago, the common lease-term of one, two, or three years discouraged investing in apartments. This has changed as inflation has become a more significant force in real estate. So, while it may be difficult to raise rents during the term of a lease, there can still be frequent rent adjustments because of its short duration. As old leases expire and new ones are entered into, the rents can be set at levels that, at a minimum, reflect current costs. As an apartment broker explained to me: "There was a time when landlords would have sold their souls for five- or ten-year leases. Not anymore. Today, with inflation, one of the attractions of apartments is the chance to renegotiate every year or two—or even more frequently."

The tax benefits of investing in apartments are also more generous than for nonresidential projects because of the liberal recapture treatment which I mentioned earlier.

If you decide to invest in an apartment project, what type should it be? There are two paramount considerations in deciding upon the type—the quality of the tenants and the size of the project.

Income level of tenants. The tenants' income level should be relatively high—ideally, a combined annual income of at least $35,000 for a family of four. This is not an attempt to equate the income of the tenants with their character, but rather a recognition of the obvious fact that the more money a person has, the more he can afford to spend on rent. Moreover, a well-to-do tenant's rent will probably be a smaller percentage of his disposable income than will that of a person at a lower income level. Accordingly, he is less likely to resist rent increases forced by rising operating costs.

Also, the project should be geared to families and older persons. They tend to be more permanent than young, unmarried tenants, and will usually renew their leases, even at higher rents. A frequent complaint of owners of the so-called swinging-singles apartments is that the tenants live up to their reputation. They do swing from one project to another; and you should avoid a project of transients, unless you are investing in a motel. In this regard, among the signs of expected and rapid turnovers are furnished apartments and projects that consist mainly of one-bedroom units.

How large a complex? On the question of size, there is a great disparity of opinion. Many people prefer to invest in a large project—one of 200 or 300 units or more—which can more easily support amenities that attract tenants, such as swimming pools, tennis courts, and other shared facilities. On the other hand, a large project requires intensive management and supervision. And if it is a multistory building, the construction and operating costs tend to be higher. Furthermore, it is not easy to fill 200 or more units, a problem that becomes more pronounced during a recession.

My preference is a 100- to 150-unit garden apartment project. Such a project strikes a balance between the economies of smallness and the burdens (and, sometimes, the inefficiencies) of large size. The amenities may be modest, but it should be possible to have at least a small swimming pool and perhaps one or two tennis courts. And management is less intricate, although not less important.

You should not overlook a smaller project. One with 50 units may not be capable of supporting more than a wading pool, but it is much less management-intensive than a larger project.

Even a small apartment building, one as small as a two-, three-, or four-family house, can be attractive. When a friend of mine was thinking about buying a two-family home in Dedham, Massachusetts, a few months ago, he was accused of lacking daring and ambition. "I wanted to move into the upstairs apartment and rent out the bottom floor. But I was told I was succumbing to my immigrant mentality—that I could only be comfortable 'living above the store.' I should never have listened. I could have gotten all of the benefits of investing in an apartment house, with very few of the worries."

Conceptually, there are few differences between a two- to four-family house and any other apartment project. You have tenants who pay rents; and, even if you live in the house, you can deduct depreciation and rental expenses (such as maintenance and repairs) allocable to the part you lease out. And if you get lulled into thinking of the house as simply your home, your tenants' complaints will probably be loud enough to awaken you to the problems of management.

I have been asked whether there are any special rules of thumb governing an investment in a two- to four-family owner-occupied home. The closest I can come to any such rule is: You are not likely to get rich on the rents.

The clearest advantage to investing in this type of house is that you'll probably be buying a better home than you could otherwise, without incurring any additional carrying costs—so long as the rents cover, as they should, at least the proportionate expenses of your tenants' apartments, including their share of the mortgage payments, utilities, and maintenance. In this situation, you should be able to reap long-term benefits of capital appreciation and equity buildup.

Take, for example, these two possibilities: You can afford to buy either a single-family home for $60,000 or a two-family home for $120,000 if you rent out one of the apartments. In today's market, the quality of a $120,000 home, even if you have to share it with another family, will probably be more than double that of a $60,000 single-family home. And this difference in quality will be translated into cash when you sell.

If you could, in either case, get an 80% mortgage at 10% interest and maturing in 25 years, your annual mortgage payments for the $60,000 home would be $6,610 ($550.84 per month), compared with $13,220 ($1,101.68 per month) for the $120,000 home. If the annual rent you can charge for the apartment in the two-family home is $6,610 plus your tenant's pro rata share of real estate taxes, utilities, and other costs of operating and maintenance, he will be paying half of the mortgage and other carrying costs. His money will, therefore, be building up 50% of your equity in the home.

You must remember, however, that your 20% down payment in this example will be $24,000 for the two-family home instead of $12,000 for the $60,000 home. Unless you can charge a rent in excess of the carrying costs for the rental apartment, you will not be getting any cash flow on your additional $12,000 down payment, although you will be getting some tax benefits through depreciation. You may, of course, be able to raise the rents if the demand for rental housing grows; and two- to four-family homes (particularly if they are owner-occupied) are often exempt from rent control laws that would otherwise limit rent increases. Whether or not you can raise the rents, you will probably be living in a more attractive home if you choose the two-family option; and you can reasonably expect to be compensated eventually for the lack of privacy and relatively low cash flow, through equity buildup and capital appreciation.

The Vacation Home

Another residential real estate investment that most people think about from time to time is the so-called vacation home—the cabin in the mountains or the cottage by the shore.

Once a year my wife and I drive down to Cape Cod and spend a weekend looking at cottages. Much to the despair of the real estate agents, it has become our annual spring hobby. We fantasize about using a beach house during the summer months and leasing it out for the remainder of the year at a rent that will cover all of our costs. This will enable us to have a "free" vacation.

"And then," I frequently hear, "there is the tax shelter. Don't forget the tax shelter." I am sorry to say, however, that you usually can forget the tax shelter if you intend to use your vacation home yourself for more than two weeks a year.

There are severe restrictions limiting the deductions you can take on a vacation home. The rules set forth in the Internal Revenue Code are amazingly complicated and could make you properly wonder about the quality of mind, and even the sanity, of whoever thought them up. Nevertheless, if you rent your vacation home for more than 14 days and if you personally use it for the greater of 14 days or 10% of the number of days the home is rented, you will not be allowed to deduct any "excess tax losses."

You can, as with any other home, take all of the ordinary home deductions without any limitation (such as mortgage interest and real estate taxes). But you will not be able to deduct any other rental expenses (such as depreciation, utilities, and maintenance) in excess of the rental income minus that portion of the ordinary deductions allocable to the rental period.

For the sake of illustration, assume that you own a vacation home and rent it for three months for $3,000. You use the home for more than two weeks. Your total "expenses" attributable to the rental period are $4,000. These consist of interest and taxes of $2,000; utilities and maintenance of $500; and depreciation of $1,500. First, you deduct the $2,000 in interest and taxes, leaving you with taxable rental income of

$1,000 ($3,000 in gross rents minus $2,000). Next, you deduct the $500 for utilities and maintenance, which brings your taxable rental income to $500. But you can only deduct $500 of the $1,500 depreciation, because your total deductions cannot exceed the rental income of $3,000 (and you've already deducted $2,500). Therefore, $1,000 of depreciation will be nondeductible.

There are other rules that apply if you rent your home for 14 days or less, or if the personal use of your home does not exceed 14 days or 10% of the number of rental days. As my lawyer told me, this series of rules had to be the invention of someone with a degree in advanced circuitry. But be sure that they are unraveled *before* you buy a vacation home, particularly if you are making the investment with the expectation of tax benefits.

How Much Should You Pay?

Whether you're considering a two-family house, a vacation cottage, an apartment project, or any other real estate for that matter, I cannot tell you the precise figure you should pay, any more than I can tell you what you should pay for stocks and bonds. The "right" price would depend upon the date of your purchase, the quality of what you are buying, and the returns you can obtain from competing investments. There are, however, certain benchmarks against which to test the investment, such as yields on long-term corporate and municipal bonds that have maturities of between 20 and 30 years.

I frequently use tax-exempt municipal bonds as a guide. If the average yield on these bonds was 9%, I would normally be looking for an initial cash return on a typical apartment project of 1 to 3 percentage points higher, or 10% to 12% (assuming a 75% mortgage). This differential, together with excess tax losses and the possibility of equity buildup and capital appreciation on the apartments, is my compensation for the risk I will be incurring and the liquidity I will be losing for not investing in municipal bonds.

Where any specific project belongs within this 10% to 12% range depends upon its quality, as judged by the several factors I have been discussing. My approach at least provides you with a starting point for deciding what to pay; and if the return you are offered falls below this guideline, there should be compelling reasons to justify the deficiency.

Cost of a new project vs. an existing one. A related question is whether you should pay less or more for a new project than you pay for an existing one. I believe that you should pay less.

You can judge an existing project on its past performance, while it will ordinarily take three to four years before you will be able to tell whether a new project will live up to its "advance billing."

Even if you accept my approach, you may still find it difficult to reconcile returns even as high as 10%, 11%, or 12% to the current high interest rates, particularly at a time when high-grade corporate bonds are selling at yields of 13% and higher. But there are several factors you should take into account.

Because of the tax benefits, most of your cash return on an apartment project will, for at least the first several years, be free of taxes; and there should be, as well, significant tax savings (see table 24). You will also be building up equity in the project through the use of someone else's money. The underlying consideration, however, is that these returns are starting points. They are not expected to remain static. You are betting on the future and the prospect that rents will go up.

This expectation is largely based upon the recent shortage of rental housing units. This shortage (attributable in part to rent control, the conversion of rental apartments into condominiums, and the high cost of construction) has exacerbated demand and, as you might expect, has allowed landlords to respond with rent increases. Moreover, this demand will grow if the cost of owning a home continues to become prohibitive for an increasing number of families.

The prospect of escalating rents attracts investors to apartments like dogs to a bitch in heat. Whether or not this prospect is fully justified (and in real estate, you must always remember, hopes escalate much faster than rents), there has been intense competition among investors for apartment projects. As a result, prices have gone up and the initial cash yields have gone down; and it may be difficult to find a project even at a return rate of 8% or 9%.

Nevertheless, if you accept a lower return you will probably be overpaying, in view of the risks you will be assuming and alternative investment possibilities. Your return may grow; but if, for example, you buy a project for an initial return of 6% or 7% ($15,000 to $17,500 on $250,000), it is doubtful that it will reach an acceptable level within a tolerable period.

I may be advising you to give up "the only game in town." But there is no point in playing it if you know at the outset you cannot win. Even the Triple Crown winner, Secretariat, would have been a consistent loser if he had been forced to begin every race several lengths behind the starting gate.

One method of increasing cash flow from an apartment project is to borrow less money (though I would resist doing so for reasons I will explain in a moment). The mortgage usually takes away a large share of the rents, particularly at a time of high interest rates. Therefore, the smaller your mortgage, the higher your cash return will be. This can be illustrated by a simple example.

The gross rents from our $1 million Texas project were $145,000 and operating expenses (exclusive of mortgage payments) were $50,000 (see table 20). This left $95,000 in net rents—$145,000 minus $50,000. Since we had to make annual mortgage payments of $75,000, our cash flow was $20,-000 ($95,000 minus $75,000), or 8% return on our $250,000 investment.

If we had invested the full $1 million in cash, without borrowing any money, we would not have had to use any of the $95,000 in net rents to make mortgage payments. Therefore, our annual cash flow would have been 9.5% instead of 8%— $95,000 on our $1 million investment.

Although we would have increased our cash return (from 8% to 9.5%) if we had not obtained a mortgage, we would have lost too much in equity buildup and tax savings by borrowing less than $750,000 (75% of our cost). These benefits are directly related to the size of the mortgage; and a 75% mortgage with a 25% cash investment provides a balanced combination of cash flow, equity buildup, and tax savings.

If, for example, we had paid $1 million in cash for the Texas project (without a mortgage), we could not have built up any equity since our cash investment would have constituted, on day one, 100% of the equity in the project. And we would have had hardly any tax savings because our only deductions would have been for operating expenses and depreciation. Without the interest deduction, our taxable loss would have been $13,000 in the first year (instead of $78,-600). By the second year, we would have had taxable income of $5,000 ($145,000 of rents minus operating expenses of $50,000 and depreciation of $90,000).

This comparison might lead you to the conclusion that the higher the mortgage, the better. As you consider the possible range from no mortgage at all to a 75% mortgage, you can see the beauty of leverage—reflected in equity buildup and tax benefits. But as the mortgage gets larger than 75% (assuming you could get one that size), you should start to beware of the curse of leverage.

At 75%, we had cash flow of $20,000. Among other things, this gave us room to make a $20,000 mistake in our projections. Only if the $95,000 in net rents dropped by more than $20,000 to below $75,000 (the annual mortgage payment) would we be in default on the mortgage. If we had obtained an 80% mortgage, our payments would have been about $80,-000, leaving a "cushion" of only $15,000. This would have made us more vulnerable to miscalculations or to adverse changes in the economy.

And beyond 80%, our margin of error would have sharply narrowed. (As I discussed earlier, most banks and other financial institutions cannot or will not lend more than 80%, but there may be exceptions, such as real estate investment trusts and other lenders not bound by legal restrictions on the amount they can lend. You may also be able to get more than 80% financing by obtaining a purchase-money second mortgage from the seller.)

Thus, a 75% mortgage gives you a balanced return. With a smaller mortgage, you may increase your cash flow, but it will be at the price of equity buildup and tax benefits. With a mortgage in excess of 75%, you may increase your equity buildup and tax savings, but your cash return will decline, along with your margin of error.

Adjustable Interest Rate and Other Commercial-Mortgage Terms

There are other features of the mortgage, in addition to its size, that you should be aware of, whether you invest in an apartment project or some other commercial property. Banks have become increasingly concerned with inflation and are looking for ways to protect themselves against its effects.

There has been a great deal of discussion among lenders recently about using a mortgage with an adjustable interest rate, which is similar in concept to the variable-rate home mortgage. While I very much doubt that lenders will abandon the fixed-rate mortgage (despite some assertions to the contrary), if the mortgage does allow for adjustments, any rate increase will eat into your future profits.

A far more typical approach is for a bank to contend with inflation by giving a mortgage under which it has the right to participate in your profits—for example, through sharing in the rent (or rent increases) and sales proceeds. An exquisitely precise rule of thumb is that the more the lender shares, the less you make.

Perhaps the most likely approach is a mortgage under which the bank, and not you, has the right to demand a prepayment after 5, 10, or 15 years. For example, the bank may give you a 25-year mortgage, but have the right to terminate it after 15 years. In this situation, you will have to pay off the unpaid principal balance of the mortgage at the end of the fifteenth year. This is similar to the home mortgage with a balloon payment, and has the same risks.

While the bankers' current concern is with inflation, they are also worried about a decline in interest rates after giving you the mortgage. If you obtain a commercial mortgage with a 15% interest rate today, a year from now the market rate may decline to 10%. This may prompt you to repay the mortgage and obtain a new one at the lower rate. In order to discourage you, the bank may require that you pay a substantial premium, or fee, as a penalty for prepaying. The bank may go further, putting a provision in the mortgage that restricts you from prepaying, even at a premium, for a period as long as ten years and sometimes longer.

The fact that a mortgage may contain one or more of these provisions does not necessarily mean you shouldn't accept it. But you should be aware, at the time of making your investment, that such restrictions may not only limit your flexibility in dealing with the property in the future but may also cut into your profits.

But whatever the terms of a commercial mortgage—whether it is for more or less than 75% and whether or not the interest rate is adjustable—make sure that the person selling you the project has actually obtained a mortgage before you invest. Many a sad tale can be told about developers who "knew" that interest rates were coming down and postponed getting a mortgage—only to be confounded by rates going up. And developers are notoriously bad in outguessing the mortgage market.

The Importance of Capital Appreciation

Most investors do not purchase apartments primarily for equity buildup or tax savings. The glamour of an apartment project, as I suggested earlier, is capital appreciation—the hope that cash flow will keep rising.

Given the present demand for rental housing, capital appreciation is a reasonable expectation and a legitimate reason for investing. When you invest for future benefits, however, you are investing in a guess. You should keep in mind that when someone conjures up a vision of spiraling rents, he is usually doing the selling, and you are doing the buying.

I recently asked an apartment-house promoter what he thought investors could look forward to as an average annual cash return over a ten-year period. He told me that "the sky's the limit, but I expect it to be somewhere around twelve-and-one-half-percent." He was not saying that the cash flow would climb to 12.5% over ten years; he was saying that it would average 12.5%. This figure has been confirmed to me by other promoters. But consider for a moment what this means.

Assume you purchased the $1 million project by investing $250,000 in cash and your initial annual return was $20,000 (8% of $250,000). In order for your average return to be 12.5% over ten years ($31,250 annually on the $250,000), it would be necessary for cash flow to go up by $2,500 each year until it reached $42,500 (or 17%) in the tenth year. This can happen, but these prophecies are more likely "such stuff as dreams are made on."

A more reasonable estimate is that the cash flow from this project may, if it is soundly constructed, properly managed, and well located, and with a push from inflation, *rise to* (not average) about 12% to 14% in ten years. This, together with tax savings, would not only be a respectable return on your money but should also enable you to make a sizable profit through a sale or refinancing of the project, since the proceeds will, ordinarily, reflect increases in cash flow.

Condominium Conversions

Another area of continuing romance is condominium conversions. This involves changing the legal structure of the project after you have purchased it. By converting the project into a condominium, you can sell the apartment units instead of leasing them. If the conversion is properly done (with professional help), you can probably make more money through the sale of individual units than by selling the entire project in a single sale. In this respect, condominium conversion is similar to subdividing raw land and selling off the separate parcels or lots.

There are, however, several problems with which you will have to contend. Conversions have been taking place so rapidly that they have become a major cause of the reduction of available rental units. This, in turn, has led tenants to resist attempts to convert their apartments. This resistance has been effective in some areas, with pressure growing for legislative action to restrict or slow down conversions. One real estate consultant I talked to warned: "You can expect the political situation to get tougher. With people finding it more and more difficult to rent and with tenants starting organized protests, the government is going to make it increasingly hard to convert."

Legal requirements. As it is, the conversion process is bound by strict and expensive legal requirements and regulations that you will have to discuss with your lawyer. Even after you have complied with the legalities, conversion will more likely be a lingering process rather than a quick one, since the units have to be sold one by one.

Tax questions. You will also have to spend money to improve and repair the units so that they are in a condition suitable for sale. Moreover, your profit, unlike the tax treatment of the gain from the isolated sale of the entire project, may be taxed as ordinary income, and not as capital gain (another matter to be checked with your lawyer).

The possibility of converting apartments to condominiums sometime in the future may be a reasonable expectation when you think about investing. But it should not be your overriding consideration. Too many things can occur to prevent it from happening, including a market decline in the demand for condominiums and inhibiting government policies. Therefore, if you decide to buy an apartment project, it should be for the simple reason that as rental housing it stands up as a viable investment.

An apartment project is not an easy or passive investment. It is management intensive; landlord-tenant relationships can be fragile; and the physical structure and location are dominant factors in success or failure.

All of this is in sharp contrast to credit real estate, where a tenant like Sears or K mart will absolve you of most of these risks and responsibilities. But in contrast to a Sears or K mart property, there is a much greater potential for growth.

Perhaps the best test of whether an apartment project is a suitable investment for you is your ability to tolerate uncertainty. More than with most other real estate opportunities, you are looking to capital appreciation. If you want only tax savings or equity buildup, a net-leased or other "tax-oriented" property (chapter 13) would be more appropriate than rental housing. If your objective is a more certain cash return than an apartment project offers, you would probably be better off with a shopping center or office building (see chapter 12).

Capital appreciation is the prime investment incentive in the case of an apartment project; and this means speculating on the future. Relying upon capital appreciation, I was once told, is "a little like fishing. It's important to be patient and prepared. You'll do better if you have the right rod and tackle. And some guys are better at it than others, but there are really no experts. You're going to be sitting on a big lake and, in the final analysis, you and everyone else will be guessing. That's why they call it 'fishing.' "

⌂ CHECKLIST

TEN POINTS TO INVESTIGATE BEFORE INVESTING IN AN APARTMENT PROJECT

Management   The project should be managed by a qualified professional management company, preferably one located near the project and familiar with the neighborhood.

Structural soundness   An independent engineer, architect, or contractor should inspect the project and evaluate the quality of its construction and its structural soundness.

Location   The project should be in an area that is not overbuilt with competing projects. However, the quality of location can change because of circumstances beyond your control.

Size   Apartment projects vary widely in size, ranging from complexes containing 300 or more units to two-family homes. I prefer a 100- to 150-unit apartment project.

Operating expenses   To the extent possible, such costs should be imposed on the tenants. Be sure that the expenses are not understated and that adequate provision has been made for vacancies and for reserves covering future repairs and replacements.

Quality and stability of tenancy   Families and older persons in upper income brackets are preferable.

Seller's responsibilities   The seller should have continuing responsibilities, particularly in the case of a new project, protecting you against structural defects and, at least in the early years, operating deficits. He should also have the financial strength to meet these responsibilities.

Seller's projections   Such estimates need to be carefully evaluated—particularly those relating to rents, operating expenses, and cash return.

Mortgage financing   Financing should generally cover 75% of the purchase price in order to get a balanced return from cash flow, equity buildup, and tax benefits.

Condominium conversion   Conversion can be a source of substantial profit. However, you should not rely primarily upon the possibility when you invest in an apartment project.

Twelve

SHOPPING CENTERS
AND OFFICE BUILDINGS—
THE MIXED TENANCIES

ONE OF MY MORE DEFLATING EXPERIENCES OCCURRED AT the end of a semester in a course I was teaching on real estate investing. In the final exam, I asked my students to analyze a new shopping center and advise a hypothetical group of clients whether or not they should invest in it.

While the exam was a pedagogical device, most of the facts (other than the names of the tenants) were derived from an actual shopping center located a few miles outside of a major urban area. I liked the center and expected the students to confirm my judgment. But after reading through their answers, I found that all but three or four disagreed with me and advised their clients not to make the investment. Since there were 80 people in the class, this was an overwhelming dissent, and I thought I had better reconsider my point of view before submitting the grades. Here are the facts, essentially in the form I presented them:

The center contains 150,000 square feet and the major tenants, K mart and Safeway, are leasing a total of 90,000 square feet of this space. The remaining 60,000 square feet are being leased to several "local" tenants, including a savings bank, a shoe store, a variety store, and a pharmacy.

The purchase price is $5,500,000, with $4,125,000 (75% of the cost) financed by a mortgage. The investors will be the co-owners of the center and will make a cash payment of $1,375,000 to cover the balance of the cost. (If, for example, there are 35 investors, each will pay approximately $39,285.)

Of the purchase price, $550,000 (10%) is allocable to the land, which is not depreciable; $4,950,000 (90%) is allocable to the building and other improvements in the center, which are depreciable.

The gross rents before operating expenses are expected to be $700,000 yearly at minimum, with K mart and Safeway paying $350,000 combined (50% of the gross rents) and the local tenants paying the other 50%. K mart and Safeway also both agree to pay additional rent each year—usually referred to as a "percentage" or "overage" rent—based upon a percentage of their gross sales over a specified dollar amount. It is estimated that together they will pay $15,000 in percentage rents, which brings the total gross rents to $715,000. A summary of the leases is set forth in table 25.

TABLE 25

Shopping Center Lease Summary

Tenant	Area Leased (in sq. ft.)	Lease Term (in years)	Annual Minimum Rent	Estimated Annual Percentage Rent
K mart	55,000	25	$200,000	$ 7,500
Safeway	35,000	20	150,000	7,500
Savings bank	10,000	10	50,000	—
Local stores	50,000	3–10	300,000	—
Total	150,000		$700,000	$15,000

The operating expenses (including a reserve for vacancies) will be $75,000, which reduces the rental income to $640,000—$715,000 minus $75,000.

Finally, the $4,125,000 mortgage will bear interest of 11.25% and will mature in 25 years. The principal and interest payments (calculated annually) will be approximately $500,000; and after making these payments, the remaining cash will be $140,000 ($640,000 in net rents minus $500,000 in mortgage payments). This will give the investors a cash return of 10.18%—$140,000 on their $1,375,000 investment. This projected summary of operations is set forth in table 26 (page 196).

After reviewing this dense set of facts, assumptions, projec-

tions, and estimates. I could understand that my students
might have been bored by the test question, but that was not
a good enough reason to reject the center. I still had a high
opinion of the investment; and I wondered whether I had forgotten to give the lecture on "How to Analyze a Shopping
Center." I felt about my students the way my mother must
have felt about me when, after I came home with another of
my dismal grade-school report cards, she cried out in mater-
nal anguish, "Where have I failed this boy?"

It was not that the students missed any of the issues and
problems. They saw them clearly enough. The local tenants
might not renew their leases, which expired within three to
ten years, and it might be difficult to replace them. They were
also financially less sturdy than K mart and Safeway, and a
recession could drive them out of business.

TABLE 26

Calculating Shopping Center Annual Cash Flow	
Minimum rents	$700,000
PLUS	
Estimated percentage rents	15,000
Total rents	$715,000
MINUS	
Operating expenses and vacancy reserves	75,000
Result—net income	$640,000
MINUS	
Mortgage payments	500,000
Result—cash flow including percentage rents	$140,000*
Cash flow excluding percentage rents of $15,000	$125,000†

* 10.18% cash return on $1,375,000 investment.
† 9.09% cash return on $1,375,000 investment.

Operating expenses would probably rise, and the students
questioned whether it would be possible to adjust the rents
quickly enough to cover these added expenses. They were
also concerned about the fact that the rents of Safeway and
K mart would remain fixed for 20 and 25 years, respectively,
except for the possibility (which was remote in their opinion)
of the payment of percentage rents.

But underlying all of their problems was their perception of this center as a hybrid. It was, with its mix of credit and noncredit tenants, somewhere between a credit and noncredit transaction, without being one or the other. Yet, it was this combination that appealed to me; and if my students saw the cup as half empty, I saw it as half full.

K mart and Safeway were the credit tenants—having national standing and strong credit ratings—and would be paying one-half of the minimum rents. They would give the center stability. I also thought that they would do enough business that they would have to pay percentage rents—if not in the first year of operation, at least within a few years thereafter. Even if the number of items they sold in their stores remained the same, the price at which they could be sold would probably go up with inflation, thereby increasing the dollar volume of sales.

These credit tenants would also act as magnets, drawing in local tenants who wanted to be near chain stores of national retail companies. This attraction would be very comforting if it became necessary to replace a local tenant that went bankrupt or refused to renew its lease.

Several of my students would have agreed with me if K mart and Safeway paid 70% or 80% of the rents. As it was, they felt that the center was relying too heavily upon the local tenants. You may find, however, that these are the tenants that will make you the most money. They pay higher minimum rents for each square foot of space than the major tenants; and since their leases are short-term, you have the opportunity, as with an apartment project, to renegotiate these rents every few years. While you run the risk of losing some of these tenants after their leases expire, they will probably want to remain in the center, even at a higher rental, if their store is performing well. Local tenants will, in most cases, also be required to pay percentage rents, although I did not include this possibility in my projections. Instead, I took the conservative position that if they were paid, they would be a bonus.

Thus, with K mart and Safeway paying 50% of the rents and the local tenants paying the other 50%, together with the possibility of percentage rents, there would be a balance between stability and potential.

There would also be a balanced return, with a mortgage covering 75% of the purchase price. While this may not be a lavish amount of financing, it allows for at least an adequate return from equity buildup and tax savings as well as, in my example, a cash yield of 10.18%. (Later in this chapter, I will analyze this composite return arising out of cash flow, equity buildup, and tax savings.)

In recommending this center as an investment, I am not suggesting that it is perfect. Since the closing of the Garden of Eden, there has been no such thing as a perfect piece of real estate. If there were, you would have to pay too much for it. This raises the first issue you should consider: purchase price.

How much should you pay? The amount you pay should, of course, depend upon the return on your cash investment. As with apartment projects, the appropriate return on a shopping center at any given time should be based upon a comparison with other investment opportunities then available. I would, in most cases, expect a lower return from a shopping center than an apartment project, because I think there is less risk. Under current market condition (as of November 1982), somewhere around 9% to 9½% seems reasonable. There is nothing sacred about this figure. In another 6 to 12 months, 10% to 10½% may be more suitable. But based upon a 9% return on the investors' $1,375,000 of cash, the purchase price of $5,500,000 is about right.

However, you would probably not hesitate to reject the center (even with tax savings and equity buildup) if the 9% return were fixed. What makes it acceptable is the possibility that, with rising rents, your average cash return over a period of 10 to 15 years will be 11% or 12%, or higher. Whether it will reach this level will heavily depend, as I pointed out earlier in regard to apartment projects, upon your initial return. If you start at 8%, you have a decent chance of reaching 11% or 12%; you have a good chance of reaching that level if you start at 9%; and at 6% or 7%, this chance drops to a hope.

In suggesting a price of $5,500,000 and 9% return on the investors' cash of $1,375,000, I am looking only at the minimum rents and am excluding the percentage rents. (If I had included the $15,000 of estimated percentage rents, remember the cash return would have been $140,000, or 10.18% on $1,375,000, instead of $125,000.) The minimum rents define, as the acquisition officer of real estate investment trust explained, "the downside risk. The percentage rents give a shopping center its 'sex appeal'. We expect to get them; and if we didn't think they were real, we wouldn't invest. But in setting the price we'll pay, we only consider the minimum rents."

Percentage rents not only help you to defend against inflation, they also give you a stake in your tenants' success. But they lack the certainty of minimum rents; and if you rely upon them in evaluating the purchase price, you may find that you will be sharing in your tenants' failures.

There are, of course, circumstances in which consideration should be given to the percentage rents. In the case of a seasoned center, for example, there may be an established pattern of tenants indeed paying these contingency rents. But this will not be true of a new center. It will usually take five or six years before a new shopping center will have sufficiently matured to produce the sales necessary to generate income under percentage-rental agreements. And my students were properly skeptical about my percentage-rent estimate of $15,000 for the K mart–Safeway center. I did not, however, have to rely upon these rents. Even without percentage rents, the cash return (assuming a purchase price of $5,500,000) was a respectable 9%—$125,000 on a $1,375,000 cash investment.

Insisting upon percentage rents but refusing to pay for them may be having your cake and eating it. But unless you carefully analyze the prospects of percentage rents, you may end up with that other digestive impossibility—pie in the sky.

How to evaluate estimates of percentage rents. In evaluating any estimate of percentage rents, you need the answers to three questions:

- How much do other companies who engage in the same business as your tenants sell in shopping centers?—that is, what are the industry standards?
- How have your tenants done in comparable centers?
- How have other shopping centers in the same geographic area been performing?

For example, if you determine that K mart and its competitors have been selling $5 million worth of merchandise in similar stores, you should forget about the percentage rents if they are contingent upon K mart's reaching, say, $7 million in sales at your location.

You should get the answers to these questions from the person selling you the center; and his information should be derived from independent sources, such as real estate consultants and analysts (who are comparable to investment advisers in the stock, bond, and other financial markets).

Cost Factors

As you saw in chapter 11, where I discussed apartment projects, the amount you pay should also depend upon operating expenses, management, construction, and location. You have to make the same kind of analysis as you'd make for an apartment project—with the central issue being: Who bears the burden of these expenses, responsibilities, and risks?

Net leases cover all expenses. It is becoming common for shopping-center tenants to enter into net leases under which they have to pay, in addition to the rent, all of the expenses arising out of the use and operation of their premises, including real estate taxes and utilities. At a minimum, the leases with your "magnet" tenants (such as K mart and Safeway) should be net. If the local tenants do not sign net leases (and it would be preferable if they did), they should at least be required to pay any *increases* in operating expenses allocable to their stores.

Operating expenses: Insist on the details. There is, however, no absolute rule or practice as to how operating expenses are to be allocated; and before you buy a shopping center, the seller should set forth these costs in detail and explain who has to pay them. Sellers will often make a financial presentation of a center without itemizing these expenses. In my exam, for example, I merely stated that they were $75,000. I was teaching my students a lesson I learned several years ago when I was sent by a client to Montreal to negotiate the purchase of a shopping center.

The developers had lumped the operating expenses together. When I asked for more information, they appeared amused and told me that they were following Canadian custom—everyone up there knew who paid for what. While I did not want to start an international incident, I telephoned my client in New York for advice. He told me: "You're doing just fine. They're trying to hide something. Tell them that the custom in the United States is not to pay any money until you see an agreement in writing accounting for every penny of cost."

Just as I returned with the message, the Canadians' secretary walked in. I apparently must have followed her across the room with my eyes, because they asked whether I liked "it." For a moment, I seriously thought they meant the city of Montreal; and I said, "Yes, it's very nice."

They were delighted and said they could "arrange something for the evening." I suddenly realized that "it" was the young lady. I was honestly stunned—offended both for myself and the secretary. It was clear, at this point, that they did have something to hide and that I was not going to reach an agreement. Within the hour, I was on an airplane heading home with neither the deal nor anything else consummated.

Vacancies. In addition to operating expenses, there may be vacancies. The center may be fully rented when you buy it, but you should assume that some tenants will move out or will be unable to pay their rents. I would suggest, as a general rule, that you apply a vacancy factor of 7% to 10% to the rents payable by the local tenants. Since the local tenants in the K mart–Safeway center are to pay $350,000 of the $700,000 in minimum rents, a prudent discount would be between $24,500 and $35,000.

Management. Every piece of real estate has to be managed, and shopping centers are no exception. A center should, however, be easier to manage than an apartment project, particularly if the tenants have entered into net leases. Compared to apartments, there are usually fewer and less diverse tenants in a shopping center, and they have experience in maintaining their stores. Nevertheless, you will probably be responsible for the parking lot and other common areas—which, at the very least, will require shoveling snow in the winter, sweeping in the summer, and collecting and disposing of trash in every season.

Structural quality: Let an expert be your judge. You have also to look into the structural quality of the shopping center. The fact that a national company is leasing space is not a warranty against poor construction.

I discovered this a few years ago when I entered into an agreement to buy a center in New Hampshire, subject only to an inspection of the site. I hate to drive and kept putting off the visit. Besides which, the major tenants were the equal of K mart and Safeway; and I felt that if they were satisfied with the construction, I had little to worry about. I was also assured by the sellers that the center was in good condition except for a minor repair, which would be taken care of promptly. After several delays (during which I ran up considerable legal fees in the review and preparation of documents), I finally took the trip and found that the "minor repair" was a roof that had caved in.

This experience not only taught me that I should have visited the site sooner, but also that I should have been accompanied by an engineer or other expert who could have examined the structure. He would have explained, among other things, that the first rule of construction in New Hampshire is to have a slanted roof so the snow can slide off. This center had a flat roof and the weight of the snow had caused it to collapse.

I did not buy the property—my ardor having been crushed along with the roof. My only solace was that I was able to drive in and out of the center quickly. It was built near the end of an interstate-highway exit ramp. Since most people have to drive in order to get to a shopping center, this was an excellent location, and it could have made the center an attractive investment if the structural problems had been remedied.

Location. Dependence upon the automobile creates some special requirements for a shopping center. It should be located within a few miles of the population center it is expected to serve, particularly in view of gasoline prices and shortages. And it must also have adequate parking facilities. Once a customer gets there, he has to have a place to put his car. Although the requirements will vary with the size and location of a shopping center, in a 150,000-square-foot center similar to the K mart–Safeway example, there ordinarily should be space for about 750 cars—five spaces for each 1,000 square feet.

Risk: new roads. The automobile also holds the center hostage to the risk that new roads may be built that will divert traffic away from the property. I do not know how to defend against this risk; and, as a real estate investor, I have always suspected that in the movie *Psycho*, Anthony Perkins was turned into a psychopathic killer not by his mother, but by the construction of a new highway that bypassed his motel.

Demographics. There are other facts that you should find out about the location. Is the population growing or contracting? What is its relative affluence? Will it, for example, be able to afford higher gasoline prices? Can the area support another center, or is there already too much competition?

The information can be put together in a demographic study prepared by the real estate consultant or analyst who answered your questions about the percentage rents. That study should also describe the performance of competing centers, and should evaluate the accuracy of the seller's rent projections, the estimates of operating costs and vacancies, and the adequacy of the parking facilities.

How to Figure Your Return

Assuming that a center can withstand the pressures of changing traffic patterns and population trends, and that it otherwise meets the standards I have been discussing, the next step is to find your composite return.

Your tax bracket will be, as with any real estate investment, a major consideration. But it will be less important in a shopping center, where so much of your return comes from cash flow. And that means, even if your tax bracket is somewhat below 40%, it may still be worthwhile.

Using the $5,500,000 K mart–Safeway center as a model, I have assumed that the minimum rents and operating expenses will remain at $700,000 and $75,000, respectively; that at the end of the fifteenth year the center can be sold at its original purchase price of $5,500,000; that the principal balance of the $4,125,000 mortgage will then be about $2,907,000; and that $4,950,000 of the purchase price will be allocable to the building (with the land value being $550,000).

Based on the 1981 tax act, the building can be depreciated over 15 years. Due to the recapture penalty for accelerated depreciation, I have used the straight-line method.

The cash flow, excluding the percentage rents, will be $125,000 each year (see table 26). The tax losses to the investors will be $1,839,000 over fifteen years, as shown in table 27. If the owners are in the 50% tax bracket, these losses will save them $919,500 (50% of $1,839,000).

TABLE 27

Breakdown of Shopping Center Tax Loss and Saving (50% Bracket)

Year	Gross Minimum Rent	Operating Expenses*	Mortgage Interest**	Straight-Line Depreciation**	Tax Loss	Tax Saving
1	$ 700,000	$ 75,000	$ 464,000	$ 330,000	$ 169,000	$ 84,500
2	700,000	75,000	460,000	330,000	165,000	82,500
3	700,000	75,000	456,000	330,000	161,000	80,500
4	700,000	75,000	451,000	330,000	156,000	78,000
5	700,000	75,000	446,000	330,000	151,000	75,500
6	700,000	75,000	440,000	330,000	145,000	72,500
7	700,000	75,000	433,000	330,000	138,000	69,000
8	700,000	75,000	426,000	330,000	131,000	65,500
9	700,000	75,000	417,000	330,000	122,000	61,000
10	700,000	75,000	408,000	330,000	113,000	56,500
11	700,000	75,000	398,000	330,000	103,000	51,500
12	700,000	75,000	387,000	330,000	92,000	46,000
13	700,000	75,000	374,000	330,000	79,000	39,500
14	700,000	75,000	360,000	330,000	65,000	32,500
15	700,000	75,000	344,000	330,000	49,000	24,500
Total	$10,500,000	$1,125,000	$6,264,000	$4,950,000	$1,839,000	$919,500

* Including vacancies
** Rounded to nearest $1,000

In determining the composite return, if the center is sold for $5,500,000 (the original cost) at the end of fifteen years and if the mortgage balance is $2,907,000, the cash proceeds from the sale will be $2,593,000 ($5,500,000 minus $2,907,-000). After taxes (assuming a 50% tax bracket), these proceeds will be reduced to approximately $1,603,000. Based upon the cash flow, tax savings, and aftertax sales proceeds, the annual aftertax return on the $1,375,000 investment is shown in table 28.

TABLE 28

Breakdown of Annual Aftertax Return on Shopping Center ($1,375,000 Investment)

Year	Cash Flow	Tax Saving	Aftertax Sales Proceeds	Total Aftertax Return
1	$125,000	$84,500	$ —	$209,500
2	125,000	82,500	—	207,500
3	125,000	80,500	—	205,500
4	125,000	78,000	—	203,000
5	125,000	75,500	—	200,500
6	125,000	72,500	—	197,500
7	125,000	69,000	—	194,000
8	125,000	65,500	—	190,500
9	125,000	61,000	—	186,000
10	125,000	56,500	—	181,500
11	125,000	51,500	—	176,500
12	125,000	46,000	—	171,000
13	125,000	39,500	—	164,500
14	125,000	32,500	—	157,500
15	125,000	24,500	1,603,000	1,752,500
Total				4,397,500

If, after fifteen years, you had refinanced the mortgage instead of selling the center, you would also have had to adjust your return. Assume that you could have obtained a new $4,-125,000 mortgage at the end of the fifteenth year, when the balance of the existing mortgage was $2,907,000. You would have had to use $2,907,000 of the new mortgage proceeds to pay off this balance. This would have left you with $1,218,-000 (an amount equal to the $1,218,000 of principal payments made on the existing mortgage over the previous fifteen years), thereby allowing you to recover your equity buildup. And you would not have had to pay any tax on these proceeds. While the $1,218,000 of refinancing proceeds would have been less than your $1,603,000 aftertax profit from a sale, you would still own the property and continue to reap its benefits.

To sell, or to refinance? Whether you should sell or refinance will depend upon conditions at the time you have to make the decision. If the interest rate and mortgage payments on a new mortgage were higher than that on the existing mortgage, you might be more inclined to sell than to refinance.

On the other hand, if it appeared that the value of the property would be rapidly increasing over the next several years, you might choose to keep the center and refinance, even though the terms of the new mortgage were more severe than those on the existing one.

In either case, if you prepay your existing mortgage because of a sale or a refinancing, you may have to pay a prepayment fee or premium to the bank.

In using the K mart–Safeway model to make this analysis, I have been assuming a $5,500,000 purchase price and a $4,-125,000 mortgage. Now, let's assume that the price had been higher, say $5,700,000.

Nevertheless, the mortgage would remain at $4,125,000. Why? If you have to buy at a higher price, and the bank was willing to give you a 75% loan, shouldn't the amount of the mortgage be $4,275,000 (75% of $5,700,000) instead of $4,125,000?

The bank's answer would probably be that when it gives you a 75% mortgage, it is based upon the price it thinks you should pay, and not necessarily upon the price you actually do pay. In making this decision, the bank looks first at the minimum rents. It wants to be sure that these rents will be sufficient not only to cover the mortgage payments, but also to provide a margin of safety in the event your projections turn out to be wrong or the center has unexpected financial problems.

Generally, the bank will insist upon at least $1.25 in minimum rents (after vacancies and operating expenses) for every $1.00 you have to pay on a shopping-center mortgage. On the $4,125,000 mortgage, the annual mortgage payments would be approximately $500,000. The net minimum rents would be $625,000 (gross rents of $700,000 minus operating expenses and vacancies of $75,000). If you divide $500,000 into $625,000, you find that each $1.00 of mortgage payments is secured, or covered, by $1.25 of minimum rents—thereby meeting the bank's requirements.

If the mortgage were increased to $4,275,000, the mortgage payments would be approximately $517,000, against the same $625,000 of net minimum rents. The ratio would decline to $1.00:$1.21 ($625,000 divided by $517,000); and it is doubtful whether the bank would give you the higher mortgage unless there were some other facts to justify an increase, such as a seasoned center in which the credit tenants pay more than 60% of the minimum rents, or a center in which there has been a long and uninterrupted history of percentage rent payments.

The Neighborhood Shopping Center

Up to now I have been dealing with the community shopping center (the type containing between 100,000 to 200,000 square feet). There are two other types of centers—the neighborhood and the regional shopping center.

A neighborhood center usually contains under 100,000 square feet, with one dominant tenant, such as a supermarket or discount retailer, and a few convenience stores, such as a shoe store, beauty parlor, or drugstore. Normally, such a center is close to the population it is serving, so its patrons don't have far to drive. And because of its size, it will probably be easier to manage than the other kinds of centers.

Nevertheless, without strong "anchor" tenants like K mart and Safeway, a neighborhood center may not be able to withstand competition of a community or regional center. One real estate analyst described the problem in these terms: "It's not just their size. It's the talent. They don't have the stars to draw in the customers or the local tenants. And when the competition gets tough, I am always afraid they will fold."

The Regional Shopping Center

By contrast, the regional center not only has "stars," it has dozens of satellites. It is usually an enclosed, self-contained trading area with as much as 500,000 to 1,000,000 square feet. It has competing national retail chains under the same roof, such as Sears, J.C. Penney, Neiman-Marcus, and Lord

& Taylor; and it usually provides the same range of merchandise that is found in downtown shopping areas, from clothing and sporting goods to large appliances and electronic equipment.

Many experienced investors believe that the regional centers have been and will continue to be the best investments in real estate. There has been spectacular appreciation in their value over the past decade, and this growth is expected to continue during the next decade, despite the shortage of gasoline and its high price. Since customers can find most of the merchandise they need within these centers, they can stock up in one trip.

These centers also draw in local and other satellite tenants, which are eager to become protectorates of the national tenants—paying rents as high as $15 to $20 a square foot for the privilege. And they, as well as the major tenants, will allow the landlord a more generous share of their gross earnings than they will in a community or neighborhood center—through the payment of percentage rents.

This rent structure and the concentration of stores in one place have given rise to the bloated claims that regional centers are both "recession and inflation proof"; and the prices investors are willing to pay for these centers testify to the sincerity, if not the validity, of these claims.

There seems to be an almost insatiable demand for regional shopping centers, and investors are often willing to accept initial cash yields as low as 5% or 6%. No shopping center is, unfortunately, immune from financial disaster, whether it is regional, community, or neighborhood. A recession, once it begins, cannot be easily controlled; and major as well as local tenants can go bankrupt, taking a center down with them.

Furthermore, because of a center's size, management can be an imposing responsibility. Managing a regional center has been compared to running a small city. These centers depend upon volume, and there has to be an almost constant series of promotional activities (from Santa Claus and the Easter Bunny to flower and automobile exhibits) in order to lure more and more patrons.

Adding to the demand for regional centers is the fact that they are in short supply; and when they are available, it takes an immense amount of cash to purchase them. A regional center in the Northeast, for example, was recently sold for a cash investment of $20 million. Consequently, these centers are accessible only to large institutional investors, such as insurance companies, pension funds, and real estate investment trusts.

As a practical matter, any investment you make in a regional center will probably have to be made indirectly—for example, by buying shares in a real estate investment trust, as I shall discuss in chapter 14.

Office Buildings: A More Complicated Investment

Office buildings belong in this chapter along with shopping centers because they often appear to be comparable investments. Both have mixed tenancies, and they are often presented to investors by real estate brokers as interchangeable alternatives. But office buildings are more complicated and require more real estate expertise.

I recently heard that the only substantive difference between an office building and a shopping center is that the shopping-center tenant may have to pay percentage rents, while the office tenant will not. This, in itself, is no small difference, since percentage rents can improve an investor's cash return during the lease term. Otherwise, he may have to wait for increases until the leases expire and new leases can be negotiated.

Mixed tenants, mostly noncredit. In fact, there are other differences that more clearly distinguish the office building, as an investment, from the shopping center. One fundamental distinction is the mix of tenancies: The office building is more heavily weighted toward noncredit tenants. Even the major tenants are likely to be local businesses, such as bank, law firm, or investment company. Although they may be strong tenants within the city or region in which they operate, they generally do not have the national recognition of a K mart or a Safeway; and this may also make it difficult to gather financial information on them—unlike the shopping center, where 50% or more of the space is usually leased to public companies with financial operations that are a matter of public record. (There are exceptions, of course. The bank could be the Chase Manhattan Bank or the investment firm could be Merrill Lynch. The office building could also be a regional headquarters of IBM or General Motors.)

Shorter leases. Office-building leases will generally be shorter than shopping-center leases, particularly in the case of the major tenants. In a shopping center, the length of the lease for a major tenant will usually be about 20 to 25 years. In the case of an office building, it will be closer to 10 years.

Whether short-term leases are good or bad, they create an atmosphere of mutual extortion. The tenant is faced with the threat of rising rents every few years, and the landlord with the threat of the tenant moving to another building. While the outcome of this contest will in part depend upon the availability of alternative office space as leases expire, the tenants have one advantage. They are usually not engaged in the type of activity that binds them to a specific location. A law firm, for example, can as easily represent a client from an office on one side of the street as the other.

More operating expenses. Although the trend in office buildings is toward net leases, they are typically not as "net" as those for shopping centers: more of the operating expenses are imposed upon the landlord. Be sure, however, that these leases contain escalation provisions requiring the tenants to pay any increases in operating expenses, particularly real estate taxes and utility costs. In addition, the rents in some buildings are tied to an index, such as the U.S. Department of Labor's Consumer Price Index, automatically rising in proportion with statistical increases.

More management. Given the nature of the tenants and the length and provisions of the leases, you can expect the management of an office building to be more burdensome than a shopping center, except, perhaps, in the case of a large regional center.

The tenants in an office building are more diverse and have different needs. In the shopping center, the tenants have a common goal—they want customers. They will act together in promoting and maintaining the center. This commonality of interest is absent in an office building except when it comes to complaining about the maintenance of the lavatories, lobbies, and elevator, and about disrepair. Moreover, with shorter leases, you will have to spend a great deal of time keeping your tenants happy so they will renew them. Failing that, you will have to expend even more effort to find new tenants to fill the empty space.

While I have an obvious preference for shopping centers

over office buildings, there are some other factors that you should consider before you choose between these two categories of real estate.

Higher cash return than on shopping centers. First, in exchange for the greater risk and more active management entailed, you should usually be able to command, initially, a somewhat higher cash return on your investment in an office building. If, as I suggested, the initial yield on a shopping center should not, as of a particular time, be below 9%, this base should be closer to 9.5% in the case of an office building (again, assuming a 75% mortgage).

Quality of tenants. Second, while the mix of office-building tenants may not be as favorable as that in a shopping center, this does not mean that office tenants are necessarily unstable or transient. Traditionally, they are established businesses that pay their rents on time, keep their premises clean, and prefer not to move if the rents are reasonable and the building is well maintained and efficiently operated.

75% mortgage. Third, you should be able to obtain a 75% mortgage on an office building—with terms, including interest rate, that are comparable to those for a shopping center.

Depreciation. The tax savings should also be comparable, since both types of properties can be depreciated over fifteen years. Again, you would undoubtedly elect the straight-line method because of the recapture penalty accompanying accelerated depreciation.

Finally, many real estate investors believe that office buildings have greater potential for capital appreciation than do shopping centers. This judgment is based upon the strong demand that presently exists for new, well-built office space (vacancy levels in some cities are below 5%). So long as this demand continues, it can be translated into higher rents and sales prices. However, there is evidence that this demand is beginning to decline. Furthermore, you should be aware that office buildings usually compete within a narrow, localized market—sometimes encompassing not more than a few city blocks. Therefore, demand may vary radically, and not only from city to city; even within the same city, variations can be startling, with one area having literally no space, while a

⌂ CHECKLIST

TEN POINTS TO CONSIDER BEFORE INVESTING IN A SHOPPING CENTER OR OFFICE BUILDING

Tenants   There should be a balanced mix of tenants, with credit tenants (those with high credit ratings) giving stability to the project and local tenants providing potential for capital appreciation.

Operating expenses   To the extent possible, the leases should be "net," which means that the operating expenses are imposed upon the tenants.

Length of leases   Those of major tenants should usually be long-term, with those of the minor or local tenants generally under ten years.

Percentage rents   Percentage rents and other provisions for rent "escalations" help protect you against inflation. They also provide some "upside" potential. However, you should be wary about relying upon percentage rents in setting the purchase price.

Quality of construction   Arrange for an independent, professional investigation. Do not rely solely upon the fact that the major tenants are satisfied.

Location   Particularly in the case of a shopping center, be sure it is easily accessible by automobile. Be aware that you are always vulnerable to overbuilding and competing projects.

Accuracy of projections   Projections about rents, operating expenses (and who pays them), and cash return should be carefully examined. As with apartment projects, adequate provision should be made for reserves to cover future vacancies, repairs, and replacements.

Seller's responsibilities   These duties should be similar to those of a seller of an apartment project: accepting liability for structural defects and operating deficits (at least in the early years of a new project). The seller should have the financial strength to meet these responsibilities.

Mortgage financing   As with an apartment project, it should generally cover 75% of the purchase price in order to get a balanced return from cash flow, equity buildup, and tax benefits.

Management   Even if the tenants have signed net leases, there will be management responsibilities that should be undertaken by a qualified professional-management firm.

nearby neighborhood goes begging for tenants. Also, the rate of vacancies may differ between new and old buildings.

Even if you are buying a building in an area with a low vacancy rate, you should find out in advance specifically who your tenants are. If it is a new building, it should be preleased. Your investment will be risky enough without speculating on unknown tenants.

Another serious problem in evaluating demand is that office buildings, like apartment projects, are extremely vulnerable to overbuilding. Developers are the joy of behavioral psychologists. Their conditioned response to the sound of the word *demand* is to salivate; and, in their rush to build, they can turn the right location today into the wrong one tomorrow.

My preference for shopping centers does not mean that I have an aversion to office buildings. Nevertheless, shopping centers, as a category, are a less complex investment and are better suited to investors who want security along with a limited involvement in the management and operation of real estate. I do recognize, however, that this is a generalization and that there will, obviously, be many situations in which a specific office building will be preferable to a specific shopping center.

This last statement may seem excessively broad-minded to those who share my obvious leaning toward shopping centers, and toward the K mart–Safeway type of center in particular. But tolerance is part of my nature, as was confirmed by one of my students. After I explained my views on the exam question, I overheard him saying, "In the scale of A to Z, his analysis is closer to Z than to A, but at least he's an easy grader."

Thirteen

NET-LEASED PROPERTIES
AND OTHER TAX SHELTERS

AT THE BEGINNING OF FEBRUARY 1980, THE FINANCIAL pages of some of the nation's most influential newspapers were filled with obituaries reporting the death of the bond market.

This was startling news, because interest rates were breaking barriers (going above 13% for United States government securities) that were thought to be more impregnable than the four-minute mile once was, and because only a few years before these same newspapers were reporting that the bond market was the only haven for refugees from the stock market.

While all of this was a reflection on the supposed omniscience of the press, it was also, to many observers, one more piece of evidence that the financial community had become mesmerized by inflation—by the belief that no matter how high interest rates climbed, inflation would eventually overtake them. If this claim were true, investors should not be buying bonds or other securities with a fixed return. And if this happened, it would be a calamity for the purest form of credit real estate—net-leased properties—because these properties are, in effect, fixed-income securities.

Net-leased property. A net-leased property is credit real estate that is leased to one tenant under a long-term net lease. The tenant typically will be a corporation with a high credit rating, having national recognition and a net worth of $50 million or more. The lease will be for an initial term of 20 to 25 years at a fixed rent; and the tenant will usually have the option to extend, after the initial term, for another 25 to 30 years at a lower rent.

Rent payable under the lease will be fixed and absolutely "net," with the tenant being required to pay all operating expenses, real estate taxes, insurance, utilities, and other expenses relating to the property. The tenant will also be completely responsible for the management and maintenance of the property—so completely that the owner, even if he wanted to, could not legally take any initiatives with respect to the property. Thus, the lease gives the tenant both full responsibility for and total dominion over the property.

Such a lease is known by many different names, including a "net, net, net lease," an "absolutely net lease," and a "hell-or-high-water lease." All of these phrases are intended to convey the point that there is no outrage the landlord can commit that will reduce the rents. But, in return, nothing can happen that will cause the rents to rise—neither inflation nor any increase in gross retail sales on the property. (There may be situations in which the tenant agrees to pay percentage rents in addition. In such cases, however, the initial, minimum rents will usually be well below the fixed rent that the tenant would ordinarily pay under the lease.)

Billions of dollars worth of properties have been net-leased to many of the country's largest corporations, including General Motors, Sears, J.C. Penney, McDonald's, Safeway, K mart, and many of the major oil companies and utilities. Among the properties under net leases are gasoline service stations, fast-food restaurants, supermarkets, free-standing retail stores, warehouses and other industrial buildings, banks, and utility facilities.

Net-leased security. From the landlord's point of view, the attraction of a net lease is the security of receiving a guaranteed return from a substantial corporation. From the tenant's point of view, it is the elimination of inflation from the rent structure.

The landlord of a net-leased property is probably more like the owner of a bond than the owner of real estate. If, for example, you had purchased a property net-leased to Sears for 25 years that gave you a 12% return on your investment (assuming no mortgage), this would be analogous to buying a 25-year bond from Sears bearing interest at 12%. In fact, these two investments are so alike that if the bond market is dead it should move over and make room in the coffin for net-leased properties. But these properties are neither dead nor comatose nor moribund. They are as alive and vibrant as they have ever been, and investors fight over the chance to buy them.

The reason for this apparent contradiction is that investors in these properties are not concerned about the fixed cash return. Indeed, they are not concerned about a cash return at all. They are usually within the 40% federal tax bracket, and they want a tax shelter; and they want it without having to worry about the real estate. (Tax shelter, as you remember from the discussion in chapter 9, arises out of the excess of interest and depreciation deductions over net rental income. This excess is a tax loss that can be deducted from your overall income, thereby reducing your taxes.)

Nothing satisfies these requirements better than a net-leased property. It is the "blue chip" tax shelter. Other tax shelters may generate more losses, but none of them has a Sears, K mart, or Safeway standing behind them. So long as your tax bracket does not decline and the tax laws do not change, there is certainty underlying the promise of tax benefits in a net-lease transaction that makes cash flow, equity buildup, and capital appreciation unimportant, if not irrelevant.

The competition for net-lease properties has grown incessantly over the last 25 years because they are the "safe" tax shelter. And this has pushed up the cost of investing in them to levels that, in many cases, make little economic sense. In order to understand why this has happened, think back to the transaction I described in chapter 9. This involved a building located in Las Vegas and net-leased to a major department store. The lease was for 25 years, and my client purchased it for $1 million.

My client financed the building with a $1 million mortgage bearing interest at 10% and maturing in 25 years. The annual mortgage payments were $110,000, and they were covered by the $110,000 in rents payable by the department store. The entire purchase price for the property was attributed to the building (it was assumed that the land had a nominal value).

If my client had purchased the building under the 1981 tax act, he would have had tax losses of $687,000 over a 15-year period. His tax savings (in the 50% bracket) would have been

$343,500 (and after the fifteenth year, the tax losses would have been used up). This is broken down in table 29 (page 219).

Thus, my client, in effect, would have made $343,500 without investing any cash because he was able to borrow 100% of the cost of the property by obtaining a $1 million nonrecourse mortgage.

While some people may question the basis of political nostalgia for the early 1960s, there is no doubt that those were the days of Camelot for my client and other persons investing in net-leased properties. If you wanted to buy this same property today, you would have to make a down payment of at least $150,000 to $200,000 (15% to 20%) and sometimes more. Obviously, something happened between 1960 and 1982 to account for this change.

First, assuming that you are in the financial position of my client, you have grown hungrier for tax shelter over these past two decades. Inflation has pushed you into a higher tax bracket, without necessarily increasing your purchasing power.

The other reason for this change is that the tenant has gotten smarter. In 1960 the department store agreed to pay enough rent ($110,000) to allow you to obtain a 100% mortgage. Banks and other lenders may lend up to 100% of the cost of a net-leased property, unlike other real estate investments. But then some alert financial officer of the department store must have questioned paying such high rent, when you, the landlord, were making no cash investment and getting such large tax savings. He must have asked himself what you would do if the tenant would pay only $95,000 in rent (instead of $110,000) for the $1 million property.

The financial officer guessed that you would still buy the property, even though $95,000 in rent would not enable you to get a $1 million mortgage. You could get a mortgage of only about $860,000, because rent of $95,000 would not be sufficient to repay $1 million over 25 years at 10% interest. (As you have seen, it takes $110,000 in rent each year to repay the $1 million mortgage.) Rent of $95,000 will support a mortgage of approximately $860,000. Therefore, you would have to make a cash investment equal to the difference between the $1 million cost of the property and the $860,000 mortgage—or $140,000. The tax losses and tax savings would

TABLE 29

Breakdown of Tax Loss and Saving on Las Vegas Investment ($1 Million Net-Leased Property)

Year	Rental Income	Mortgage Principal Repayment* (nondeductible)	Mortgage Interest*	Straight-Line Depreciation*	Tax Loss	Tax Saving (50% Bracket)
1	$110,000	$10,000	$100,000	$67,000	$57,000	$ 28,500
2	110,000	11,000	99,000	67,000	56,000	28,000
3	110,000	12,000	98,000	67,000	55,000	27,500
4	110,000	13,000	97,000	67,000	54,000	27,000
5	110,000	15,000	95,000	67,000	52,000	26,000
6	110,000	16,000	94,000	67,000	51,000	25,500
7	110,000	18,000	92,000	67,000	49,000	24,500
8	110,000	19,000	91,000	67,000	48,000	24,000
9	110,000	21,000	89,000	67,000	46,000	23,000
10	110,000	24,000	86,000	67,000	43,000	21,500
11	110,000	26,000	84,000	67,000	41,000	20,500
12	110,000	29,000	81,000	67,000	38,000	19,000
13	110,000	31,000	79,000	67,000	36,000	18,000
14	110,000	35,000	75,000	67,000	32,000	16,000
15	110,000	38,000	72,000	67,000	29,000	14,500
Total					$687,000	$343,500

* Rounded to the nearest $1,000.

220   **THE REAL ESTATE BOOK**

be about $719,000 and $359,500, respectively, over 15 years;
but this time you would be paying $140,000 for them. (As I
have suggested in the preceding chapters, you would not have
to put up the $140,000 by yourself. In most situations, you
will be able to participate with other investors in buying the
property, as I'll explain in the next chapter.)

As it turned out, the financial officer guessed correctly, because you and other investors continued to covet the
property. But he was not, as yet, completely satisfied; and he
decided to go a little further. He wanted to see if you would
invest if he lowered the yearly rent to $88,000. This would
mean that you could get a mortgage of about $800,000
($88,000 being the annual amount necessary to repay ap-
proximately $800,000 over 25 years at an interest rate of
10%). You would have to make a cash investment of $200,-
000 (the $1 million property cost minus the $800,000 mortgage); and your tax losses and savings would remain almost
the same.

This was becoming a less appetizing return, but investors
still flocked to the property. If you did not want it, they were
eager to take your place—and, in many cases, were willing to
pay even more than $200,000. And that was because new
techniques had been conceived to conjure up even more tax
benefits—more than those shown in table 29. Let me tell you
about a few of them and show you their effect. Bear in mind
that I will be tinkering with the numbers, but the property,
the tenant, and the form of lease will remain the same.

The basic technique has to do with how the rents are allocated to interest and principal on the mortgage.

Increasing tax benefits. The rents are the source of all payments to be made on the mortgage. The greater the proportion of these rents applied to interest, the greater your tax
losses will be, since interest is deductible. On the other hand,
there is no deduction for that portion of the rents used to repay principal; it is a nondeductible expenditure. So, one way
of getting more tax losses is to increase the proportion of
rents that are applied to interest, and this can be done by de-
ferring or delaying the repayment of principal.

More to interest, less to principal. To understand this, take
another look at table 29. It shows the typical payment pattern
of a mortgage: the amount of principal being repaid increases each year. The interest deductions, at the same time,

decline by the same amount. For example, in the first year, $100,000 of the $110,000 in rents is applied to interest and $10,000 is applied to principal. That creates a deduction of $100,000—an amount equal to the interest payment. Over time, the interest deduction gets smaller because a larger portion of the rents has to be used to repay principal.

If I could, in this example, delay the repayment of principal, I could significantly improve your tax position; and this may be possible in a net-lease transaction.

Banks may postpone payment of principal. When the rents payable by a credit tenant under a net lease are part of the security for a mortgage, a bank may be willing to postpone the repayment of any principal for as long as ten years. This means that you have to pay only interest (of 10%) over the 10-year period, or $100,000 each year (10% of $1 million). In this case, the rents can also be reduced to $100,000 (instead of $110,000), because they only need be sufficient to cover mortgage payments.

Moreover, these rents, since they're being applied entirely to interest, will be fully deductible. From a tax perspective, the interest deductions are neutralizing the rental income.

The effect of this approach is to increase your tax losses over the ten-year period by the amount of the principal that is being deferred. In the example, $159,000 of the principal was repaid by the tenth year. If this $159,000 can be deferred, your tax losses will go up by the same amount. This is illustrated in table 30.

During the last 15 years of the mortgage, however, all of the principal will have to be repaid—the repayment period for the principal portion having been compressed from 25 to 15 years. As a result, both the mortgage payments and the rents will have to climb to about $131,500 starting in the eleventh year.

Thus, the tenant will be paying $100,000 annually over the first 10 years of the lease and $131,500 annually over the last 15 years, rather than a flat $110,000 for the entire 25-year period. The tenant will usually agree to this two-tiered arrangement because during the first 10 years it will save $10,-000 yearly in rent (the difference between $110,000 and $100,000). The saving compensates the department store for the escalation in rent after the tenth year—based upon the universal principle that a dollar saved today is worth more

TABLE 30

Breakdown of Tax Loss on Las Vegas Investment Using Deferred Principal Repayment

Year	Rental Income	Mortgage Principal Repayments	Mortgage Interest	Accelerated Depreciation*	Tax Loss	Increase in Tax Loss over Tax Loss in Table 29
1	$100,000	0	$100,000	$60,000	$60,000	$ 10,000
2	100,000	0	100,000	56,000	56,000	11,000
3	100,000	0	100,000	53,000	53,000	12,000
4	100,000	0	100,000	50,000	50,000	13,000
5	100,000	0	100,000	47,000	47,000	15,000
6	100,000	0	100,000	44,000	44,000	16,000
7	100,000	0	100,000	41,000	41,000	18,000
8	100,000	0	100,000	39,000	39,000	19,000
9	100,000	0	100,000	37,000	37,000	21,000
10	100,000	0	100,000	34,000	34,000	24,000
Total						$159,000

* Rounded to nearest $1,000.

than a dollar that has to be paid 10 years from now. In other words, $100,000 in annual rent for 10 years followed by yearly rent of $131,500 for 15 years is, when you factor in the timing of the payments, roughly equivalent to $110,000 for 25 years.

How should you feel about all this? You should be delighted. Even though you are not building up any equity during the first ten years, you have increased your total losses for those years by $159,000. And it is the rare investor, indeed, who would not eagerly give up equity buildup for more tax losses.

After ten years, your annual tax saving will decline as a result of the increase in principal payments. In the eleventh year, for example, the principal payment will be $31,500, as compared with $26,000 if you hadn't deferred principal repayments (per table 29). Nevertheless, this should not dilute your pleasure. Since you are getting your tax savings sooner, they are worth more.

The balloon payment. There is another device that can be used to defer repaying principal. In chapter 3 I discussed a "balloon payment" on the mortgage of a home. The bank will frequently give a modified version of this type of mortgage on a net-leased property. The bank may, for example, require that you repay only 85% of the principal ($850,000 on a $1 million mortgage) during the term of the mortgage. This would leave a 15% ($150,000) balance, or "balloon," due at maturity. This means that the repayment of $150,000 of the principal is being deferred for 25 years, and over this same period you will increase your tax losses by $150,000.

These techniques appear to have the sanction of the Internal Revenue Service. There are, however, other devices that ar being used to increase or accelerate tax savings that may prove to be less acceptable to the IRS. Among these are mortgage arrangements that defer so much of the principal that there will be a "balloon" of 40% or 50% ($400,000 to $500,000 on a $1 million mortgage). This will, in turn, substantially cut into your equity buildup.

Methods have also been devised that purport to enable you to deduct your entire cash investment almost immediately. In an ordinary transaction, most of the cash you invest is deductible over fifteen years at the same rate at which the property is being depreciated. But by some imaginative, convoluted, and questionable manipulation of numbers and the tax laws (such methods are almost as difficult to explain as they are to invent), the deduction of your cash investment may be compressed into the first year or two of the transaction. Before you invest, however, make sure that such a deduction has the blessing of your accountant.

These mortgage arrangements and other devices are known by a variety of names, including "wrap-around mortgage," "deferred and accrued interest," "rent abatement," and "transaction services." But their aim is the same—to increase and accelerate tax losses.

When all these methods are used in a single transaction (as they have been from time to time), they have been likened to a symphony climaxing in a crescendo or a Victorian novel in which all the characters come together and meet in the closing chapters. I think, however, that they represent a frenzied effort to increase tax losses in order to justify the high prices being charged for net-leased properties. But too much of this increase is artificially induced (being, as I said earlier, merely a manipulation of numbers and the tax laws); and you must consult with your lawyer in order to determine how many of these "creative" benefits will pass muster with the IRS.

Caution: Watch out for the IRS. If these devices strike a discordant tone, the IRS may become aroused. Tax officials may also become hostile if the overall economic benefits are so emasculated that all you are left with is tax savings. In a transaction in which you have, for example, only a nominal current cash return and your equity buildup is being exchanged for increased interest deductions, your general economic benefits may become so diluted as to make the IRS suspect that your reason for investing is limited solely to tax savings—which can be fatal. When you invest in a property only for tax savings and sacrifice other economic benefits in the process, the Internal Revenue Service may take the position that you are not really the owner because you do not own anything of economic substance. If the Service prevails with this argument, the deductions you have claimed may be disallowed, and the tax savings for which you have paid so dearly may be lost.

Land as a Liability

Stripping a property of its economic substance can go even further. Land may be excluded. Land (as I discussed in chapter 10) is not depreciable. For tax-shelter purposes, it is a liability rather than an asset. In the example of the $1 million property, it was assumed that the land had only a nominal value. But what if its value were $100,000 (10% of the total cost), and the value of the building itself were $900,000? In this situation, your depreciation deductions would have been reduced by 10% ($100,000 over 15 years) because only $900,000 of your cost could have been depreciated.

In many transactions, in order to improve your tax position, you will be able to buy simply the building—a depreciating asset—and not the land upon which it is located. In such situations, you will have a right to use the land; but it is a finite right that will eventually terminate (usually within 40 to 60 years). At that time the land will revert back to the person who sold you the building.

Incredible as it may seem, this may be a better deal for you—when measured by the myopic standard of tax savings—even though your cash investment will be about the same as what you would have made if you had bought both the land and the building. But from an economic point of view, you will be losing capital appreciation. After your right to use the land terminates, you will have to surrender the land to the owner, and he will be the ultimate beneficiary of any increase in value.

Furthermore, your ownership of the building is illusory. Once you lose the land, you can keep the building only if you can take it with you.

Fixed rents can cut capital appreciation. There is one other feature of these transactions that can deprive you of capital appreciation: the fixed rents payable by the net-lease tenant. In an apartment project, shopping center, or office building, if the value of the property increases, you expect to be able to charge higher rents, which will reflect this increase. This cannot happen in a net-lease transaction. Not only are the rents fixed for the term of the lease (25 years in the example), but the net-lease tenant will customarily have the option to renew, or extend, the lease for additional periods of time.

A renewal lease might lower rents. The renewal periods may be as long as 25 or 30 years, during which time the rents will not only be fixed but will usually be lower than the rents payable during the initial 25-year term. This reduction (to an amount agreed to at the time you and the tenant enter the lease) is often 50% or more, even though the property may have increased in value. For example, if the rents were $110,-000 during the initial term, they might be $55,000 during the renewal periods.

Fixed rents limit selling price. Fixed rents will also limit the amount you can receive from a sale or refinancing of the property. They partly determine the selling price and the amount of the new mortgage. The value of your property may, in the abstract, have gone up tenfold over 25 years; but you cannot sell an abstraction. Even if you sell or refinance, the net-lease tenant will have the right to continue leasing property at the fixed rents specified in the lease. This effectively puts a ceiling on the selling price and the amount of the refinancing. Simply stated, the price at which you can sell a property will be lower if the rents during the renewal periods are $55,000 instead of $110,000.

A bind: when your tax losses become taxable income. As a practical matter, the rents under a net lease define the actual value of your property, and this can become an acute problem when you have exhausted your tax benefits. As I explained in chapter 9, the tax losses will eventually run out. In the example shown in table 29, this occurs after 15 years. After that, you will have taxable income, but you will have no cash from the property with which to pay the taxes (all of the rents will be going toward the mortgage payments). You will probably be unable to raise enough money to cover your tax liability through a sale or refinancing, because, as I just explained, the amount you can raise will be limited by the net-lease tenant's fixed and declining rents.

It is important to be aware of another distinction, contained in the Internal Revenue Code, between net-leased properties and other real estate projects: In a net-lease transaction, the interest deduction may not be fully available.

Interest deduction may be limited. The Code contains a restriction on the amount of interest you may deduct on a mortgage of a net-leased property. (This restriction may also apply to interest on a mortgage of raw land—see chapter 10. While it does not usually relate to other kinds of real estate, it may have to be considered when you invest in a property having several tenants, such as a shopping center, if one or more of the tenants have entered into net leases. However, it is unlikely that the restriction will apply to this type of property or, if it does, that it will have any material effect on your tax savings.)

A net lease shelters investment income only. While this is a complex, technical issue, you can assume that you may not make full use of the interest deduction in a net-lease transaction in order to "shelter" personal-service income, such as your salary. This deduction may be used to its fullest only if the income you intend to shelter is "investment income," which includes dividends; interest on savings accounts, bonds, and other securities; and rents and royalties. This explains why net-leased transactions are often referred to as "investments for the gentry"—for those with clean fingernails.

This interest-deduction limitation may not, however, be as restrictive as it first appears, because you will probably not be buying the entire project alone, but participating with other investors. If you are purchasing a one-tenth interest and paying a tenth of the total purchase price, you will be entitled to a tenth of the tax losses, including those derived from the interest deductions. So long as you have sufficient investment income against which to apply your limited share of the total interest deduction, this will be a viable investment. Nevertheless this is another time when you should ask your lawyer whether, given the source of your income, it makes sense for you to invest in a net-leased property.

Some Net-Lease Advice

Based upon all of these considerations, I offer the following recommendations:

Consult with your lawyer in order to be sure that you are buying *real estate* and not just tax losses. Otherwise, you may find, when you meet with a representative of the IRS, that you have bought neither.

You should be in at least the 40% tax bracket in order to take proper advantage of the tax losses that stem from a net-lease tax shelter.

The price you pay for a net-leased property (or any other tax shelter) should depend upon the projected tax losses. In the case of a net-leased property, you should expect to pay around $1.00 for each $3.50 of projected losses. For example, if your cash investment were $100,000, the losses before the tax benefits disappear should be about $350,000. Of these losses, $200,000 should come within at least the first five or six years of the transaction—$2.00 for each $1.00 you invest.

You should be wary of the sources of these losses. Stay away from transactions where losses are derived from devices that will deprive you of substantially all of the other economic benefits and thus invite a challenge from the IRS. Your lawyer's advice is indispensable here.

I would also be reluctant to invest in a property in which the land is excluded, because you'd be surrendering the ultimate economic advantage—perpetual ownership.

Do not invest if the renewal-period rents are too low. Although you may have to agree to some reduction in rents when a net lease is renewed, I would draw the line at 50%; but I would also urge you, when you negotiate the original transaction, to fight for no reduction at all.

Make sure, because of the IRS limitations on the interest deduction in net-lease transactions, that the income you intend to shelter is "investment income" and not your salary.

Other Tax Shelters for Other Income

If net-leased properties are tax shelters for the gentry, there is a group of properties that will shelter the income you earn by the sweat of your brow.

Whether your income is personal-service income (such as your salary) or "investment income" (such as dividends), you can generally make full use of the interest and depreciation deductions when you invest in government-assisted projects for new and rehabilitated housing (often referred to as "subsidized housing"), properties that are classified as "historic structures", and nonresidential commercial properties at least 30 years old.

There is usually no limitation on the amount of interest you can deduct, but as with any other tax-oriented investment, you should be in at least the 40% tax bracket.

Moreover, since such properties have a precise social purpose, you can not only bathe yourself in tax benefits but also cloak yourself in virtue. By investing in subsidized housing (whether new or rehabilitated), you are providing rental apartments for low-income families; and by investing in "historic properties," you are helping to preserve our national heritage.

Subsidized housing. "Subsidized housing" refers to apartment projects leased to persons with "low income," which is a sanitary phrase meaning that they are poor—earning below the overall median income of residents in the areas in which the projects are located. Such projects are assisted in one or more ways by the federal, state, or local government; and the purpose of this assistance is to keep the rents low and to insure that they will be paid. While there are several government programs (with many of them, at times, overlapping in the same project so as to create a chaos of benefits), they have several elements in common.

Long-term, low-interest-rate government mortgage. First, the government generally provides the mortgage, which will typically have a 40-year maturity and a below-market interest rate. These terms can be translated into low rents, since the mortgage payments will be considerably less than the payments you would have to make on a conventional mortgage provided by a bank. A 40-year maturity spreads out the period over which principal has to be repaid.

For example, on a normal $1 million bank mortgage with a 10% interest rate and a 25-year maturity, the annual mortgage payments will be about $110,000, and the rents will have to be at least sufficient to cover these payments. However, on a $1 million government mortgage with a 40-year maturity and an interest rate of less than 10%; say 8%, these annual payments will be approximately $84,000. Thus, the rents required to cover this mortgage will be $26,000 less than would be necessary to meet the payments on the bank's mortgage—$110,000 minus $84,000.

The government may help more directly by making "housing-assistance payments." Such payments supplement the rents payable by the tenants. If a family cannot afford to pay the full amount of rent for an apartment unit (and, in some cases, the tenants are not required to pay more than 15% of their income in rent), the government may agree to make up the difference.

Government limits on rents and cash flow. In return for these very generous subsidies (the long-term, low-interest-rate mortgage and the housing-assistance payments), there are usually statutory ceilings on the rents that can be charged and on the amount of cash flow an investor can receive. As a practical matter, you ordinarily should not expect more than 2% or 3% of your investment. But like the net-leased property, you are not investing for a cash return. You are investing for tax benefits—and they can be considerable.

Accelerated depreciation at a higher rate than other properties. The sources of these benefits are the same as those for any other real estate—depreciation and interest deductions. You can depreciate a subsidized project at an accelerated rate that begins at 13% of your cost, as compared with 12% for other buildings. If the project cost were $1 million (assuming a nominal land value), accelerated depreciation in the first year would be $130,000—13% of $1 million. Over the first five years, the depreciation deductions using the accelerated method would add up to $520,000 (52% of $1 million). For other buildings, the deductions would total only $460,000.

When you sell a subsidized project, the recapture rules are comparable to those for conventional housing for the first eight years and four months, with only the excess of accelerated over straight-line deductions being subject to recapture. However, if you hold the subsidized project for more than eight years and four months before selling, the amount that will be recaptured will decline by 1% each month.

Slow principal repayment. The 40-year maturity enables you to slow down the rate at which you repay principal. You can see this by comparing two $1 million mortgages having the same interest rate (10% for example) over a 20-year period —one mortgage that matures in 25 years, and the other in 40 years. On the 25-year mortgage, approximately $580,000 of the principal will have been repaid after 20 years, while on the 40-year mortgage, the principal payments will add up to about $130,000.

Therefore, over the first 20 years, only a small portion of the rents on the 40-year mortgage will be used to pay principal: most of the rental income will be applied to interest. As a result, over this 20-year period there will be $450,000 more in tax losses with the 40-year mortgage than with the 25-year mortgage ($580,000 minus $130,000—the difference in the amount of principal that has been repaid).

When you combine this benefit of the extended mortgage maturity with accelerated depreciation, there is an abundance of tax savings. The negative side is, however, that the cash return is so small as to be irrelevant, and the pace of the principal repayments is so slow that the buildup of equity, at least for the first 20 years, becomes inconsequential.

In addition, the limitations on the amount of rents you can charge provide you with little hope of realizing capital appreciation, either through increased cash flow or by a sale or refinancing. And the government may also impose restrictions on your right to sell or to refinance the mortgage.

Be Aware of the Real Estate Risks

While subsidized projects are unabashedly tax shelters, they are still housing projects, and you have to be concerned with the real estate risks I discussed in chapter 11. As with conventional apartment projects, there are problems of management, operating expenses, construction, and location.

Expert management required. Management of subsidized projects requires a specialized expertise and experience. There is, too often, a perception that because the tenants are poor, they are also unintelligent or incompetent. However, if a project is being abused by the tenants, you will probably find that the problem is not their intelligence, but their inexperience.

A few years ago, a project in which I had invested was, in the words of our manager, "hopeless. Hell, we can't even get these people to put their garbage in the incinerator. They throw it in the corridors, and then don't want to pay the rent because the place stinks."

The new management firm, which we promptly hired to replace this man, understood the situation immediately. The tenants had never seen a garbage incinerator before. They were shown how to use it, and classes were held on the use of the other facilities in the building, such as the washing and drying machines, the stoves, and the refrigerators. After that, most of the problems disappeared; and a project that was literally on the verge of financial and physical collapse was salvaged. But it required patient, intelligent, and intensive management.

The government's say in operating expenses. This same sort of patience is necessary when it comes to operating expenses —not only when dealing with the tenants, but also with the government.

In a democracy, operating expenses theoretically go up for the rich and poor alike. But if you own a subsidized project, usually you will have to obtain government consent before raising rents to cover such costs. This can take time, and even if you do get the approval, the tenants may resist making the payments. To some extent this problem can be obviated if the government agrees to increase its housing-assistance payments in order to meet the increased costs.

Construction considerations and developer's responsibility. The government will also be involved in the construction and maintenance of the project, establishing standards that have to be met and maintained. But you should not be looking solely to the government for assurance of quality construction. The developer from whom you are purchasing should be experienced and financially responsible.

Furthermore, if you purchase during construction, you will be able to deduct certain construction-period expenses currently that would have to be deferred in the case of other kinds of real estate.

You should also demand from the developer the same financial guarantees I discussed in chapter 11—in regard to completing construction, making structural repairs after completion, and paying operating deficits during the early years of the project.

You not only have to be concerned with how the project is constructed, but with where it is constructed.

Location is controversial. The location of a subsidized project is an extremely sensitive issue. One of the sociological theories underlying these projects is that they can upgrade an economically depressed area. However, you may find that the project will quickly deteriorate to the level of the area unless it is part of a comprehensive renewal program, rather than an isolated thrust into a slum.

A project located in a middle- or upper-middle-class suburb may, on the other hand, benefit from the neighborhood, but it may not be greeted benevolently by its neighbors.

A few years ago, there was a bitter debate in the town in which I live over a proposed government-assisted housing project. People whom I had always assumed to be civic-minded and "liberal" strained their imaginations to find obstacles that would block locating the project in the town. They were worried about the impact on water levels, the effect on parking, the increase of pollution, and overpopulation.

Finally, one man came forward with the truth: "We don't want these people here. Why don't they put the damned project where they are wanted?"

This lack of receptivity may be a dismal fact, but it is a fact nonetheless. And you should insist that the developer obtain all of the necessary government approvals, including those from the town in which the project is to be located, before you advance him any money.

Subsidized housing for the elderly. A subsidized project that is designed for the elderly is often more acceptable in suburban areas. There seems to be a common view that elderly poor taint the quality of life less than middle-aged or younger poor. Without examining the sociological merits of this point of view (or the psychological difficulties of those who hold it), the elderly—rich or poor—do generally provide a more stable tenancy, since they are less likely to move from one project to another.

Tax benefits. Based upon the price you will have to pay for subsidized housing, the tax benefits will be reasonable, although not generous. Over a period of 15 years, you can expect about $3.25 to $3.75 in losses for each $1.00 you invest (between $325,000 and $375,000 on a $100,000 cash investment). Of these losses, you should receive $2.00 for every $1.00 over at least the initial 5- or 6-year period ($200,000 on $100,000 invested).

Other benefits. Furthermore, subsidized projects are usually financially stable. Because of the low rents, there are usually few vacancies, and you will rarely lose a project because of default.

These projects are also, in most cases, well built. There is a misconception that they are "low-cost" housing. This is inaccurate. The cost of the bricks, mortar, and labor will be about the same as that for a luxury apartment building of similar size on Fifth Avenue in New York City. (The subsidized project's land will cost less, since it will be located in a less affluent neighborhood.)

The basic difference between luxury and subsidized projects is the income of the tenants, the size of the rooms, and the extent of the amenities offered tenants. As President Kennedy once remarked "Life is unfair"; the rich do live better than the poor. They have larger rooms, thicker carpeting, bigger swimming pools, and better parking facilities. But in terms of the actual quality of construction and structural soundness, the similarities between luxury projects and subsidized ones will be more striking than their differences.

Rehabilitated Housing

Government subsidy programs for rehabilitated housing (for "low-income" families) are similar to those for new projects. They provide long-term mortgages with low interest rates as well as housing-assistance payments. There are, however, two major differences.

The first, of course, is that the rehabilitation programs apply to existing buildings that are renovated and turned into rental units for low-income families. The buildings can be old apartments that are being restored, or they can be warehouses, factories, or offices that are being turned into apartments. (Such government-assisted housing programs do not, however, apply to personal residences.)

Depreciation over five years. The other difference is the method of depreciation (the term used in the Internal Revenue Code is *amortization*, but it means the same as *depreciation*). The costs of rehabilitation (up to $40,000 for each housing unit) can be deducted over the first five years.

Assume you buy a building for $500,000 and you incur rehabilitation costs of another $500,000, for a total of $1 million. You can depreciate the $500,000 in rehabilitation costs at the straight-line rate of $100,000 annually for 5 years. The other $500,000 in costs can be depreciated over 15 years, using either the accelerated or straight-line method. If you use accelerated depreciation, your total deductions over the first 5 years will be $760,000—$500,000 allocable to the rehabilitation costs plus $260,000 (52% of $500,000) allocable to your initial purchase price.

Base the cost on losses. Despite this abundance of tax benefits, the price you pay for rehabilitated housing will still be a function of the potential losses. Currently, as with subsidized housing, you should pay about $1.00 for each $3.25 to $3.75 in losses, and should get the bulk of these losses over five years.

After the five-year period, your depreciation deductions will sharply decline, since you will have fully depreciated the rehabilitation costs. This decline will make it difficult, at best, to sell the project at the end of five years (assuming that you can obtain government approval of a sale), because you will be subject to an overwhelming tax on the gain.

If you refer back to the calculations I made in chapter 9 (table 18), you will see that your taxable gain is the difference between your selling price, including the mortgage, and your undepreciated cost in the property. Since you have depreciated, in the present example, $760,000 after five years, your undepreciated cost is now $240,000 (your original cost of $1 million minus depreciation of $760,000). If you sell for $1 million (your purchase price plus rehabilitation costs), your taxable gain will be $760,000—$1 million minus your undepreciated cost of $240,000.

Gain is partly taxed as ordinary income. Worse yet, remember, is the fact that part of this gain will be taxed at ordinary income-tax rates. This amount is equal to the excess of accelerated over straight-line depreciation, which is "recaptured" and taxed as ordinary income and not as capital gain.

What this means, as a practical matter, is that you may not be able to afford to sell. Therefore, you should be setting aside some of your tax savings during the first five years in order to fund your tax liabilities in the later years—along the lines I suggested in chapter 9. As with new subsidized projects, however, you will escape the full impact of recapture if you hold the project for more than eight years and four months.

Additionally, the difference between straight-line and accelerated depreciation, as you saw in chapter 9, will be "tax preference," and may subject you to the alternative minimum tax. Before you invest, you should ask your accountant whether you will have to pay this alternative tax if you go into this type of transaction.

These two problems, the tax upon a sale and the "tax preference," are present in any real estate transaction (including a new subsidized project) in which you use accelerated depreciation. But they are magnified in the case of rehabilitation housing because of the increased rate of depreciation. Nevertheless, these are problems worth tolerating so long as you have sufficient income to be sheltered in the early years of your investment (otherwise the losses will be wasted). These problems, it is clear, have not discouraged investors, who have eagerly rushed to invest in these projects.

A special caution: Under existing law, the right to depreciate the rehabilitation costs over five years will expire on January 1, 1984, except for costs incurred on projects where the rehabilitation work began before January 1, 1984. Based upon past experience, however, you can expect Congress to extend the program for another two or three years.

Historic structures and old nonresidential commercial properties. Other tax shelters that have caught the fancy of investors are "historic structures" and nonresidential commercial properties (such as warehouses and office buildings) that are at least 30 years old.

You are entitled to a tax credit (not merely a deduction) equal to a percentage of the rehabilitation expenditures for those buildings. It is a one-time credit, usually to be taken in the year in which you complete the rehabilitation.

A tax credit is subtracted from your tax liability *after* you have figured out your tax. For example, if you have taxable income of $100,000, after deductions, your tax in the 50% bracket would be $50,000. If you have a tax credit of $20,-000, that would reduce your taxes to $30,000—$50,000 of taxes minus the $20,000 credit. (There is a limit on the amount of the credit. It cannot exceed, in any year, $25,000 plus 85% of your tax liability in excess of $25,000.)

The credit for historic buildings is 25% of your rehabilitation expenditures. For buildings at least 40 years old it is 20%, and for those at least 30 years old it is 15%.

Historic structures are broadly defined, and they include not only buildings that are national landmarks (such as Faneuil Hall in Boston and Sonoma Mission outside of San Francisco) but also buildings that contribute to the "historic significance" of an historic district. Historic districts, in turn, frequently encompass large sections of a town or city.

Special requirements. An historic structure normally has to be at least 50 years old (although in special situations, it can be less than 50 years), and to qualify for these tax benefits, it must be a commercial property—a property to be used in trade or business or held for the production of income, such as an apartment project, retail store, or office building. The law does not permit you to apply these benefits to your own home, even though it may be an historic structure.

The rehabilitation work must also meet several requirements, but the basic standard is that the building be restored to a "compatible use" without impairing its architectural or historical integrity.

This standard is liberally interpreted. For example, a "compatible use" is not the same as "original use." A building that was originally a factory does not have to remain a factory. It can be turned into an apartment project or an office building.

Another consideration is that the tax benefits are conditional upon your obtaining from the appropriate local, state, and federal agencies certifications that, first, the property is an historic structure, and, second, that the rehabilitation work complies with the standards of the agency administering the program.

While these agencies (including the United States Department of the Interior, which is responsible for this program at the federal level) are generally cooperative and expeditious in issuing these certifications, you should not invest until they have been obtained.

In the case of older buildings (at least 30 years old), they have to be *nonresidential* commercial properties in order to get the credit. The credit is not available for apartment projects.

Credit reduces depreciation. In addition to the credit, you can depreciate these buildings, historic or otherwise, over 15 years. However, for the thirty- and forty-year-old buildings the amount to be depreciated must be reduced by the credit. For historic structures, the reduction in depreciation is 50% of the credit.

Take, for example, a warehouse you buy for $400,000, on which you spend another $600,000 to rehabilitate, for a total cost of $1 million. If it is 30 years old, you get a credit of $90,000 (15% of $600,000). You can also depreciate your cost of $1 million minus the $90,000 credit, or $910,000. For a 40-year-old building the credit would be $120,000 (20% of $600,000) and the depreciable amount would be $880,000— the $1 million cost minus the $120,000 credit.

With an historic structure, you would be entitled to a $150,000 tax credit (25% of $600,000). The depreciable amount would be reduced by one-half the credit, or $75,000, so you could depreciate $925,000—$1 million minus $75,000.

There are no restrictions on the rents that can be charged for these older buildings, including historic structures. That means you can obtain extraordinary tax benefits and, at the same time, avail yourself of the full economic benefits you would receive by investing in any other commercial real estate. The government will not, however, provide the mortgage or any assistance payments to supplement the rents (unless, of course, the project is also subsidized housing); you will have to get the mortgage from a bank.

The return on your investment in any of these properties will, therefore, be a combination of tax savings and other economic benefits. Your cash return will, however, probably be less than that from a comparable property not entitled to such abundant tax benefits.

There are, however, some conditions that have to be met in order to qualify for the credit.

First, there has to be a substantial rehabilitation. The rehabilitation costs have to exceed the greater of $5,000 or the acquisition cost of the building less any depreciation deductions you have taken before beginning the rehabilitation work. If your initial cost (minus depreciation) was $400,000, your rehabilitation expenditures would have to be more than $400,000 for you to be eligible for the credit.

Second, you have to incur the rehabilitation expenditures within a 24-month period (although it can be 60 months in certain situations).

Third, some of your expenditures may not get the credit. You will not, for example, get the credit if you replace more than 25% of the external walls of the building in the course of rehabilitation. Ask your lawyer about the qualified expenditures.

Fourth, all or part of the credit will be recaptured if you sell within five years. One hundred percent of the credit will be recaptured if you sell in the first year, 80% if the sale is in the second year, and 60%, 40%, and 20% if it is in the third, fourth, and fifth years, respectively. If you sell after the fifth year, none of the credit will be recaptured.

When there is recapture of any part of the credit, the amount is added to your tax bill. If, for example, you got a $100,000 credit and sold in year two, 80%, or $80,000, would be recaptured and would be added to your taxes.

Fourteen

BUYING IN

THE MANAGER OF A SPECIALTY STORE IN ACTON, MASSA-chusetts, told me just before Christmas that computer and electronic games have brought a major technological break-through in the game business over the past few years. Perhaps —but the novelty of these games is at least matched by the marvel of Monopoly and its continuous popularity. It is one of the "games of all time"—not just a passing fancy but an enduring passion. And what is it all about? Real estate, of course—a horizontal board measuring about two feet by two feet on which all the dreams and fantasies of becoming a real estate tycoon can be played out.

The representatives of many institutional investors (such as banks, insurance companies, and pension funds) that are ac-tively engaged in acquiring real estate would have you believe that unless you can invest $1 million or more, you should confine your real estate activities to the Monopoly board.

Their rather patronizing point of view arises from the fact that real estate is not a small investment. In real estate terms, a small project is one that costs between $1 million and $2 million. The saying that one man's money is as good as an-other's is questionable when speaking of such grandiose amounts. At first glance, it might appear that real estate has to be the lone province of institutions with huge amounts of capital to invest.

You will find, however, that the real estate market is filled with investment opportunities for individuals too, even if you have a relatively small amount to invest—as little as $1,000 or $2,000. By participating with other investors, you can ac-quire projects of almost any size and type.

Brokers

Real estate traditionally has been sold through brokers. These men and women, acting as "middlemen," bring together sellers and buyers.

The simplest illustration is the broker who arranges for the sale or purchase of your home. A broker also performs the same function in the area of commercial real estate—apartments, shopping centers, office buildings, and so forth. However, unless you are prepared to buy an entire project yourself, a broker may be reluctant to deal with you. This is not an attitude arising out of disdain—brokers show great respect for anyone's money. It is simply that the typical broker is not in a position to assemble a group of investors.

Investment Firms

This has led to the birth of another layer of middlemen, who do put together investor groups. They are large investment firms—including Merrill Lynch and Shearson/American Express and other giants of the securities industry—as well as several smaller firms that specialize in real estate. A real estate broker will frequently offer a project to one of these firms, which will, in turn, find the investors.

If you have $1,000 to $50,000 to invest, your first step should be to get into contact with an investment firm. You can do this by telephoning your investment adviser or securities broker (the same person you would call if you wanted to invest in the stock market) and explaining what you are looking for. I would be surprised if, within 24 to 48 hours afterward, you were not offered at least two or three investments. In fact, the response may be so quick as to make you feel as if the Merrill Lynch bull or someone else's buffalo or elephant has come crashing through your front door. Extending the animal metaphor a bit further, you may have become, in the words of the investment community, "a pigeon"; but it is hoped that after reading this chapter, you will know when to roost and when to fly away.

When the investment firm puts you together with other investors, it will not be a social event. It is more than likely that you will not know any of your co-investors and will never get to meet them. You and your anonymous colleagues will become members of an entity formed and sponsored by

the investment firm in order to own one or more properties.
In most cases, this entity will be a private or public limited
partnership or a real estate investment trust—as it is commonly called, a "REIT"—all of which I will consider in this
chapter.

In joining with other investors, you will be buying more
than real estate. When you jointly participate in the ownership of a property, whether through a limited private or public partnership or a REIT, your fractionalized interest is, as a
matter of law, a security—as if it were a share of stock in a
corporation.

The designation of your interest as a security has legal consequences that run throughout the transaction. When an investment firm sells you a security, it must comply with
federal and state laws and regulations, which can be expensive and time-consuming; and the cost of complying with
these laws and regulations is like a sales tax—it will be
passed along to you as part of the price of your investment.

Private Limited Partnerships

There is, however, an exception: A private limited partnership is exempted from many of the burdens imposed by the
securities laws and regulations. The basic legal tests of
whether a real estate partnership is "private" is the number
and financial qualifications of the investors. As a general matter, it will be deemed to be a private partnership if it has 35
investors or less, each of whom meets certain financial standards. Among the most important are that he or she be in at
least the 40% to 50% tax bracket and have a substantial net
worth in relation to the size of his or her investment. The
investor must also be capable of evaluating the investment or
must have retained a professional, such as a lawyer, accountant, or investment adviser, who can do it instead.

With so few investors, the private partnership is usually organized to own one specific property, such as the K mart–
Safeway shopping center I discussed in chapter 12. To see
how such a private partnership works, take another look at
the center.

As you may recall, the total purchase price was $5,500,-
000; $4,125,000 was financed with a mortgage, requiring a
cash investment of $1,375,000. Even with an inflated and in-

flating dollar, this is a prodigious amount of money for you or any one person to have to invest. But if you could share the cost with others, the center might be within your grasp. At this point the investment firm steps in.

It will form a private limited partnership in which you and 34 other persons become members. Therefore, each of you will have to invest approximately $39,285 ($1,375,000 divided by 35), and you will each own a 1/35 interest in the center—including 1/35 of the cash flow, tax savings, equity buildup, and capital appreciation.

An investment of $39,285 is still large. But you can usually spread your payment out over three to five years. If you could, in the K mart–Safeway transaction, make your investment in four annual installments, each would be in the amount of approximately $9,821. Moreover, the actual timing of these payments could be tied to standards of performance—for example, the completion of construction and the leasing of sufficient space to produce a minimum cash return.

General partners. This private limited partnership will have two classes of partners—general and limited partners. The general partner will normally be the investment firm or one of its affiliates or subsidiaries. The developer of the project may also be a general partner. The general partner or partners will manage the partnership and will be responsible for the operation of the center. The general partners will also be personally liable for any damages or expenses incurred by the partnership because of negligence, breach of contract, or violation of the law. They will also be responsible for arranging the mortgage financing (and you should not invest until it is obtained). Thus, the full burden of ownership will fall upon them.

Limited partners. You and your colleagues will belong to the other class of partners—the limited partners. Your financial responsibility will be limited to your $39,285 overall investment; you thus have "limited liability"—like the stockholder of a corporation, all you can lose is the money you have committed yourself to invest. But in return for this insulation from liability, you cannot, as a matter of law, operate or manage the property or (except within very narrow bounds) make any decisions regarding such operations and management. Those are the rights and responsibilities of the general partners; and this legal fact makes the selection of these partners a matter of paramount importance, as you'll see.

Tax benefit of partnership. While limited liability is a feature of both a limited partnership and a corporation, the partnership (as distinct from its partners), whether private or public, has the added advantage of not being subject to federal income taxes.

If, instead of a limited partnership, a corporation had been organized to acquire the K mart–Safeway center, all of the taxable income and loss from the center would belong to the corporation in which you and the other investors were stockholders. It would have to pay taxes as if it were an organic being. Moreover, any taxable income distributed to you by the corporation would be a dividend on which you would also have to pay a tax. In effect, the income from the center would be taxed twice—first, as ordinary income to the corporation and, second, as dividend income to you.

The limited partnership escapes this "double" tax. If there is taxable income from the center, only the general and limited partners, and not the partnership itself, have to pay the tax. More important, if there are tax losses (because interest and depreciation exceed the rents), they go directly to the partners; and these losses can be used by them to shelter their other income (see chapter 9).

Since the K mart–Safeway center had a tax loss of $169,-000 in the first year (see table 27), your share would have been about $4,829 ($169,000 divided by 35). Thus, the limited partnership acts as a conduit of both taxable income and loss to its partners. A corporation, on the other hand, could not pass these losses along to its stockholders, and they would go to waste if the corporation itself did not have other income against which to apply them. Because of this, an investment firm rarely forms a corporation to own real estate. (There is an exception for Subchapter S corporations, but because of certain restrictions it will not, ordinarily, be used in a real estate transaction.)

You should now be getting suspicious. If you get the limited liability and most of the income and loss from the center, you might well ask, "What is in it for the general partners?" The answer is: Money.

General partners' fee. The general partners receive a variety of fees (referred to as organizational, promotional, and acquisition fees) out of which they get most of their profit as well as the money to pay the expenses of putting the transaction together. In a private partnership these fees will generally amount to about 20% of your investment. If you and your co-investors pay $1,375,000 in cash for the K mart–Safeway center, at least $275,000 (20% of $1,375,000) will probably go to the general partners. Therefore, only $1,100,-000 ($1,375,000 less $275,000) will actually be invested in the center; and some part of this $1,100,000 will be paid to the developer (whether or not he is a general partner) as his profit for building and selling the complex.

In addition, there are some transactions in which there are continuing management, administration, and incentive fees, as well as "disposition fees" when the project is sold or refinanced. These fees come out of the cash generated by the project and, as a result, will reduce your cash return.

General partners' ownership. The profit of the general partners may not come solely from this conglomeration of fees. While you and the other limited partners may be providing all of the cash necessary to buy the center, the general partners will share the ownership with you. They may own as much as 10% to 15% of the property—leaving the limited partners with an interest of between 85% and 90%. Furthermore, their share may graduate to somewhere between 25% and 50% after several years. This switch in the respective ownership interests of the general and limited partners will usually occur when you and your co-investors each have received cash from the center (whether through cash flow, refinancing, or sale) equal to the amount you have invested—$39,285 in the example—plus some return on your investment.

The general partners will justify this readjustment by telling you that it gives them an incentive. By having a financial stake in the center's success, they will be motivated to work harder and to concentrate more closely on the project. Whatever the motivational effect, however, you should not invest, as a general rule, if the readjustment would give more than a 25% interest to the general partners, unless they guarantee exceptional performance, such as doubling or trebling your money over five to ten years.

The prospectus. The extent of the general partners' participation in the project and the amount of the fees payable to them will be set forth in the selling documents—usually referred to as the "prospectus" or "placement memorandum" —prepared by the investment firm. These documents are required by law to be submitted to you before you invest, and they purport to explain what you are buying. However, they are often a hundred or more pages in length, and trying to calculate and sort out who gets what and when can be as difficult as trying to learn a foreign language; you will need your lawyer or investment counselor to act as your translator.

The prospectus is also supposed to disclose all of the risks involved in the transaction. This is usually done in fine detail; but too frequently it appears that there's a democracy of risks: no serious attempt is made, in listing them, to discriminate between the probable and the improbable ones. After reading a prospectus, you may feel as I often do—that vacancies are as likely to be caused by the reemergence of the plague as by an increase in competition.

The statutory design behind all of this detail was, originally, to alert you, the investor, about what could go wrong with your investment, so that you could make a proper evaluation. But this purpose has been corrupted, and the prospectus is now used as much to protect the general partners as to protect the investors.

The general partners can hide behind the prospectus, claiming that since you have been made fully aware of all of the pitfalls in the transaction, you have no cause to complain if anything goes wrong. And one can properly wonder, without being a reactionary or a robber baron, whether the laws promulgating these statutory requirements are more effective in obfuscating than in disclosing what you are getting for your money.

The private limited partnership, as I said earlier, usually acquires a specific property. It is also the entity most commonly used to own tax-oriented real estate, such as net-leased properties and government-assisted apartment projects.

Because of the small number of limited partners, the minimum cost of investing through one of these partnerships is usually around $25,000. This is, for most investors, an imposing amount; and if you want to invest less money and have a more diversified real estate portfolio, you should look to the public limited partnership or the REIT.

Public Limited Partnership

The legal structure of the public limited partnership is the same as that for the private partnership. The investment firm (or one of its affiliates) that organizes and sponsors the partnership will usually be the general partner. The investors will be the limited partners and will have limited liability. And the partnership per se will not be subject to federal income taxes.

But the public partnership will have many more than 35 limited partners. It may have as many as 10,000, 20,000, or 30,000; and the size of each partner's investment will typically be between $2,500 and $7,500. (This investment is not made in installments.) The public partnership can, therefore, raise a great deal of money. If it has 10,000 limited partners, with each investing $5,000, it will have capital of $50 million. This will enable the partnership to buy not one, but thirty or more K mart–Safeway centers.

The prospectus. Before you invest through a public partnership you will receive a prospectus. Throughout this book I have urged you, as I did in connection with the prospectus for a private partnership, to consult with your lawyer. This time I not only offer you this advice, but I defy you to get through a public partnership prospectus without the help of a lawyer. Even if you have enough technical background to untangle the prose, you will not be able to survive the boredom.

This prospectus will be a tour de force of obscurity, but you should be looking for two things:

• *What properties are you buying?*
• *How much you are actually paying for them?*

Strange as it might seem, neither of these basic facts will be easy to uncover.

The public partnership will be a newly organized entity. It will not be operational until you invest, since it is your money that the general partner is going to use in order to find and acquire the real estate; and it would be suicidal, the general partner would argue, to commit to spend $50 million on real estate before you had agreed to invest.

Drawbacks of public limited partnerships. On the other hand, this means that you will not know precisely how your money will be spent. If this seems like a "chicken-or-egg" problem, it has been resolved: in favor of the general partner. Quite simply, most of the properties are usually not identified until after the investors have paid their money.

Trying to put together a group of investors in a private partnership in order to buy just one property at a time can be a frustrating experience. And it has prompted me, at one time or another, to join the chorus of promoters in reciting the words, "If only I had some money to play with, I could do so much more for my investors and myself." The money I am talking about playing with, however, is yours—not mine.

Even if you have an irresistible impulse toward generosity, you should use every effort to curb it. You should not hand your money over to me or any other promoter until he can describe to you the properties, or at least most of them, he intends to acquire. At minimum, you should withhold your investment until two-thirds of the partnership capital is matched with specific real estate.

As to the balance of the capital, the prospectus should set forth the criteria that will be used in acquiring the remaining properties—information such as:

- the types of properties (whether they will, for example, be shopping centers, office buildings, or apartment projects);
- the standards of selection, including construction and location;
- the maximum amount to be paid for any one property;
- the percentage of mortgage financing for each property; and
- the expected source of return from each property.

Unfortunately, the prospectus is not always clear or precise with regard to future acquisitions. If this is the case and you invest anyway, you are giving the promoter too much discretion over your money. Indeed, you are investing blindly. That's why many of these partnerships have been labeled, quite aptly, "blind pools."

Another troublesome fact about public partnerships is that too much of the capital may be diverted from the properties into fees and expenses of the general partners. In some cases, this can amount to a shocking 30%, which means that if $50 million is raised from the limited partners, only $35 million will be invested in the real estate. Part of this money has to be used to cover the costs of organizing the partnership, marketing the limited-partnership interests, and complying with the federal and state securities laws that I discussed earlier, but this still leaves layer upon layer of fees for the general partners. While the sponsors of some of these partnerships may be offended by my saying this, I would not invest unless there was a limit of 20% to 25%; and it would be far preferable if the general partners' profit were closely tied to the performance of the real estate. But whatever limitations are placed upon these fees and expenses, you can generally assume that they will be greater than those paid under a private partnership—which means that your return will be smaller.

REITs: Real Estate Investment Trusts

The other major form of joint ownership of a diversified real estate portfolio is the real estate investment trust.

Whenever the word *REIT* is mentioned, you may be able to hear, if you listen closely, the groans of those who invested so heavily through REITs in the mid-1970s. The REIT originally grew out of the same need that, in my judgment, gave birth to the public partnership—the need to satisfy the appetite of promoters for a large pool of money that they could use, at their discretion, to buy real estate.

With the cost of buying a share of a REIT as low as $10 to $25, these entities were able to attract billions of dollars of capital, not only from institutional investors but also from small individual investors who might not otherwise have been able to invest in real estate.

By 1973, the proliferation of REITs had reached a point where it seemed unthinkable for any self-respecting real estate promoter not to form his own REIT and sell to a public clamoring for "a piece of the action."

Eventually, as happens with any fad, the market became saturated. Some of the REITs were poorly managed, and others became financially overextended. By the mid-1970s, when the real estate industry went into a deep recession, the REITs were among the casualties; and they have not, as yet, regained their status in the marketplace.

Despite this rueful experience, some distinctions should be made. There have been some good REITs, some bad ones, and some in between. Generally speaking, those that have survived the 1970s are sound and provide another way for you to participate in the ownership of real estate.

The REIT setup. A REIT can be organized as a corporation or as an unincorporated association or trust. It is governed by a board of trustees or directors. The investors, who must number at least 100, are the owners of the REIT shares, and they have limited liability and limited control over management and operation of the REIT. You can buy REIT shares from an investment firm, just as you would interests in a private or public limited partnership.

Under the Internal Revenue Code, the REIT has been given a significant tax advantage. It is not subject to a corporate "double" tax. So long as the REIT distributes its income to its shareholders, only they (and not the REIT) have to pay an income tax. The REIT acts simply as a conduit of income.

Because of the low entry cost (REIT shares still sell for about $10 to $25), the REITs are well suited to the small investor; and billions of dollars have been invested through REITs. As a result, many REITs have been able to acquire an impressive array of properties (in terms of size at least)—with some REITs having assets totaling more than $250 million.

But when you buy into a REIT, reconcile yourself to the fact that it is a relatively passive entity. It is an organization, as my investment adviser put it, "without much action." This is a result of the constricting statutory requirements under which a REIT is governed.

Restrictions on REITs. Most of the income of the REIT must be derived from real estate assets, and the REIT must distribute at least 95% of its annual taxable income to its shareholders. Therefore, it cannot accumulate income and create a capital base that can be used to make future acquisitions. If it wants to buy new properties, it must go back into the marketplace and find new investors or, alternatively, incur debt. Nor can it put aside any of its income to protect against future hard times or poor performance.

The REIT cannot actively manage or operate its real estate. Rather, it has to delegate these responsibilities to an independent management firm. Nor can it be a developer or a real estate trader. With some very limited exceptions, the REIT must purchase real estate for investment and not for the purpose of resale.

Finally, while the income the REIT distributes to its share-

holders will be undiluted by taxes at the REIT level, any tax
losses (resulting from an excess of deductions for interest
paid and depreciation over rental and other income) cannot
be passed along to them.

Cash return. A REIT has been described to me as "a rather
tame creature. Despite the market gyrations in the cost of its
shares during the 1970s, its income comes from tame sources
—primarily lease rents." Since this is true, a REIT should
be evaluated primarily on its record of distributing cash to its
shareholders. And if you decide to invest in a REIT, you
should analyze its assets from this point of view: *Are the assets capable of generating an adequate cash return?*

Unlike the public limited partnership, you will usually
know what the REIT's assets are. Almost all of the REITs
available to you will have been in existence for several years
and will have completed their investment portfolios (although
there can, of course, be changes in these portfolios from time
to time).

When you examine a REIT's properties, you should be
sure that they consist primarily of real estate equities—that
is, ownership positions in real estate and not mortgages.
While a REIT must, as a practical matter, invest almost ex-
clusively in real estate, it is allowed to include real estate
mortgages among its assets. Unless you want to be bound to
fixed-income investments, you should avoid those REITs
whose assets are predominantly mortgages. They are like
banks; and if that is your preference, you would probably do
better with the real thing (invest in a bank).

Management fees. You should also be aware that your cash
return will be diminished by management or "advisory" fees
paid out by the REIT. The REIT's investments will customarily be managed by advisers (who are often the sponsors or
originators of the REIT). Their compensation is more likely
to be based upon a percentage of the REIT's assets than upon
performance. To the extent that this is the case, these man-
agers or advisers will be paid their fees irrespective of how
well you may have fared.

Although cash distributions are probably the best measure
of a REIT's performance, many investors have purchased
REIT·shares for another reason: It has been a way for them
to play the stock market.

Usually REIT shares are publicly traded in the same manner as the common stock of a corporation, and they can be bought and sold in a public market. As with common stock, the price of these shares may, at times, have only a remote connection with the value of the REIT's properties. The shares often seem to be commodities in themselves—disembodied from the assets they are supposed to represent.

I became aware of this discrepancy when I bought some REIT shares for $10.00 each. About a year later, I sold them for $12.50. But between the time I bought and sold, the REIT portfolio had remained static. No new properties had been acquired, and none had been sold. Nor had there been any appreciable change in the value of these properties. In effect, I had played the market successfully. But this is a hazardous game, because it is too easy to lose. I was fortunate. But as many investors who suffered through the 1970s found out, speculating in the price of REIT shares can turn into a disaster if the marketplace fails to discriminate properly between sound and unsound REITs.

Liquidity of REIT shares. Nevertheless, the ability to buy and sell the shares quickly is a decided advantage of REITs. It gives you liquidity, which is absent in the case of limited partnerships. The right to sell your interest in one of these partnerships will be tightly restricted, whereas you can sell a REIT share with relative ease.

The Property Is What Counts

The lack of direct connection between the values of REIT shares and REIT assets raises what is perhaps the key issue when you decide to invest in real estate through any of the entities I am looking at in this chapter.

At the height of the REIT craze, investors seemed to believe that the REIT interposed some mystical insulation between the real estate and them. But they discovered, to their sorrow, that the REITs did not afford much protection during the 1974–1975 recession; and they shared, along with the REITs, the misfortunes of the real estate industry.

None of the joint-investment entities can protect you from the actual real estate they invest your money in—and the real estate itself is the ultimate test of your investment. You should be prepared to analyze each of the properties owned by a REIT or a partnership as if you were acquiring it directly—applying the principles I have been discussing throughout this book. To paraphrase an old real estate saying: The three most important things about investing through a REIT or partnership are the real estate, the real estate, the real estate.

Actually, I can go one step further. It is no longer fatuous, given the handsome profits made by unscrupulous promoters on fictitious tank cars and imaginary salad oil, to suggest that you be sure that the property you are buying actually exists.

When I made one of my early forays into real estate promotion, I worked with an investment firm that found the limited partners for private partnerships. In order to illustrate to the firm's salesmen how these partnerships were to be structured, I made up a prospectus describing a nonexistent property located in an outcast area of the United States. The prospectus was covered with the words "*A Hypothetical Transaction—For Illustration Only.*" Several of the salesmen called to ask how they should go about signing up customers who were interested in the property. It was not that they were rapacious or dishonest. Perhaps they did not know the meaning of the word *hypothetical*. But salesmen and promoters are enthusiasts. They do not make a living by urging caution; they live by making sales.

Check on the Sponsors

Moreover, you should look into the experience and background of the sponsors of the partnerships and REITs you are considering. Since they will be using your money, there are a number of things you want to know about them.

They may be experts in the general field of investing, but what do they know about real estate? They should be willing to stand behind their projections and have the financial strength to meet their obligations. For example, they should provide adequate guarantees that construction will be completed (in the case of a new project) and that operating deficits will be funded by them at least in the early years. And some of the sponsors' profit (the more the better) should be deferred until the performance of the real estate reaches the level of their promises.

All of these matters should be set forth in the prospectus. The prospectus should also tell you whether these sponsors have other real estate interests that may conflict with your investment; in other words, find out whether they own other properties that will be competing with your project.

⌂ CHECKLIST

**EIGHT POINTS TO CONSIDER WHEN
INVESTING THROUGH A PARTNERSHIP
OR REIT**

Appropriate entity   What's appropriate will depend primarily upon how much you have to invest. If you have $25,000, you should be able to invest through a private limited partnership. Otherwise, you will probably have to invest through a public limited partnership or a REIT.

Proper organization of entity   Unless it is properly organized, you may lose the tax benefits you are expecting.

Source of return   In the case of a private or public limited partnership, your return will consist of cash flow, equity buildup, capital appreciation, and tax benefits. A REIT cannot distribute "excess tax losses" and your decision to invest in a REIT should be based primarily on its capacity to generate a cash return.

Identification of properties   The holdings will usually be identified in the case of a private limited partnership and a REIT. They may not be named (or only a small percentage may be) in the case of a public limited partnership.

Quality of real estate   Don't lose sight of the fact that whatever entity you invest through, the ultimate test of your investment will be underlying assets. Neither a private or public limited partnership nor a REIT protect your investment from the real estate.

Actual cost of properties   Find out how much of your investment is going into the real estate and how much is being paid to the sponsors of these entities for profits and expenses.

Qualifications of sponsors   Find out how knowledgeable the sponsors are about real estate and whether
they are willing (and have the financial strength) to
stand behind their projections.

Finding the entity   Ask your broker or financial adviser.

Consult Your Attorney

If you want to avoid being that "pigeon" I referred to earlier, you should take the prospectus to your lawyer and review it with him. As he wades through it, he should also look
into the tax aspects of the transaction.

In previous chapters, I warned you to be wary about projections made as to the source and timing of certain deductions. When you invest through a partnership or a REIT,
there is a more basic issue.

These entities must be organized to conform with certain
statutory standards in order for them to entitle you to the tax
advantages I described. Unless your lawyer can assure you
that these standards have been met, you should invest elsewhere. Otherwise, most of the tax benefits you are expecting
will be lost.

Despite these several caveats, the private and public limited
partnerships and the REITs can give you a place in the real
estate investing community.

It may be that the making of great fortunes in real estate
for you and others who are characterized as "small investors"
will still be limited to the Monopoly board; but by investing
with others, you can be a force in the marketplace. Real estate promoters are increasingly aware of this, and are looking
at the small investor and his growing interest in real estate
with greater affection than was true in the past.

After all—taking some liberties with Mr. Lincoln's statement—"God must have loved the small real estate investor.
He made so many of them."

GLOSSARY

GLOSSARY

accelerated depreciation   *See* depreciation.

alternative minimum tax   A tax that will be payable if it exceeds, in any year, your regular tax. The more tax preferences you have, the more vulnerable to this tax you will be.

alternative mortgage instrument (AMI)   A mortgage that is a variation on the standard, conventional mortgage—such as a variable-rate, roll-over, graduated-payment, or reserve-annuity mortgage.

alternative use of money   Comparison of the return on different types of investments, such as a home, stocks, or bonds.

amortization   The gradual repayment of the principal (as opposed to the interest) of a mortgage. Also, under the Internal Revenue Code, the five-year write-off of rehabilitation expenses allowed for subsidized rehabilitated housing.

balloon payment   A lump sum, or balance, of principal that remains unpaid (and that you will have to pay) on the maturity date of a mortgage.

blanket mortgage   A mortgage covering the entire building in a cooperative, as distinguished from separate mortgages on the individual dwelling units.

capital appreciation   The increase in the market value of a property over the price you originally paid for it.

capital gain   The portion of your taxable profit realized upon the sale of a property that is *not* taxed at your ordinary income-tax rate. Capital gain is taxed at a rate that is 40% of your ordinary income-tax rate. If, for example, you are in the 50% income-tax bracket, your capital-gain rate will be 20% (40% of 50%). You have to own the property for more than 12 months in order to get this capital-gain treatment.

carrying costs The ongoing expenses, which you usually pay monthly, of running or operating your home or other property, such as mortgage payments, real estate taxes, and charges for utilities, insurance, maintenance, and repairs.

cash flow The current cash return on your cash investment (exclusive of the mortgage) made in a property.

closing costs Your incidental costs and expenses (in addition to the down payment) of buying your home or other property. They are customarily paid when you "close the deal." In the case of a home, they include attorney's fees, title-insurance premium, survey cost, recording fees, appraisal cost, inspection fees, and mortgage application fees.

collateral Property securing the repayment of a loan. Your home is the bank's collateral on a mortgage.

common areas The areas in a condominium, cooperative, or other building that you and your neighbors share the use of, such as corridors, elevators, and recreation areas.

condominium An apartment project in which you and your neighbors each directly own the individual apartment units and share ownership of the common areas.

cooperative An apartment project that is owned by you and your neighbors indirectly. The project is usually directly owned by a corporation (or other entity), and the residents each own shares of stock in the corporation. In addition to the shares of stock, you have a "proprietary lease" on your apartment unit.

credit real estate Properties leased under long-term net leases to nationally known tenants having high credit ratings. A free-standing retail store net-leased to K mart would be an example of credit real estate.

default The failure to comply with terms of the mortgage on your home or other real estate, including the failure to pay interest and principal as they become due.

depreciation A tax concept that allows you to deduct the cost of a commercial building from your taxable income, generally over 15 years. If depreciation is deducted in equal amounts, this is known as "straight-line depreciation." For example, on a $1 million building, your annual depreciation deduction will be approximately $66,667 ($1 million cost divided by 15).

Accelerated depreciation is a method of depreciation enabling you to deduct your cost at a faster rate than straight-line. On a $1 million warehouse, for example, your depreciation deduction would be $120,000 (12% of $1 million) in the first year.

down payment   Your initial cash investment (excluding the closing costs) in a home or other real estate. If the purchase price of your home were $100,000 and you obtained an $80,000 mortgage, your down payment would have to be $20,000.

equity   Your down payment on a home or other property plus an amount equal to the principal you have repaid on the mortgage.

equity buildup   The increasing value of your ownership in a home or other property that occurs as you repay the principal of the mortgage. In other words, your equity gradually grows, or builds up, by the amount of the mortgage principal you pay off.

FHA mortgage   A low-down-payment mortgage on your home insured by the Federal Housing Administration. The maximum amount available under an FHA mortgage on a single-family home is usually $67,500 (although it can be higher in certain areas of the country).

government-assisted housing (subsidized housing)   A new or rehabilitated apartment project leased to low-income families and economically assisted in one or more ways by the federal, state, or local governments. Because of the low cash return and large tax benefits, such housing is usually a tax shelter investment.

graduated-payment mortgage (GPM)   A home mortgage on which you have to make relatively low installment payments (of both interest and principal) in the early years. These payments rise each year and eventually exceed the installment payment amount on a comparable conventional mortgage. This type of mortgage appeals primarily to younger persons.

ground (or land) lease   A legal agreement conveying use of the land underlying and surrounding a building from the owner of the land (the lessor), to the owner of the building (the lessee). In the case of a condominium, the landowner is frequently the developer.

historic structures   A national landmark or other building (usually at least 50 years old) that contributes to the significance of a historic district. You can get very generous tax benefits by investing in a historic structure.

installment payment   The periodic payment (usually monthly) of interest and principal on a mortgage.

interest   The cost of borrowing money.

land lease   *See* ground lease.

leverage   The use of borrowed money to pay for part of the purchase price of a property. For example, if you purchased a $1 million property by using $250,000 of your own cash and by borrowing $750,000, you would have leverage of 3 to 1—that is, for every $1 you put up, you are borrowing $3.

liquidity   The speed at which an investment can be converted into cash. For example, a share of common stock of a corporation listed on the New York Stock Exchange can ordinarily be sold for cash more quickly than a home and is, therefore, more liquid.

maturity date   The date by which the principal and interest on a mortgage must be paid in full.

mortgage   A legal document that secures the money you borrow in order to finance part of the purchase price of a home or other property. The mortgage gives the lender a claim against your property in case you default in repaying the money (plus interest) you borrow.

mortgage company (or banker)   A financial intermediary that originates mortgages and, normally, sells them to various lending institutions and government agencies.

net lease   A long-term lease (usually 20 to 25 years) under which the tenant agrees to pay a fixed minimum rent and also all operating expenses, including real estate taxes, insurance, utilities, and cost of repairs and maintenance.

noncredit real estate   Property, such as an apartment project, that is leased to several tenants who do not have high credit ratings or national reputations. The leases are usually for a relatively short term (one to five years) and are not, customarily, "net" of all operating expenses.

nonrecourse morgage   A mortgage that does not make the borrower personally liable. If you default in repaying the money you borrow (plus interest), the lender's recourse is limited to recovering the property; and if the value of the property is less than the amount outstanding on the mortgage, the lender cannot collect the deficiency from you.

percentage-interest   Your proportionate share of ownership in the common areas of a condominium or cooperative.

percentage rent   Rent that is contingent upon (and based upon a percentage of) a commercial tenant's gross dollar volume of business on a property and that is paid in addition to the fixed minimum rent agreed to in the lease. Also called "overage rent."

points   Payments you may have to make to a lender at the
time you obtain a mortgage. Each point is equal to 1% of the
mortgage amount and is, in effect, a form of interest. For example, one point on a $1 million mortgage would be $10,000.

prepayment   The repayment of the principal of a mortgage
prior to its maturity. One of the most important reasons to prepay is to take advantage of lower interest rates. For example, if
you are paying 15% interest on a mortgage and the available
interest rates drop to 10%, you may want to prepay the 15%
mortgage and get a new one at 10%.

principal   The actual amount you borrow when you obtain a
mortgage. For example, when you get a $1 million mortgage, the
principal amount is $1 million.

private limited partnership   An entity formed to enable a
small group of investors (usually not exceeding 35) to participate
together in the purchase of a property. The investors are usually
the limited partners of this entity; their liability for any obligations of the partnership is limited to their cash investment. The
limited partners are also entitled to receive most of the tax benefits from the property. The minimum cost of investing through a
private limited partnership is usually about $25,000.

privately insured mortgage   A home mortgage that is insured by a private mortgage-insurance company. Because it is
insured, you can usually make a low down payment (typically
between 5% and 15%).

proprietary lease   A legal agreement that gives you the right
to us your dwelling unit in a cooperative.

public limited partnership   An entity whose legal structure
and purpose are similar to that of a private limited partnership.
The major distinction is that there can be as many as 10,000 to
30,000 investors, each typically investing between $2,500 and
$7,500. The public limited partnership has to comply strictly with
federal and state securities laws and regulations.

real estate investment trust (REIT)   An entity enabling large
numbers of investors to participate in the ownership of real estate.
The investors do not acquire the real estate directly; rather, they
buy shares in the REIT, which owns the real estate. The REIT
is well suited to the small investor, because a REIT share can be
purchased for as little as $10 to $25. The REIT cannot pass along
tax losses to the investors, but the REIT itself will not be taxed
on any income distributed to them.

recapture   The amount of gain on the sale of a property that is taxed at your ordinary income-tax rate (instead of at capital-gains rates). Recapture usually occurs if you elect the accelerated method of depreciation. The recapture rules are more liberal for housing projects than for other types of commercial properties.

recreation lease   A legal agreement conveying use of a condominium's recreation facilities, such as a swimming pool and tennis courts, from the owner (the lessor) of these facilities to the condominium association (the lessee). The owner of these facilities is frequently the developer.

refinancing   Prepaying your existing mortgage and replacing it with a new one. For example, if you want to refinance your $1 million mortgage that has been paid down to $750,000, you would get a new mortgage and use the proceeds to pay off the $750,000 balance of the existing mortgage. If the new mortgage were also for $1 million, then you would have $250,000 in cash left over after prepaying the existing mortgage. You may want to refinance in order to take advantage of lower interest rates.

reverse-annuity mortgage (RAM)   A home mortgage under which you receive an annuity instead of a lump sum at the time you obtain the mortgage. You are not required to repay the mortgage until the maturity date. This type of mortgage is geared to elderly persons.

roll-over mortgage (ROM; renegotiable-rate mortgage)   A home mortgage that has a short initial term (usually three to five years) and that can be extended at your option (and not the bank's) for additional periods. The interest rate is renegotiated and adjusted at the time of each such extension. If you accept this type of mortgage, you will be gambling against the bank on the movement of interest rates.

second mortgage   A supplementary mortgage that "ranks below" the mortgage you get from your bank. For example, if you obtained a $75,000 mortgage from your bank on a $100,000 home plus a $10,000 mortgage from someone else (such as the seller), the $10,000 mortgage will usually be a second mortgage and subordinated to the bank mortgage. Thus, if you default, claims stemming from the bank mortgage would be repaid first, before those involving the second mortage.

straight-line depreciation   *See* depreciation.

subsidized housing   *See* government-assisted housing.

tax credit   An offset against your income tax. For example, if you are entitled to a $1,000 credit and your income tax would otherwise be $10,000, the credit would reduce your tax to $9,000.

tax losses   The excess of deductions from your taxable income (taken for mortgage interest, depreciation, and operating expenses, including real estate taxes) over the rental income from a property.

tax preference   The excess of accelerated over straight-line depreciation deductions taken each year, and the 60% capital gains exclusion when you sell a property.

tax saving   The amount of money you save in taxes because of the tax losses from a property.

tax shelter   A real estate investment that generates income-tax deductions in excess of the rental income. These excess deductions, which arise primarily out of depreciation and interest payments on the mortgage, can be offset against (deducted from) your taxable income, enabling you to save, or "shelter," money you would otherwise have to pay in taxes. Net-lease properties and subsidized housing are examples of tax shelters.

title insurance   Coverage that protects you from potential losses arising from irregularities in the legal title to your home or other real estate.

VA mortgage   A home mortgage that is guaranteed, sometimes up to $27,500, by the Veterans Administration. Because of this guarantee, you may not have to make any down payment. This type of mortgage is available to eligible veterans.

variable-rate mortgage (VMR)   A home mortgage that is similar to the roll-over mortgage, except that the adjustments in the interest rate are made more frequently (usually once or twice a year).

write-off   The depreciation or amortization taken on a commercial property.

INDEX

Business Guides from MENTOR and SIGNET

Buy them at your local
bookstore or use coupon
on next page for ordering.

All About Business from the MENTOR Library